ADVANCES IN
GROUP PSYCHOTHERAPY:

Integrating Research and Practice

ADVANCES IN
GROUP PSYCHOTHERAPY:

Integrating Research and Practice

edited by
ROBERT R. DIES, Ph.D.,
and
K. ROY MacKENZIE, M.D.

Monograph 1
AMERICAN GROUP PSYCHOTHERAPY ASSOCIATION
MONOGRAPH SERIES

Series Consulting Editor:
Fern J. Cramer Azima, Ph.D.

INTERNATIONAL UNIVERSITIES PRESS, INC.
New York

iv

Copyright ©1983, American Group Psychotherapy Association

Library of Congress Cataloging in Publication Data
Main entry under title:

Advances in group psychotherapy.
    (Monograph series/American Group Psychotherapy
Association; monograph 1)
        Bibliography: p.
        Includes index.
        1. Group psychotherapy.   2. Group psychotherapy — Research.
I. Dies, Robert K., 1940–   .   II. MacKenzie, K. Roy, 1937–
III. Series: Monograph series (American Group Psycotherapy
Association); monograph 1.
[DNLM: 1. Psychotherapy, Group.   2. Research. W1
M0559PU monograph 1 / WM 430 A244]
RC 488.A62 1983   616.89'152   83-206
ISBN 0-8236-0107-2

Manufactured in the United States of America

Contents

Contributors

Beck, Ariadne P., M.A.
: Private Practice, Chicago and Indian Head Park, Illinois.

Bond, Gary R., Ph.D.
: Associate Professor, Clinical Psychology Program, Department of Psychiatry and Behavior Sciences, Northwestern University, Chicago, Illinois.

Coché, Erich, Ph.D.
: Private Practice, Philadelphia, Pennsylvania.

Dies, Robert R., Ph.D.
: Professor, Department of Psychology, University of Maryland, College Park, Maryland.

Dugo, James M., Ph.D.
: Director, Group Psychotherapy Institute, Lutheran Medical Center, Park Ridge, Illinois.

Eng, Albert M., M.S.W.
: Graduate Student, Clinical Psychology, Northwestern Medical School, Chicago, Illinois.

Lewis, Carol M., M.A.
: Staff Psychologist, Community Guidance Clinic, Mercy Hospital, Chicago, Illinois.

Lieberman, Morton A., Ph.D.
: Professor, Department of Behavioral Sciences (Human Development) and Department of Psychiatry, University of Chicago, Chicago, Illinois.

Livesley, W. John, M.B., Ph.D.
: Associate Professor of Psychiatry, Faculty of Medicine, University of Calgary, Calgary, Alberta, Canada.

MacKenzie, K. Roy, M.D., F.R.C.P.(C)
: Professor of Psychiatry, Faculty of Medicine, University of Calgary, Calgary, Alberta, Canada

Peters, Lana N., Ph.D.
: Consulting Psychologist, DuPage County Health Department, Wheaton, Illinois.

President's Preface

The publication of this first volume in the Monograph Series of the American Group Psychotherapy Association in the Association's fortieth anniversary year marks a major milestone in its development. It brings to mind earlier milestones, such as the birth of the *International Journal of Group Psychotherapy* in 1951, together with its Silver Anniversary issue in 1975; the *Brief History of the American Group Psychotherapy Association: 1943–1968;* as well as the *Guidelines for the Training of Group Psychotherapists* and the *Consumer's Guide to Group Psychotherapy.* All stand as testimonials that we have remained true to our primary mission of enhancing quality training, together with furthering the knowledge base of clinical group psychotherapy and that of the broader field of "people-helping" groups.

Since we have frequently been criticized for being unduly steeped in the subjectivity of clinical practice, it is especially gratifying that our first monograph is devoted to group psychotherapy research. We are thus underscoring the fact that the American Group Psychotherapy Association, while comprising mostly clinicians, remains ever mindful of the need to subject both what we *think* and what we *do* to objective scrutiny!

In addition to Dr. Fern J. Azima, Consulting Editor of the Series and Chairwoman of the AGPA Publications Committee; Drs. Robert R. Dies and K. Roy MacKenzie, co-editors of this monograph; and Dr. Zanvel A. Liff, Editor of the *International Journal of Group Psychotherapy;* many people, too many to name here, had a role in the creation of this volume. In thanking them for their efforts, I would also like to express our gratitude to Dr. Norman A. Neiberg, currently Retiring President, under whose administration the idea for the AGPA Monograph Series was hatched. Last but not least, there is Marsha S. Block, the Association's Chief Executive Officer, whose guiding spirit hovers over all its undertakings.

Saul Scheidlinger, Ph.D.
President, American Group Psychotherapy Association

Consulting Editor's Preface

The Monograph Series of the American Group Psychotherapy Association will serve as the companion publication to the *International Journal of Group Psychotherapy* and will answer the mandate of the Association to bring its membership publications of the highest quality in group psychotherapy. The series provides a parallel way of publishing a number of articles devoted to a single topic that has special importance to the theory, technique, and research in the field of group psychotherapy. Thus, the monographs will address issues that should enable clinicians to upgrade standards of practice, further specialized training, and provide a better understanding of research implications.

The present volume, edited by Drs. Robert R. Dies and K. Roy MacKenzie, is an important contribution by them and their co-workers on clinical research and group therapy. It is a fitting commencement for the series as we move into an era of empirical assessment of clinical group practice.

Fern J. Cramer Azima, Ph.D.
Consulting Editor, AGPA Monograph Series
Chairwoman, AGPA Publications Committee

Foreword

It is an extreme pleasure to welcome this first volume in the new Monograph Series of the American Group Psychotherapy Association. Its topic is especially pertinent as group psychotherapy moves into the mainstream of contemporary mental health treatment, with accountability and quality control increasingly becoming central issues.

Superbly edited by two outstanding research scholars and clinicians, Drs. Robert R. Dies and K. Roy MacKenzie, this volume serves its purpose more than well. In my view, its threefold mission has been successfully accomplished — it presents up-to-date research findings in the group field, it raises standards for new research despite innumerable complex variables, and it cultivates and develops a more inquiring research attitude in everyday work with groups by non-research-oriented practitioners. Its focus on process, outcome, and leadership research is especially important since our future direction lies in deeper probings of both the internal and external interactional fields, between patients themselves as well as patients and group leaders.

We are all concerned with improving group psychotherapy practice. But this can only come about with hard data and replicable research findings. In this issue the frontiers of both our methodology and our evidence move many steps forward.

Zanvel A. Liff, Ph.D.
Editor, *International Journal of Group Psychotherapy*

Introduction

Critical reviews of the group psychotherapy research literature have consistently concluded that a principal problem with the field is the failure of researchers and clinicians to collaborate in their efforts to understand group phenomena. Practitioners have been characterized as lacking interest in empirical findings and being too preoccupied with clinical theory and unsystematic speculation. Researchers, on the other hand, have been depicted as overly concerned with experimental rigor and thus failing to appreciate the practical realities of the clinical setting. Nevertheless, there is a growing recognition that the perspectives of the clinician and the researcher are not incompatible, and that there is some hope for rapprochement between their two positions. Indeed, many would argue that the field of group psychotherapy cannot continue to flourish without a narrowing of the gap between research and practice. The insights of the practitioner and the systematic investigations of the researcher must be integrated if the field is to forge ahead and develop a more sophisticated understanding of the unique curative processes inherent in group interaction.

With this monograph, we hope to encourage further communication within the field. The contributors are all group psychotherapists who are keenly aware of the advantages of incorporating a research perspective into their clinical work. Each author has attempted to furnish practical guidelines for improving group treatments through empirical methods. In the first chapter, Robert R. Dies summarizes the basic controversies defining the split between group psychotherapy practitioners and researchers. He suggests that the schism results, in part, from stereotyped views, and that the actual differences between empirical and applied work are not so dramatic. Dies proposes that a common meeting ground may be in the intensive study of single groups through evaluative or N = 1 research. These methods underscore the importance of using empirical measures for understanding group treatment. Dies illustrates how instrumentation to investigate group leadership, process, and outcome has many practical advantages for the clinician and may ultimately serve to narrow the gap between research and practice.

In the second chapter, Dies focuses on group psychotherapy leadership. The importance of instrumentation for understanding this aspect of group treatment is highlighted by a survey of self-report, client-rating, and observer-rating measures of leadership published during the 1970s. Based on this review of the literature, Dies outlines a model of short-term group psychotherapy. He stresses the role of the group psychotherapist as a model-setting participant and technical expert who provides therapeutic structure and guides the development of a meaningful and positive learning environment, which can then be used to promote change in the individual group members.

Erich Coché (Chapter 3) continues the emphasis on instrumentation by providing an overview of basic outcome measures. He begins by describing the CORE Battery, an outcome self-evaluation kit for practitioners, recently published by the American Group Psychotherapy Association. A multiperspective, multimeasure approach to treatment evaluation is recommended. Coché illustrates the practical use of the CORE Battery and highlights the benefits to the clinician of systematic assessment of client change. He then suggests a number of additional objective, projective, and behavioral outcome measures, and discusses the evaluation of group treatments in a variety of inpatient, outpatient, and private practice settings.

The remaining six chapters shift the emphasis of the monograph to an understanding of group process. K. Roy MacKenzie and W. John Livesley present a developmental model for brief group psychotherapy (Chapter 4) and discuss the emergence of social roles within the framework of their developmental model (Chapter 5). These two chapters are largely theoretical, but they are based on an extensive program of research. MacKenzie and Livesley reason that there are consistent rules guiding the sequential development of groups and that groups will not progress constructively until they have resolved earlier developmental hurdles. They delineate specific interactional dimensions characteristic of each developmental stage, and suggest that a developing group may be viewed as a series of social contexts, which have a differential impact on members according to their characterological structure. Livesley and MacKenzie argue that personality dynamics and system requirements interact to define social roles. Thus, viewed in social system terms, the significant issue regarding social roles is not whether behaviors cluster in the individual, but rather whether these behaviors occur at critical points in the group's development. The system needs varied roles just as the individual needs to acquire role flexibility.

Chapter 6, by Ariadne P. Beck, James M. Dugo, Albert M. Eng, Carol M. Lewis, and Lana N. Peters, addresses similar developmental and social role issues, but with a different theoretical emphasis. Beck has pioneered in her efforts to bring some coherence to the literature on stage development, and has published extensively in this area. Beck and her co-workers provide rich observational data concerning stage characteristics, with particular emphasis on the contributions emerging leaders make in facilitating stage shifts. They demonstrate the value of empirical methodology for understanding clinical material. At the same time, their measures are based on the intensive analysis of group interaction.

In Chapter 7, MacKenzie provides an alternative approach to group process with his Group Climate Questionnaire, which asks members to reflect on important dimensions of group interaction. This instrument is highly adaptable to clinical practice and complements the leadership and outcome measures discussed by Dies and Coché. MacKenzie has refined his Group Climate Questionnaire through sophisticated statistical techniques, but has not lost sight of the practical implications of his work. The use of such measures can do much to bridge the gap between research and practice.

Gary R. Bond (Chapter 8) also relies on client reports to evaluate group process. He offers an objective method for measuring clinically observed phenomena of norm regulation, deviancy, and risky behavior in group psychotherapy. In contrast to MacKenzie's unidimensional portrayal of group process in terms of interpersonal behavior, however, Bond adds an evaluative component. In his two-component model, he states that norm regulation is dually determined by the shared evaluation and shared behavioral expectation of group members. A precondition for norm regulation is that a consensus agrees that the behavior is either acceptable or unacceptable. Without this consensus, the behavior is considered lacking in norm regulation, regardless of the expectations of members.

In the final Chapter, Morton A. Lieberman investigates change mechanisms through an instrument designed to assess client preceptions of helpful therapeutic events. His research findings show that group system properties have a major influence on the type of events or experiences participants report as being useful. Lieberman debates the relative advantages and disadvantages of phenomenological and observational approaches to investigating group process, and challenges researchers to devise more sophisticated measures. He suggests that group members give us answers only for the questions we as researchers ask. Do we, then, end up studying reflections of our own theories rather than clinical reality?

Throughout this monograph there is a consistent concern for the appropriate use of instrumentation to evaluate group treatments. The contributors agree that the field would be further along if researchers and clinicians cooperated in their efforts to develop more sensitive and creative measures.

Although the editors are solely responsible for the contents of this monograph, this volume could not have been completed without the active support of the American Group Psychotherapy Association. We are especially grateful to Drs. Fern J. Cramer Azima, Zanvel Liff, and Saul Scheidlinger and to our very competent Chief Executive Officer, Marsha Block, for their efforts.

1

Bridging the Gap Between Research and Practice in Group Psychotherapy

ROBERT R. DIES, Ph.D.

An appeal for greater collaboration between researchers and practitioners has been echoed for over three decades throughout the group treatment literature, with little evidence that progress has been made toward forging an effective alliance (Dies, 1979). As Parloff recently noted, "the twin fields of psychotherapy and psychotherapy research have emerged, developed, and flourished in essentially untrammeled independence of each other" (1980, p. 279). Discouraged by the complexities of group therapy research, investigators have generally taken refuge in isolated environments in which control of experimental variables is more feasible; research on nonpatient groups and small-scale investigation of a limited range of variables have been the most fashionable retreats (Dies, 1979). Practitioners, on the other hand, have persevered in their efforts to understand group phenomena without consulting the researcher; they have dismissed the bulk of empirical work on groups as irrelevant or, at best, only tangentially related to actual clinical practice.

Recent developments both within and outside the field make it clear that clinicians and researchers can no longer afford to maintain such mutual dissociation. Parloff (1980) and Strupp (1979) argue convincingly that the very survival of psychotherapy as a profession rests on the active integration of research and practice. These two luminaries in the field of psychotherapy research suggest that legislators, insurance companies, and patient-consumers are increasing their demands to know about the efficacy, safety, and cost-effectiveness of psychological treatment. Unsubstantiated assurances and pronouncements about the value of psy-

1

chotherapy are no longer sufficient. What the policy-makers, health care underwriters, and consumers require is empirical documentation that continued support of mental health services is worth the investment. Although present threats from external sources of funding have precipitated a renewed interest in a negotiated settlement between scientists and practitioners, it is evident that the pressures for greater collaboration do not emanate exclusively from the outside. The snail-paced progress and comparative naiveté regarding group treatments have prompted many professionals within the field to insist on a more cooperative relationship between clinicians and researchers. I have elsewhere urged that the respective aptitudes and skills of practitioners and researchers must be synchronized if we are to achieve much progress toward understanding the complexities of various group processes and the complicated nature of therapeutic change for individual group members (Dies, 1979). Similarly, Bednar and Kaul (1979) have stated that a greater integration of the practitioner's insights and the researcher's controlled investigations is mandatory for each to achieve a higher level of professional development.

Lately, we have witnessed some hopeful indications of a growing rapprochement. Writers have addressed the anti-research biases that characterize practitioners and group participants (Bennis, 1960; Lakin, 1972), but now recommendations are being formulated to overcome this obstacle (Dies, 1978; Weigel and Corazzini, 1978). To facilitate communication, several new journals that publish both clinical and research papers have appeared in recent years, and the conventional group journals now publish more research-oriented manuscripts (Dies, 1979). The American Group Psychotherapy Association (AGPA), an organization traditionally limited to practicing group psychotherapists, recently introduced a new membership category for researchers. Moreover, AGPA supported the publication of the CORE Battery, a set of outcome measures for clinicians to use in evaluating their own practice (MacKenzie and Dies, 1982), and it is now sponsoring the present monograph on bridging the gap between research and practice. These and other signs are encouraging, but it is obvious that even more attention must be directed toward creating a harmonious relationship between researchers and clinicians. Simple entreaties for collaboration apparently have had only limited impact (Bennis, 1960; Dies, 1979; Parloff and Dies, 1977), so it would seem that more concrete recommendations are in order. I shall therefore attempt to build on the suggestions that are appearing with increasing frequency in the group psychotherapy literature. Before I offer specific proposals for reducing the gulf between research and practice, however, a broader appreciation of the problem is needed.

THE EXISTING GAP BETWEEN
RESEARCH AND PRACTICE

Recently I asked a number of group psychotherapists to evaluate the impact of group therapy research on their own clinical practice and to indicate why research did not have an even greater influence.[1] These practitioners reported that research had only a moderate effect on their therapeutic activities (the average rating on an 11-point scale, which ranged from "extremely little impact" to "substantial impact," was 5.8). Altogether, 132 reasons were listed to explain the modest impact of group psychotherapy research. Table 1 summarizes the findings.

These informal results demonstrate that a majority of the clinicians (77.3%) questioned the relevance of group psychotherapy research. Comments describing research as "esoteric," difficult to translate into clinical practice, and often focused on "narrow" or "superficial" problems are consistent with other reports in the literature. Hartman (1979) has observed, for example, that the "efforts made by the researcher to concretize variables, to control for factors of change, and otherwise to bring the group situation into line with scientific standards may leave the clini-

TABLE 1
Impact of Research on Group Therapy Practice

Explanations for Limited Effect	Number of Items Listed (N = 132)	Number of Raters Listing (N = 47)
Limited clinical relevance of research	52 (39.4%)	34 (77.3%)
Inadequate quality of research	32 (24.2%)	23 (52.3%)
Poor communication between researchers and clinicians	14 (10.6%)	12 (27.3%)
Limited time for reading	13 (9.8%)	13 (29.5%)
No access to publication outlets	9 (6.8%)	8 (18.2%)
Personal limitations	6 (4.5%)	5 (11.4%)
Miscellaneous	6 (4.5%)	6 (13.6%)

[1]The brief questionnaire was distributed at a meeting of the Board of Directors of the American Group Psychotherapy Association. Forty-seven voting and nonvoting board members (e.g., committee chairpersons, affiliate society representatives) responded.

cian feeling deprived of the richness, complexity, and, perhaps, the essence of the clinical enterprise" (p. 454). Bednar and Kaul (1979) note that even though many studies are technically proficient, they are conceptually bankrupt. Too many investigators focus on the individual in the group and neglect the most salient dimensions of group process. Much of the research takes an either-or perspective regarding group process and outcome. The failure to link therapeutic change to specific parameters of group process yields research with limited applicability for the practicing clinician.

More than half the respondents (52.3%) in my informal survey complained about the quality of group research, e.g., the "insufficient samples," "limited methodological controls," "inappropriate instrumentation," and the "lack of creativity" of the research in general. Reviewers of the group treatment literature have offered similar evaluations (Bednar and Lawlis, 1971; Lewis and McCants, 1973). The research is characterized as deficient in conceptual and methodological uniformity. Although investigators have studied a variety of techniques, the treatment groups are seldom adequately described (Parloff and Dies, 1977), there are generally few consistent procedures to evaluate outcome or process, and the instruments employed are frequently homemade and of questionable validity (Hartman, 1979). This makes it difficult to compare findings across studies and makes the field appear disjointed and confusing to most readers (Coché and Dies, 1981). The technical language of many empirical reports is frustrating to practitioners, who may understand basic statistics and research design but are unprepared to comprehend the "esoteric" technical discourse in some research (Coché and Dies, 1981). Then, too, the investigator's reliance on statistical significance as the criterion of "meaningful" effect leaves many clinicians disappointed. The group comparisons required by most statistical tests may obscure clinically meaningful change in *individual* group members.

Table 1 reveals that many clinicians (27.3%) expressed dissatisfaction with the nature of communication between researchers and practitioners. These findings are not surprising. Over two decades ago, Bennis (1960) commented, "Presumably social scientists who conduct research on small group behavior and psychotherapists who conduct groups observe and are concerned with similar phenomena. And yet, for the most part, they do not read the same journals, usually do not attend the same meetings, and more usually appear to have a difficult time communicating with each other" (p. 65). Contemporary writers confirm that these observations are still valid (Bednar and Kaul, 1979).

Coché and I have revealed that while empirical reports are published in over a dozen professional journals, most of these outlets are not devoted to group methods, or if they are, they allocate comparatively few pages to research (Coché and Dies, 1981). In this regard, Table 1 shows that a number of clinicians in our sample (18.2%) expressed concern about the inaccessibility of publication outlets. Moreover, Weigel and Corazzini (1978) have castigated researchers for their failure to exercise adequate responsibility in reporting their research findings. They suggest that "'Piece workers,' i.e., those who publish multiple articles from a single investigative study, have contributed to the negative research halo" (p. 194). Coché and I have also impugned researchers for not making the practical implications of the research sufficiently explicit, and for failing to invite their practitioner colleagues to play a more active role in the planning and implementation of their research: "Considerable friction could be alleviated if researchers were more responsive to the group members' needs and helped the clinician to introduce the research to their clients, and further to enlist their cooperation based upon a clear understanding of the potential personal and scientific merits of the research" (Coché and Dies, 1981, p. 414). In this way, both group therapists and members might experience research projects as less of an imposition, thereby improving the overall climate for research.

Over the years, many practitioners have come to distrust research because the findings directly challenged the effectiveness of group treatments, and therefore contradicted what clinicians knew to be true, namely, that their therapeutic efforts were indeed worthwhile. However, the continued disenchantment with research is no longer warranted on these grounds. There has been a noticeable increment in the quality of group research, and the results clearly support the efficacy of group treatments (Bednar and Kaul, 1978; Dies, 1979; Gazda, 1978). Moreover, there are numerous reviews of the research literature with definite implications for therapeutic practice, e.g., pregroup structuring (Bednar, Melnick, and Kaul, 1974), patient selection (Woods and Melnick, 1979), group composition (Melnick and Woods, 1976), negative outcome (Dies and Teleska, in press), and leadership style (see Chapter 2).

Whether or not the practitioner's attitude toward research will improve in light of the researcher's increased sophistication and current efforts to make empirical findings more practical remains to be seen. The stereotyped view of research as "nonrelevant" and fraught with methodological imperfections is quite pervasive and firmly entrenched. At this point it is too easy for clinicians to automatically dismiss research without weighing its potential contribution, and to hold the researcher responsible for the schism within the field. This is a grave mistake. Clinicians must examine their own contributions to the gap between research and practice. The responsibility for the breech cannot be placed entirely at the doorstep of the researcher.

Bennis (1960) suggested long ago that the practitioner's presumed opposition to research often represents "powerful unconscious resistances" (p. 75). The possibility that research findings might confront therapists with their own ineffectiveness or that group members (and research-oriented colleagues) might disapprove of how the therapy group was conducted should not be disregarded too casually. To many practitioners, such a possibility presents a serious threat to their personal and professional identity. Many clinicians also experience research as a disruptive inconvenience, an additional strain on a heavily taxed schedule (e.g., Table 1, limited time for reading), and a potential loss of personal income. Furthermore, many clinicians do not feel comfortable with the research and are uncertain about their role (e.g., Table 1, personal limitations). They might agree to participate in the study but still feel uneasy about its implementation: What if group members object to the data-collection procedures or ask questions the clinician feels unable to handle? Frequently, group psychotherapists feel caught in the middle between the researchers and group members, in part because the research is introduced by an outside evaluator who is unkown to the group members. On the other hand, this outsider role is extremely difficult for most researchers, particularly when the clinicians themselves do not welcome the external interventions. This insider-outsider dichotomy poses enormous obstacles for research unless a clear understanding is established among the various participants in the project—the group members, the psychotherapist, the researchers, and the administrative and support personnel within an agency—if this is where the research is being conducted (Dies, 1978). Finally, Lakin (1972) notes that just as group members' subjectivity during the treatment session leads them to resist evaluation, the personal commitment of many therapists to group process makes them impatient with the need to objectify their experience through the tools of research (e.g., questionnaires, self-ratings, etc.). This creates a situation in which "the researcher in the small group field is appalled by the lack of commitment to look systematically at what is occurring in personal change groups and to subject the enterprise to examination in quantifiable and replicable terms" (Hartman, 1979, p. 458).

In the face of substantial difficulty in gaining entry into the clinical setting, and practitioners' apparent aversion to empirical methods, many researchers have adopted a stereotyped view of clinicians as unsystematic and overly speculative. As a result, we have a situation in which researchers and practitioners reject each other because of perceived attitudinal differences. Bednar and Kaul (1979) submit, however, that "the polarization of therapy-softness and research-rigorousness is artificial and does not represent a complete picture of what is required for high level clinical service" (p. 318). They suggest that effective clinical service and effective research productivity require highly similar dispositions and intellectual functions. For example, the abilities involved in understanding the empirical literature and in formulating meaningful research are not dissimilar from the operations involved in comprehending group process and planning interventions to facilitate clinical change. Kiesler (1981) reports that practitioners and scientists employ identical processes: "Both start with empirical observations (systematically measured or not) from which generalities are abstracted and treatment or manipulative hypotheses are deduced, applied and subsequently validated empirically (through systematic observations or not). Both the science and practice of psychotherapy involve at their core a hypothesis-testing procedure" (pp. 213–214).

As group psychotherapists, we first observe group members' interactions within the treatment sessions and listen to their reports about interactions occurring outside the sessions. Then we generate conceptualizations of our clients' behaviors and of the group process, from which we derive intervention strategies to promote constructive change. We might note, for instance, that several group members seem rather hesitant to participate openly in the group discussions, and formulate a plan to confront the contratherapeutic norms underlying the apparent reluctance to risk personal sharing. We might then intervene to encourage resolution of the therapeutic impasse, followed by an evaluation of the effectiveness of our intervention. Thus, we move from conceptualization, to intervention, and then to validation (observing the impact of our therapeutic interventions). Throughout group treatment, therapists continually move back and forth between their conceptualizations of client behavior (and group process) and the data base of what clients do in and outside of their sessions. "The very practice, then, of psychotherapy is a scientific event encapsulating the application, whether systematic or not, of scientific methodology to the single case," Kiesler (1981, p. 214) states. He explains that what has differentiated the researcher from the practitioner is (1) whether the inductive-deductive logical process operates implicitly or explicitly and (2) whether systematic or unsystematic observation occurs. "Accordingly," he argues, "to make his/her efforts scientific, the only additional steps required of a practitioner are to explicate the client conceptualizations and to apply some form of empirical measurement so that the data base will be objective and replicable and thus in the public domain" (p. 214).

Unfortunately, the vast majority of group psychotherapists have been unwilling to take the additional steps to build instrumentation into their clinical practice. For some practitioners, the reluctance is based on a genuine conviction that the use of research tools will not advance clinical service. For others, however, the reservations represent a form of personal resistance (e.g., limitations of time, unfamiliarity with the research tools, and fear of client retaliation). In the following pages, specific recommendations are offered to help those clinicians who are willing to move beyond their uneasiness to explore the value of instrumentation in their group work. My goal is not to transform clinicians into researchers, but to demonstrate how it is quite possible to incorporate systematic observation into one's clinical practice and thereby improve the quality of service delivery. I also hope to show that the stereotyped view of research as "irrelevant" to group treatment is fallacious.

BUILDING INSTRUMENTATION INTO CLINICAL PRACTICE

Many practitioners think only in terms of research with a "capital R"—i.e., random, representative, and/or robust samples, rigorous methodological controls, refined statistical operations, and resplendent computer technology. Oetting (1976a, 1976b) argues, however, that all research is not traditional scientific inquiry; he proposes that an acceptable alternative may be evaluative research. In his opinion: "Scientific inquiry is aimed at the advance of scientific knowledge. There is little need for such research to be immediately useful or practical, but there must be great concern for making sure that any contribution that is made is stated as accurately as possible and that the exact relationship between independent and dependent variables is known. Evaluative research has a different purpose. It is aimed at collecting data that will help in making decisions about programs" (1976a, p. 11).

Suppose, for example, that a psychotherapist is interested in symptomatic change in the members of an outpatient group. This clinician selects a suitable symptom checklist and administers the scale before and after treatment to evaluate the degree of client improvement. From the standpoint of scientific research, this study is fundamentally flawed; the lack of an appropriate control group and the small sample size make it impossible to generalize about treatment effects. From the viewpoint of the practitioner, however, this simple study may prove to be quite beneficial. Assuming that a valid measure of symptomatic expression was employed, the results might help the clinician to understand the significance of client change more concretely. It may not be possible to correlate specific changes with precise parameters of group process, but the fact that the clients are reporting remediation of symptoms, or the finding that certain clients remain unchanged or even deteriorate slightly, gives information to the practitioner which may have been overlooked without the empirical measurement. The value of this initial investigation would be enhanced if the therapist included some assessment of group process, and requested clients to speculate on the relationship between their experiences within the sessions and the therapeutic results. Although this informal "experiment" still may not yield publishable results in the absence of appropriate controls and replication, tapping client perceptions in this manner may provide rich material for modifying therapeutic interventions. Later in this paper I shall illustrate how simple studies can be refined even more to produce information of considerable potential benefit for clinical practice.

According to Oetting (1976a), evaluative research favors short-term, immediate, and practical benefits. As a consequence, it is generally more relevant to treatment goals. Although evaluative research may not eliminate all the crucial alternative explanations of results (the goal of scientific inquiry), it will at least reduce the number of alternative interpretations of practical importance, and permit generalization to the same or similar target groups.

The use of instrumentation in evaluative research is critically important and offers a distinct advantage over scientific research in that the evaluator is afforded greater flexibility in constructing instruments to fit the particular treatment context. For instance, psychotherapists may not be able to find appropriate measures of group process to match their specific needs, and may therefore devise instruments more in keeping with their treatment goals. Such scales are *verboten* in rigorous scientific inquiry, but in evaluative research this option is often highly desirable. Oetting (1976a) reports that evaluators can often construct instruments with a high degree of face validity: "if the instruments are short and simple and seem reasonable, the client is likely to feel more like cooperating and may even take the trouble to do ratings very carefully. If the instrument seems to make little sense, the client may refuse or mark at random or use any of the other innumerable techniques for showing irritation" (p. 13).

Closely related to Oetting's description of evaluative research is the idea of the single-case study or N = 1 research, which has been touted as an effective way to bridge the gap between research and practice (Barlow, 1981). In the case study method or, in our situation, the investigation of a single group, the clinician intensely studies the group through systematic and repeated observation throughout the course of treatment, to monitor possible connections between certain process variables and therapeutic outcome. This intensive examination is facilitated by the careful application of empirical measures. Kazdin (1982) proposes that single-case research designs "provide a methodological approach well suited to the investigation of individuals, single groups, or multiple groups of subjects" (p. vii). In a recent issue of the *Journal of Clinical and Counseling Psychology* entitled "Empirical Practice and Realistic Research," a number of research-oriented clinicians emphasize the value of instrumentation. Hayes (1981), for instance, states that clinicians are already doing evaluations of potential scientific merit, but that they could improve their treatment work by specifying their methods more precisely and by introducing systematic and repeated measurement into their clinical work. Nelson (1981) offers practical guidelines for implementing data-collection procedures into empirical clinical practice. Among other things, she suggests that clients' problems should be assessed in specific terms, measures should be selected that accurately and sensitively reflect the therapeutic objectives, several different measures should be used with each client, monitoring of dependent variables should begin early in the course of treatment, and the same measures should be given before, during, and after treatment. Nelson also outlines realistic dependent measures, including self-monitoring, self-ratings, questionnaires, observational methods, and indirect methods.

As I noted earlier, the Research Committee of the American Group Psychotherapy Association has recently developed the CORE Battery, an outcome evaluation kit for group psychotherapists who wish to objectify their assessment of change in their group members (MacKenzie and Dies, 1982). The CORE Battery manual summarizes the principal advantages and disadvantages of instrumentation in the group setting.

Following the lead of Pfeiffer, Heslin, and Jones (1976), it identifies ten benefits of instrumentation:

1. Encourages client involvement in the treatment process.
2. Fosters open reaction to personal feedback.
3. Clarifies client goals and facilitates contracting for new behavior.
4. Increases the objectivity of measuring client change.
5. Provides for comparisons of individual clients with normative groups.
6. Facilitates longitudinal (before, after, follow-up) assessment of therapeutic change.
7. Sensitizes clients and therapists to the multifaceted nature of therapeutic change.
8. Gives clients the sense that their therapist is committed to effective treatment.
9. Improves communication between clients and therapists.
10. Allows the therapist to focus and control the group more effectively.

An equal number of disadvantages are listed, relating primarily to client and therapist defensiveness, the misuse of the measures, and the interference with treatment precipitated by the measures. Yet MacKenzie and I furnish extensive guidelines for avoiding these potential problems. In general, our recommendations focus on legitimizing the use of instruments with group members by fully explaining their potential value, removing the mystique surrounding measures by describing their contribution to understanding group process and therapeutic outcome, and assuring clients that every precaution will be taken to guarantee responsible use of the findings.

Up to this point, I have attempted to show that the systematic use of empirical measures holds considerable promise for improving the quality of group treatments, but I have not yet established that instrumentation will necessarily narrow the gap between research and practice. It would seem to follow that when group psychotherapists begin to incorporate the tools of research into their clinical practice, they may also develop a more positive attitude toward research activities. Stereotypes about research as "irrelevant" are likely to fade as practitioners recognize that empirical investigations within their own treatment setting are not only possible, but potentially beneficial as well. As clinicians learn that data-collection procedures are not always time-consuming and inconvenient, and that clients do not invariably experience empirical investigations as intrusive, their personal resistance to research may diminish.

Moreover, as group psychotherapists participate in their own evaluative or N = 1 research, they may modify their misconception that all empirical investigations must be of the "capital *R*" variety, and discover that research no longer has to be a "dirty word." Positive experiences with research instruments may actually encourage clinicians to explore additional measures for investigating their group treatments and thus bring them into closer contact with the empirical literature. As clinicians develop an increased openness to research findings, they may feel more inclined to invite their research-oriented colleagues to collaborate in devising more sophisticated instruments for investigating group treatments. It is to be hoped that as group psychotherapists increasingly recognize the potential contribution of research (and researchers) to clinical practice, the gulf between empirical and clinical modes of understanding will indeed be reduced. Later, I shall mention additional steps toward forging an effective alliance between researchers and practitioners, with an eye to the researcher's role in opening the doors for greater communication. Clearly the problem is not the sole responsibility of the group therapist; researchers must become aware of their own contributions to the split within the field. At this point, however, I should like to focus on how, specifically, clinicians can build instrumentation into their group treatments.

ILLUSTRATIONS OF INSTRUMENTATION IN CLINICAL PRACTICE

In the following clinical illustrations the practical benefits of instrumentation will be highlighted. The goal is to introduce group psychotherapists to empirical measures in a way that will encourage them to adopt the instruments in their clinical practice. As I indicated above, it is hoped that clinicians' firsthand experience with research tools will result in a greater appreciation of empirical methodology and an eagerness to explore additional methods. Thus, although the following presentation is largely geared to improving clinical service, its ultimate objective is a reduction of the scientist-practitioner split within the field.

Outcome Measures

Earlier, I used the example of a group psychotherapist who administers a symptom checklist before and after treatment to evaluate client improvement. This illustration can be expanded to show how one can collect meaningful information without meeting (or necessarily violating) the stringent requirements of scientific inquiry. In the simplest version of pre/post-testing, the clinician can select an instrument of demonstrated validity to assess clinical improvement. The Self-Report Symptom Inventory (SCL-90-R), for example, is a standardized instrument with extensive norms and a broad foundation of empirical work to support its utility in investigating clinical change (Derogatis, 1977).[2] Clients can complete the test on their own time, and the instrument can be scored quite easily by the group therapist or by an administrative assistant. Thus, the SCL-90-R does not disrupt the treatment sessions, nor does it require much time from the clinician. Group members are usually quite willing to complete the inventory since it is brief and has obvious face validity. Post-testing with the SCL-90-R is experienced by group members as an obvious extension of the initial assessment. The principal advantage of the test is that it allows clinicians to assess group members against normative standards, thus providing a reasonable framework for evaluating levels of psychopathology along a variety of symptom dimensions. A major shortcoming is that individualized treatment goals may not be tapped by such a standardized measure. To offset this disadvantage, the clinician may incorporate a "target-goals" approach, requiring group members to identify specific and personal treatment goals which can be evaluated in terms of their achievement later in therapy (Coché, Chapter 3; MacKenzie and Dies, 1982). The target-goals approach is highly compatible with routine clinical practice and thus is readily acceptable to most group members.

At this point, then, the clinician has integrated two important methods into the group treatment program which offer considerable potential for clarifying the nature of client improvement. This has been accomplished without an enormous investment of time or extra resources on the part of the group therapist. The intrinsic benefits of a systematic assessment of change should be quite apparent, but there are other advantages as well. The administration of such empirical measures encourages clients to establish concrete goals for change, and provides a common denominator for therapists and clients to communicate about the change process. What may be regarded as a problem of "pre-test sensitization" in group psychotherapy research (Bednar and Lawlis, 1971), i.e., the observation that testing itself may influence clients to respond in certain ways, can be viewed as a distinct advantage in the clinical setting. Whether this potential bias is regarded as a limitation (the "capital

[2]The SCL-90-R is described more extensively by Coché in Chapter 3, to which the reader is referred for an elaboration of its symptom dimensions.

R" researcher's perspective) or a refinement of clinical service depends on the nature of the contract established between the psychotherapist and the group members. Clearly, whenever group therapists decide to incorporate research tools into their clinical practice, the instrumentation should be an essential component of the therapeutic contract since the measures will serve partially to structure the group treatment (Dies, 1978). Clinicians who are familiar with research on the various measures will be in a better position to utilize instruments in their treatment groups. Weigel and Corazzini (1978) have recommended that practitioners should do some basic "homework" before they begin their data-collection procedures. They encourage clinicians to become aware of (1) previous research with the instruments they plan to incorporate into their intensive group study, (2) possible variations in data-collection strategies, and (3) alternative approaches to instrumentation. These goals may be achieved most effectively with the assistance of a research consultant, one who is aware of the pragmatic problems inherent in group treatment (e.g., dropouts, missing data, test biases, etc.).

This clinician/researcher might also help the group psychotherapist to add further refinements to the evaluative or N = 1 research project. Additional outcome measures can of course be incorporated besides the SCL-90-R and Target Goals Procedure. Coché, in Chapter 3, summarizes a range of outcome instruments with wide applicability, and he recommends several resource materials for identifying even more empirical measures. MacKenzie and Dies (1982) offer a number of criteria for selecting a suitable change-measures package. They recommend that the ideal battery should include:

1. Multiple measures, due to the complexity of therapeutic change.
2. Both objective and subjective viewpoints evaluating subjective impressions and behavioral observations.
3. A combination of individualized and standardized measurements.
4. Assessment of various areas of functioning, e.g., self-esteem, interpersonal and social role functioning.
5. Measures from varying sources of information, including the therapist, client, and significant others.
6. Instruments that represent a reasonable compromise between comprehensiveness and realistic time demands.

Thus, refinement of the simple pre/post study can be gained through the use of additional outcome measures. However, since neither the clinician nor the group members want to be overwhelmed by the instrumentation, it is generally best to employ only a few, carefully selected measures. The decision as to which measures are most appropriate depends on whether the clinician wishes to focus on symptoms, attitudes toward self, interpersonal style, or some other area of functioning. In the face of time or resource limitations, clinicians may adopt different strategies with particular groups. In one setting the focus may be on symptomatic remediation, whereas with a different group the target may be changes in social role functioning. Ideally, the group therapist will be able to incorporate multiple measures within the same group.

The problem with many of the instruments used in group research is that they are often not relevant to clients' experiences within the sessions. Too often investigators using pre/post designs have assumed that as long as they can demonstrate the efficacy of their interventions, it makes little difference what happens during the sessions. It has become increasingly important, however, to evaluate outcome from the standpoint of general group processes or in light of the individual's unique experiences within the treatment sessions. A preliminary step can be taken in the direction of linking outcome to process by administering change measures during the course of treatment instead of using a simple pre/post design. The repeated assessment will serve to keep group members task-oriented and provide regular monitoring of client progress throughout treatment. This modification of the basic design does not add new instruments; it merely increases the number of times existing ones are applied. Replication of the measures allows group psychotherapists to note continuous changes reflected on the outcome instruments and to integrate their findings into the treatment process.

For example, clients may be encouraged to discuss the implications of change scores during the meetings and to share their impressions about important group events contributing to shifts on the outcome measures. Repeated assessment may give the group psychotherapist more information than is typically gathered because clients complete the measures on their own time and are thus given an extra opportunity to express themselves. Although the level of commitment to instrumentation increases, the demands on the clinician's time are not significantly altered, nor is there any interference with the treatment process. If anything, a valuable approach to improving the quality of group treatment has been introduced. From the standpoint of "pure scientific inquiry," an unpardonable sin has been committed by allowing instrumentation to "contaminate" the treatment, thereby biasing results, but from the practitioner's point of view treatment effectiveness has been potentially enhanced. Evaluative and N = 1 research are far more tolerant of such lapses in methodological rigor (Oetting, 1976a, 1976b).

One of the problems of small-scale research, however, is that it is difficult to determine the significance of change on the various empirical measures. In most cases, scores will reflect individualized patterns of outcome, with scores on some measures showing improvement; others, no change; and still others, apparent deterioration. MacKenzie and I have offered several guidelines to interpret the *clinical* implications of change (MacKenzie and Dies, 1982). Obviously, group therapists would hope to identify fairly sizable changes, reflecting clinical improvement, and to show that there is a uniform pattern of change across measures, and that therapeutic benefits are highly relevant to treatment goals. In actuality the clinician may find that the various change indices fail to reflect a consistent pattern, or even that results are mixed or seemingly contradictory (Strupp and Hadley, 1977). The group therapist will then have to consider carefully the constellation of results and weigh the relative number and magnitude of changes which show a clear positive direction against those which suggest deterioration or are less clearly interpretable. Clinical judgment will have to be used to integrate the complex results since many clinicians may question the value of calculating the statistical significance of change, especially with their small sample sizes. The magnitude of the difference between pre- and post-test scores required for statistical reliability is a complicated issue relating to the particular outcome measure used, the test-retest reliabilities of the instruments, and the unique context of testing. The ultimate criterion of the clinical significance of therapeutic outcome may be common sense. Thus, change on several measures is probably more meaningful than change on a single measure, especially if the multiple change scores reflect a clear pattern that can be linked to specific treatment goals. The more consistent the pattern of change scores across the various measures, and the greater the magnitude of the changes, the more confidence can be placed in their clinical significance. If both the therapist and the client agree on the nature of the therapeutic results, and particularly if a significant other such as a family member also concurs, then even greater trust can be vested in the identified change scores. Finally, more stock can be placed in changes obtained on individualized outcome measures (e.g., target goals) that are corroborated by corresponding changes on standardized instruments.

In many small-scale investigations, research-oriented colleagues can help practitioners to devise statistical methods for determining the meaningfulness of clinical findings. Appropriate statistical tests may be available or, if not, the data-collection procedures can be planned to permit reliable assessment of therapeutic outcome, even with the small sample sizes (Kazdin, 1982). Moreover, it is always possible to accumulate outcome data over a number of groups over time, or to pool information with other clinicians who are also interested in understanding the efficacy of their therapeutic interventions. With the active collaboration of a research consultant and other practitioners, it is quite possible to build a data base that will permit valid comparisons of therapeutic results in a particular treatment setting.

Process Measures

The goal of integrating group process and therapeutic outcome is more effectively achieved when process measures are incorporated into the intensive N = 1 study. At an elementary level, a clinician could use a critical-incidents approach and request group members to spend a few moments after each session recording their perceptions of helpful therapeutic events. This widely employed technique has been found to be of considerable value in facilitating the understanding of group phenomena (Lieberman, Yalom, and Miles, 1973; MacKenzie, Chapter 7). Frequently, group members are willing to share material that is difficult to disclose during the sessions due to the pressure of time or personal inhibitions. When the critical-incident cards are completed anonymously (an interesting option to use periodically), the answers occasionally reveal rather surprising hidden agendas. A brief perusal of this material following the session may give the group psychotherapist important leads for structuring subsequent meetings.

Many clinicians will want to build more systematic and readily scorable measures into their treatment programs. Several of the contributors to this monograph describe quantifiable process instruments. In Chapter 7, for example, MacKenzie presents empirical data on his Group Climate Questionnaire (GCQ), a 12-item measure of important interpersonal behavior perceived by group members within the treatment sessions. The GCQ is well suited to the group treatment setting: it is face-valid, brief, easily scored, and assesses key dimensions of group process (e.g., engaged, avoiding, conflict). MacKenzie shows how his scale may be used as a sensitive barometer of group developmental phenomena. Responses of individual group members may be combined to plot shifting perceptions of interpersonal behaviors as the group moves through important developmental hurdles (MacKenzie and Livesley, Chapter 4). Aside from their information-gathering value, instruments such as the GCQ may actually improve group treatments. The measures serve to structure the therapeutic enterprise by encouraging clients to focus on critical dimensions of group interactions, and they facilitate continuity across sessions. One variation that may have substantial therapeutic value is for the group members to discuss their scores within the sessions. As I have shown elsewhere (Dies, 1982, 1983), it is possible to use instrumentation to enhance group process and to improve therapeutic outcome for individual group members. To illustrate: clients can complete measures relevant to evolving group themes, such as member/leader role expectations, group norms, self-disclosure, and interpersonal feedback. Clients can even devise their own instruments to evaluate their group experience. The use of empirical measures need not be viewed as an unwanted external intrusion; it can become a vital component of the therapeutic program. Clinicians who are aware of research methodology and test construction principles can help their group members to design interesting and informative measures. Moreover, it is possible to consult with research-oriented colleagues, who can assist in constructing process instruments which are more suitable to the group psychotherapist's own treatment setting. Many of the existing measures are of limited utility because they reflect the test developer's idiosyncratic therapeutic biases, or they are so poorly designed that group members find them objectionable. One of the greatest potential benefits of improved communication between practitioners and researchers is the creation of more appropriate instrumentation.

Group process instruments such as the GCQ can be evaluated in terms of their implications for individual group members in linking process to outcome. Certain clients, for example, may have a considerably different experience of the treatment sessions because they have played rather unique roles within their group. In Chapter 5, Livesley and MacKenzie describe the "divergent" role, characterized by a challenging and questioning interpersonal stance, which is frequently seen as nonconforming. Such a member may eventually become an angry outcast from the group and manifest this through personal disengagement and perceptions of considerable group conflict on the GCQ. Beck and her colleagues (Chapter 6) have used a sociometric technique to identify deviant group members, and then coordinated their findings with developmental issues. Examination of the deviant member's responses on the various outcome measures (e.g., SCL-90-R, Target Goals Procedure) may reveal an exacerbation of symptoms rather than clinical improvement. With Teleska, I have reviewed the literature on therapeutic casualties and linked divergent group roles with negative outcomes (Dies and Teleska, in press). The use of process measures to identify members who are having a nonconstructive group experience may increase the clinician's capacity to prevent contratherapeutic effects. Research findings have indicated that group psychotherapists are not sufficiently sensitive to those group members who are likely to have a detrimental group experience (Lieberman et al., 1973). The proper use of empirical measures may compensate for this clinical insensitivity. Indeed, many would argue that this is precisely why there is a pressing need for a stronger working alliance between practitioners and researchers, i.e., to devise measures that can identify potential therapeutic casualties before they actually occur.

Several other contributors to the present monograph report on additional measures of group process which may have considerable merit. Lieberman (Chapter 9) outlines empirical findings on change mechanisms in groups based on client perceptions of helpful therapeutic events (e.g., universality, catharsis, altruism, support). Research on curative factors across a range of clinical settings demonstrates that therapeutic outcome is influenced by the clients' experience of group treatment (Butler and Fuhriman, in press). The use of a curative-factors instrument provides another approach to understanding group process. Bond (Chapter 8) provides still another alternative with his emphasis on norm regulation in group psychotherapy. He reports findings from an inventory designed to appraise the acceptability and likelihood of certain behaviors occurring within the group sessions. Bond discusses the clinical implications of his measure in terms of increasing members' sensitivity to normative expectations and helping group psychotherapists to enhance their treatment effectiveness.

Any one of the foregoing measures (GCQ, critical incidents, sociometric, curative factors, and perception of norms) can be integrated into the basic outcome study described earlier. For example, it is possible to conduct an N = 1 study using the SCL-90-R and target-goals procedure as outcome measures and then assess process through the GCQ and critical-incident approach. At this point, it should be clear that the measures are based on clients' self-reports. Beck and her colleagues (Chapter 6) illustrate the use of observational techniques. They demonstrate that evaluation of verbal behavior and level of "experiencing" from transcripts of group treatment sessions may provide useful empirical anchors for defining phase boundaries across group sessions. Their methodological advances in studying group phenomena have important clinical implications, but their instrumentation will be of limited utility to the general practitioner, due to the extensive time commitment required to analyze the data. In fact, this is a major drawback of many observational systems for evaluating group process.

Lieberman (Chapter 9) discusses the pros and cons of both observational and phenomenological approaches. He shows that self-report methods have distinct advantages because the phenomenological information can be generated quickly, the methods are comparatively low in cost, and they adequately reflect the range of mechanisms theoretically linked to therapeutic outcome. Although self-report or phenomenological procedures also have several drawbacks, many clinicians will decide to use them because they do not have the time or the inclination to turn to the more time-consuming and cumbersome observational models. For this reason, the present discussion has been restricted to self-report measures. Readers who are interested in observational methods are referred to my chapter on leadership (Chapter 2). Techniques such as the Hill Interaction Matrix, Interaction Process Analysis, Reinforcement-Prompt Code, Training Style Scoring System, and many others, are cited in the appendix to that chapter.

Group psychotherapists who wish to apply observational methods in investigating their group work might invite their empirically minded colleagues to collaborate in the project. In fact, many researchers would welcome the opportunity to collect group process information using observational techniques, and would be more than willing to record and analyze the data simply to have access to clinical material. Many researchers are reluctant to intrude on the clinician's domain without an open invitation.

Leadership Measures

The final component of the N = 1 study is a measure of group leadership. In Chapter 2, I shall summarize a wide range of self-report, client-rating, and observer-based systems. The most popular approach to evaluating group psychotherapists has been through client ratings. Despite inherent weaknesses in this approach, a majority of practitioners will undoubtedly find client reports to be the most convenient (economical, time-efficient) and perhaps even the most pertinent source of information about treatment. Client measures range along two principal axes: unidimensional/multidimensional and behavioral/impressionistic. Multidimensional and behaviorally descriptive instruments are regarded as the most useful, but there must also be an appropriate framework for judging the relative and absolute levels of the group psychotherapist's interventions. Since I elaborate on leadership instrumentation in the following chapter, at this point I shall offer only a few observations to show how client ratings of the group psychotherapist may be used to (1) generate feedback about leadership style, (2) to enhance understanding of the group members' needs and experiences, (3) to influence group process, and (4) to link client experiences within the sessions to their therapeutic outcome.

Practitioners may use a variety of instruments to gather information on how they are perceived by their group members. Bolman (1971), Lieberman et al. (1973), and Lundgren (1971) have all used leadership measures that reflect a number of general dimensions (e.g., conceptual input, conditionality, openness, caring, activity level). Other investigators have introduced more focused scales: self-disclosure (Dies, Mallet, and Johnson, 1979), helpfulness (Donovan, Bennett, and McElroy, 1979), and amount of influence (Peters, 1973). Use of any of these instruments will provide group psychotherapists with feedback which may be used to correct faulty assumptions about their leadership style. In the absence of regular feedback from one's professional colleagues (co-leaders, observers, or consultants), this format may furnish an effective form of self-supervision. The instruments can be modified to focus the feedback on those areas in which the clinician feels most in need of self-reflection. The accumulation of this information throughout treatment can provide valuable insights into perceptions of the leadership role in relation to the phase of group development. Compilation of the data across a number of groups will strengthen the possibility of generalization, and may in fact produce a highly publishable study. In Chapter 2, I indicate that very few investigators have replicated their measures throughout group treatment; most researchers use a post-group-only design. This simple illustration demonstrates that the gap between research and practice need not be a wide one. Any clinician can gather meaningful empirical data.

Leadership instruments may be adapted to provide rather interesting information. For example, clients may be requested to complete a therapist self-disclosure measure twice, once in terms of how they actually perceive their therapist during the sessions, and again in light of how they would prefer their therapist to interact. This will not only give general information about client satisfaction with the therapist's interventions, but also provide clues as to how particular group members view their therapist's contribution. Thus, leadership measures may be used to enhance understanding of group members. If, for instance, clients are asked to rate their group psychotherapist on a "contribution to group norms questionnaire" (Luke, 1972), inspection of the responses may shed light on which group norms are viewed as the most central, and reveal whether the leader or group membership is regarded as most influential. Some clients may be found to idealize their therapist's contributions whereas others may strongly repudiate the leader's input. Research has demonstrated that clients who show disappointment or significant disapproval of their therapist's style often become either dropouts from the group or therapeutic casualties (Dies and Teleska, in press). Early detection of these negative attitudes on the research measures might serve to decrease the possibility of deleterious treatment effects.

The group members' responses to the leadership instrument may be incorporated into the content of the treatment sessions on a general basis. Without revealing the identity of individual raters, the therapist may lead a discussion on the therapeutic implications of attitudes toward the group leader. Distortions can be clarified, projections interpreted, and realistic evaluations analyzed in light of the clients' needs and stages of group development. Periodically, group members might be requested to report on a critical-incident card their impressions of what is needed for the next session. The information can be particularly revealing of group members' preoccupations, serve to introduce continuity and effective timing across sessions, and augment the clients' sense of control about what happens during treatment.

Finally, I should note that the use of leadership measures may facilitate the clinician's understanding of therapeutic outcome. The various outcome and process measures recommended earlier in this chapter may be examined against the leadership findings. Clients who show significant therapeutic gains may be contrasted with those who show little or no improvement to determine whether or not these clients have divergent perceptions of their leader or the group process. Reviews of the group psychotherapy research literature generally conclude that one of the principal shortcomings in the field is the failure to integrate process (including leadership) and outcome information (Bednar and Kaul, 1978; Dies, 1979). Although the efficacy of group treatment has been clearly established, the field is only on the threshold of identifying the unique process parameters contributing to therapeutic change. Group psychotherapists who begin to collect this more comprehensive information, and particularly those who collaborate with researchers to develop a broader foundation of findings based on a number of treatment groups, can provide a significant service to the field by sharing their results.

The illustrations of how leadership instruments may be employed are endless. It is clear that empirical measures can be used in a highly flexible fashion to furnish feedback to group psychotherapists on their own contributions to the group process, on how clients' needs and experiences within the group sessions may shape their impressions of the leadership role, and on how leaders can modify their interventions to improve the overall quality of their treatment program. Nevertheless, the practical advantages of leadership measures should not overshadow the importance of using instrumentation to reduce the gap between research and practice. As clinicians increasingly recognize the advantages of research tools, it is hoped they will take a more active interest in the empirical literature, and in working with researchers to devise more sophisticated instruments and more refined methods for understanding group treatment.

FURTHER RECOMMENDATIONS

Certainly group psychotherapists can do much to narrow the gap between clinical and empirical modes of understanding. Nevertheless, little will be accomplished unless researchers also modify their stance and begin to explore more vigorously how they can work to reduce the schism within the field.

Kiesler (1981) has suggested that the most effective way to dissolve the scientist-practitioner split is to overhaul our training programs. Similarly, I have offered a number of recommendations for improving the attitudes toward research by building instrumentation into the various phases of group psychotherapy training (Dies, 1980). The didactic portion of group training can be improved by having trainees complete a variety of empirical measures oriented toward group leadership technique (Wile, 1972), personal aspects of leadership (Dies, 1977), or personality attributes relating to one's interactional style (Schutz, 1967). The observational component of training can be enhanced by encouraging trainees to record their perceptions of ongoing groups. Use of the instruments may significantly improve the trainees' learning by sharpening their observational skills and by introducing them to systematic procedures for understanding group process. The experiential component of group psychotherapy training can be improved by having trainees complete measures to evaluate their own group experience. And, finally, instrumentation can be incorporated into the supervisory aspect of training by requiring trainees to build research measures into their groups and then to discuss client perceptions with their training consultants.

Modification of group therapy training models through instrumentation may require researchers to take a more active role in introducing the tools of their trade into therapy training programs. Researchers and clinicians, then, need to coordinate their efforts to design an effective training sequence (Dies, 1982, 1983). This planning may be easier said than done, unless researchers change their own stereotypes about effective research. It has been shown that scientific inquiry is only one alternative to empirical investigation. Researchers who cling dearly to their extreme "capital *R*" perspective may find it difficult to communicate with practitioners who find that the case study and evaluative research approaches are much more congruent with their pragmatic interests.[3] Researchers may have to venture forth, out of their experimental strongholds, and enter the practical world of the clinician. They can no longer write just for their scientific colleagues, but need to spend more time contemplating the clinical implications of their findings (Coché and Dies, 1981). To accomplish this effort toward bridging the gap, researchers must spend more time observing and interacting with clinicians, who in turn must be prepared to invite their empirically minded colleagues to participate in evaluating their treatment interventions. Only with greater collaboration can we make significant strides toward achieving an integrated clinical-empirical approach to group treatment.

Research and practice do not have to exist as dichotomous activities;

---

[3] Recently I administered a questionnaire to 40 researchers, asking them to rank the relative importance of 60 recommendations for improving the quality of group psychotherapy research. Inspection of item content revealed that the most important requirements of sound research related to basic methodology; namely, making sure that raters are well trained, independent, and unbiased; that leaders are experienced; that sufficient treatment is provided to adequately assess therapeutic outcome; and that measures are appropriate. The least important items related to various client-related considerations (e.g., interviewing clients about the impact of experimental interventions, controlling for communication by subjects, reporting on expectancy changes throughout the study, etc.). The forgotten variable in group psychotherapy research seems to be the participant. It appears that researchers and clinicians differ in their concern for the client. The therapist must focus directly on clients and their needs, whereas researchers have traditionally ignored clients and their reactions to research interventions (Dies, 1978).

they can be merged to achieve a harmonious alliance. Similarly, researchers and practitioners do not have to be two different breeds of professionals with totally discrete identities. Effective clinicians in a sense must be clever researchers, and skillful researchers must be sensitive clinicians. The two roles are not inherently incompatible.

REFERENCES

Barlow, D. H. (1981), On the relation of clinical research to clinical practice: Current issues, new directions. *J. Consult. Clin. Psychol.,* 49:147–155.

Bednar, R. L., & Kaul, T. J. (1978), Experiential group research: Current perspectives. In: *Handbook of Psychotherapy and Behavior Change: An Empirical Analysis,* ed. S. L. Garfield & A. E. Bergin. New York: Wiley.

———— ———— (1979), Experiential group research: What never happened! *J. Applied Behav. Sci.,* 15:311–319.

———— & Lawlis, G. F. (1971), Empirical research on group psychotherapy. In: *Handbook of Psychotherapy and Behavior Change,* ed. A. Bergin & S. Garfield. New York: Wiley.

————, Melnick, J., & Kaul, T. J. (1974), Risk, responsibility, and structure: A conceptual framework for initiating group counseling and psychotherapy. *J. Counsel. Psychother.,* 21:31–37.

Bennis, W. G. (1960), A critique of group therapy research. *Int. J. Group Psychother.,* 10:63–77.

Bolman, L. (1971), Some effects of trainers on their T groups. *J. Applied Behav. Sci.,* 7:309–325.

Butler, T., & Fuhriman, A. (in press), Curative factors in group therapy: A review of the recent literature. *Small Group Behav.*

Coché, E., & Dies, R. R. (1981), Integrating research findings into the practice of group psychotherapy. *Psychother.: Theory, Res., Prac.,* 18:410–416.

Derogatis, L. R. (1977), *The SCL-90-R: Administration, Scoring and Procedures Manual I.* Baltimore: Clinical Psychometric Research.

Dies, R. R. (1977), Group leader self disclosure scale. In: *The 1977 Annual Handbook for Group Facilitators,* ed. J. E. Jones & J. W. Pfeiffer. LaJolla, Cal.: University Associates.

———— (1978), The human factor in group psychotherapy research. In: *Group Therapy 1978: An Overview,* ed. L. R. Wolberg, M. L. Aronson, & A. R. Wolberg. New York: Stratton Intercontinental Medical Book Corp.

———— (1979), Group psychotherapy: Reflections on three decades of research. *J. Applied Behav. Sci.,* 15:361–373.

———— (1980), Group psychotherapy training and supervision. In: *Psychotherapy Supervision: Theory, Research, and Practice,* ed. A. K. Hess. New York: Wiley.

———— (1982), Using instrumentation to facilitate group process and to enhance client change. Workshop presented at meeting of Canadian Group Psychotherapy Association, Montreal, October.

———— (1983), Using instruments to facilitate group process and to enhance client change. Workshop presented at meeting of American Group Psychotherapy Association, Toronto, February.

————, Mallet, J., & Johnson, F. (1979), Openness in the coleader relationship: Its effect on process and outcome. *Small Group Behav.,* 10:523–546.

———— & Teleska, P. A. (in press), Negative outcome in group psychotherapy. In: *Above All Do Not Harm: Negative Outcome in Psychotherapy and What to Do about It,* ed.

D. T. Mays & C. M. Franks. New York: Springer.

Donovan, J. M., Bennett, M. J., & McElroy, C. M. (1979), The crisis group—an outcome study. *Amer. J. Psychiat.,* 136:906–910.

Gazda, G. M. (1978), *Group Counseling: A Developmental Approach,* 2nd Ed. Boston: Allyn & Bacon.

Hartman, J. J. (1979), Small group methods of personal change. *Ann. Rev. Psychol.,* 30:453–476.

Hayes, S. C. (1981), Single case experimental design and empirical clinical practice. *J. Consult. Clin. Psychol.,* 49:193–211.

Kazdin, A. E. (1982), *Single-Case Research Designs: Methods for Clinical and Applied Settings.* New York: Oxford University Press.

Kiesler, D. J. (1981), Empirical clinical psychology: Myth or reality? *J. Consult. Clin. Psychol.,* 49:212–215.

Lakin, M. (1972), *Interpersonal Encounter: Theory and Practice in Sensitivity Training.* New York: McGraw-Hill.

Lewis, P., & McCants, J. (1973), Some current issues in group psychotherapy research. *Int. J. Group Psychother.,* 23:268–273.

Lieberman, M. A., Yalom, I. D., & Miles, M. B. (1973), *Encounter Groups: First Facts.* New York: Basic Books.

Luke, R. A. (1972), The internal normative structure of sensitivity training groups. *J. Applied Behav. Sci.,* 8:421–437.

Lundgren, D. C. (1971), Trainer style and patterns of group development. *J. Applied Behav. Sci.,* 7:689–709.

MacKenzie, K. R., & Dies, R. R. (1982), *The CORE Battery: Clinical Outcome Results.* New York: American Group Psychotherapy Association.

Melnick, J., & Woods, M. (1976), Analysis of group composition research and theory for psychotherapeutic and growth-oriented groups. *J. Applied Behav. Sci.,* 12:493–512.

Nelson, R. O. (1981), Realistic dependent measures for clinical use. *J. Consult. Clin. Psychol.,* 49:168–182.

Oetting, E. R. (1976a), Evaluative research and orthodox science: Part I. *Personnel Guidance J.,* 55:11–15.

_____ (1976b), Planning and reporting evaluative research: Part II. *Personnel Guidance J.,* 55:60–64.

Parloff, M. B. (1980), Psychotherapy and research: An anaclitic depression. *Psychiat.,* 43:279–293.

_____ & Dies, R. R. (1977), Group psychotherapy outcome research 1966–1975. *Int. J. Group Psychother.,* 27:281–319.

Peters, D. R. (1973), Identification and personal learning in T-groups. *Human Relations,* 26:1–21.

Pfeiffer, J. W., Heslin, R., and Jones, J. E. (1976), *Instrumentation in Human Relations Training,* 2nd Ed. LaJolla, Cal.: University Associates.

Schutz, W. C. (1967), *The FIRO Scales.* Palo Alto: Consulting Psychologists Press.

Strupp, H. H. (1979), Foreword In: *Group Psychotherapy Research: Commentaries and Selected readings,* ed. H. B. Robach, S. I. Abramowitz, and P. S. Strassberg. Huntington, N.Y.: Robert Kriegel.

_____ & Hadley, S. W. (1977), A tripartite model of mental health and therapy outcomes. *Amer. Psychologist,* 32:187–196.

Weigel, R. G., & Corazzini, J. G. (1978), Small group research: Suggestions for solving common methodological and design problems. *Small Group Behav.,* 9:193–220.

Wile, D. B. (1972), Nonresearch uses of the group leadership questionnaire (GTQ-C). In: *The 1972 Annual Handbook for Group Facilitators,* ed. J. E. Jones & J. W. Pfeiffer. LaJolla, Cal.: University Associates.

Woods, M., & Melnick, J. (1979), A review of group therapy selection criteria. *Small Group Behav.,* 10:155–175.

2

Clinical Implications of Research on Leadership in Short-Term Group Psychotherapy

ROBERT R. DIES, Ph.D.

Far too many practitioners believe that the gap between research and practice in group psychotherapy cannot be bridged. They assume that the preponderance of empirical work on groups is simply irrelevant. Researchers are viewed as a strange breed, preoccupied with rigorous experimental design and methodological control, and thus failing to appreciate the complexities of intensive group interaction. Clinicians see researchers as having so trivialized group process and therapeutic outcome as to render them virtually meaningless. Even the language of the researcher is foreign to practitioners who are not conversant with such jargon as "analysis of covariance," "varimax rotations," and "stepwise discriminant function analyses." Then, too, researchers rarely address clinicians; they seem more interested in communicating with their fellow empiricists. Results are seldom reported in a manner that encourages translation from research to practice. Furthermore, findings are offered piecemeal and are not integrated effectively with previous research or clinical theory so that the literature lacks coherence. No wonder clinicians look askance.

But research *is* relevant to clinical practice! In this chapter, I shall examine the research on leadership in group psychotherapy to show, for instance, that empirical findings *can* be translated to fit the therapeutic setting. My purpose is to provide an outline for a model of short-term group psychotherapy based on clinical research.

My conclusions are founded on a careful review of the empirical literature spanning a decade of research on leadership in a variety of change-oriented groups, including treatment, encounter, and T-group experiences. Integrative reviews published during this ten-year period (1970–1979) and more recent surveys of the research literature on group leadership are also considered. What at first glance may appear to be a simple and relatively straightforward exercise has proved to be a cumbersome and time-consuming process. The wide range of publication outlets and the fact that many empirical findings derive from projects not specifically focused on leadership made it difficult to identify appropriate research. Unfortunately, there is no convenient reference volume such as *Index Medicus* or *Psychological Abstracts* which catalogs the pertinent materials under the heading of group psychotherapy leadership with any degree of thoroughness. Consequently, a few studies may have escaped my attention despite my efforts to conduct an exhaustive review.

Since this chapter is written for the practitioner rather than the researcher, an extensive critique of the research literature is not offered. Critical reviews of the various conceptual, methodological, and design inadequacies characterizing the group literature appear quite regularly (e.g., Bednar and Kaul, 1978; Diamond and Shapiro, 1975; Dies, 1978; Parloff and Dies, 1978). My focus is more practical or applied. However, before we examine the research on group leadership, we should place this body of literature in proper perspective.

EMPIRICAL FOUNDATION

In a recent review of research trends in group psychotherapy (Dies, 1979) I reported that nearly 20% of the 400 to 500 articles published in the group literature each year are empirical studies. Over the years confidence has been growing in the efficacy of group treatment, due in part to an increment in research sophistication and an accumulation of supportive results. Nevertheless, we are still largely naive about many of the specific mechanisms of change. We know that group treatments represent potentially powerful and unique sources of learning, but we are hard-pressed to particularize the processes and leadership interventions that contribute to therapeutic outcome. The principal goal of the present review is to identify salient results and coherent themes among the diverse studies of leadership and to suggest therapist styles or behaviors that might account for therapeutic progress as well as therapeutic deterioration.

Nature of the Studies

I have identified 95 separate investigations published during the 1970s. Most of these studies were based on short-term groups; nearly all examined treatments lasting 30 sessions or less. It is thus immediately apparent that any conclusions derived from this review must be considered as mainly applicable to short-term group treatment.*

A variety of patient populations are represented in the research, although nearly two-thirds (64.3%) of the studies use nonpatient samples or participants in various encounter, personal growth, or T-group experiences. Most reviewers of the group treatment literature integrate the findings from these varying group experiences in their attempts to understand therapeutic process and outcome (Bednar and Kaul, 1978; Dies, 1979; Lieberman, 1976). Lieberman, (1975) has pointed out that the goals of these various group experiences, and even the individuals who participate in the groups, are highly similar. Indeed, he found substantial overlap among the members in his comparison of therapy and encounter group formats. Most surveys, including the present one, exclude results based on task-oriented groups and other group situations in which the goal is not specifically personal change through intensive group interaction. A final stipulation for inclusion in this current review is that studies had to have clear implications for the therapist's behavior; in some cases, it was necessary to eliminate studies contrasting two types of group structure when the findings did not have distinct implications for leadership.

Instrumentation

A wide latitude of measures has been used to assess leadership effects. These measures can be grouped into three general perspectives: (1) leader self-reports, (2) ratings from group members, and (3) judgments from independent raters who either observed the group process or evaluated transcripts or recordings of treatment sessions. A compilation of instruments used to evaluate leadership has never been published, so

---

Editors' Note: A word of caution is in order regarding the leadership literature reported in this chapter. Much of it is based on quite brief groups and the techniques are not necessarily applicable in quite the same manner in all group settings. Dies limits his findings to "short-term" group psychotherapy, but this is an ambiguous phrase covering everything from six-session assertiveness training programs to dynamically oriented therapy of 30 or 40 sessions. For example, Dies suggests later that "advice" is a useful therapist behavior. This would not be surprising if resolution of specific current problems is the objective, but may be questionable if introspection to induce characterological change is expected.

it has been difficult for clinicians to find instruments that might be of value in their clinical practice, and virtually impossible for researchers to become aware of the range of techniques available. For this reason, tables summarizing the various instruments used in the 95 published reports are contained at the end of this chapter (pp. 64–72). The measures are divided into the three perspectives on leadership: self-report (Table 1), client ratings (Table 2), and observer ratings (Table 3). Within each table the measures are further separated into those addressing personal aspects of leadership (e.g., relationship variables, self-disclosure, positive or negative feelings between the therapist and group members), those highlighting therapeutic technique (e.g., structure, reinforcement, cognitive input), and finally those covering both personal and technical aspects of leadership.

The most popular approach to understanding leadership is through ratings furnished by group members (46.3% of the studies), followed by observer ratings (41.1%), and then by therapist self-reports (27.4%). A majority of the studies (72.8%) utilized only one perspective to assess leadership, while 19.8% used two perspectives (usually self-reports and client ratings), and 7.4% employed all three perspectives. Fourteen of the studies covered in this review did not incorporate formal measures of leadership, but merely looked at the effects of contrasting therapist styles on group process or outcome.

The self-report measures summarized in Table 1 range from a focus on general personality variables (e.g., 3, 5, 8, 14), interpersonal or interactional style expressed before group involvement (e.g., 16, 17, 28, 29), to reports on actual behavior within the group setting (e.g., 13, 22, 25, 26). The latter instruments have proved the most popular and indeed most germane to our knowledge of leadership effects, although measures administered before the group, focused on behaviors central to group interaction, have also been of some merit. The general personality and attitude scales, however, have not shed much light on the clinical implications of leadership.

The client and observer rating systems summarized in Tables 2 and 3 also range in their focus. Many of the techniques represent a single dimension of leadership whereas others portray multiple dimensions, and some of the measures are more behaviorally-oriented while others are more inferential. The more popular approaches appear to be multidimensional and impressionistic. Thus, the Hill Interaction Matrix (Table 3: 23), the Relationship Inventory (Table 2: 20), and the bipolar-adjective approach (Table 2: 4) have received the most attention. Unidimensional and behaviorally-anchored methods (e.g., Table 2: 7, 11; Table 3: 20, 31) have not been as common, but they have yielded results bearing substantially on our understanding of leadership.

Methodological Note

An issue of utmost importance that has been continually ignored by investigators in this field concerns the proper framework for judging therapeutic interventions. With Mallet and Johnson, I have shown, for example, that the impressions of a group leader's behavior will vary dramatically as a function of the method of assessment (Dies, Mallet, and Johnson, 1979). In our study of therapist self-disclosure, we found that ratings on a simple seven-point scale gave the impression that the group therapists were all quite open and revealing because group members consistently placed them on the "highly self-disclosing" end of the continuum. Yet when these same group members were asked to rank-order their therapists compared with co-members, many of the leaders were characterized as among the least disclosing of the participants. Moreover, when group members were requested to furnish examples of the most self-disclosing comments offered by their therapists, it was evident that many of these leaders were indeed quite nondisclosing. Thus, the three perspectives on group therapist openness — ratings, rankings, and examples (Table 2: 11, 12, 13) — gave completely different impressions of the relative and absolute levels of therapist behavior.

In using measures of leader behavior, therefore, practitioners and researchers alike must be mindful of this problem and establish an appropriate reference point for judging therapeutic interventions. Ideally, there should be standardized scores based on normative data gathered from a large sample of practicing group psychotherapists. Given the lack of replication and the small-scale nature of the research in this area, this goal remains a pure fantasy. Hence, clinicians and researchers must consider other standards for evaluating leadership. Every effort should be made to avoid "floating reference points," such as simple impressionistic scales that are not anchored in behavioral terms or methods that do not demonstrate adequate interrater reliability. It is always possible to use within-group comparisons of leader behavior and ask group members to rank-order their leader in reference to fellow group members on such dimensions as activity level, self-disclosure, supportiveness, and confrontation. Multidimensional scales may also be used with leaders serving as their own controls. In this case, the question becomes one of judging the relative incidence of a variety of leadership behaviors.

The extensive list of instruments in the tables in this chapter furnishes an overview of what has been accomplished. It is hoped the tables will be of value to clinicians who wish to explore the possibility of using instruments in their own clinical practice, and to investigators who are contemplating leadership research. These tables will be referred to throughout the subsequent generalizations about leadership. The discussion is divided into personal and technical aspects of leadership, with only the most salient findings highlighted. Thus, only those areas are reviewed in which there appears to be some consensus across a number of studies, a range of assessment strategies, and diverse perspectives on leadership.

PERSONAL DIMENSIONS OF LEADERSHIP

This section on the personal aspects of leadership covers three general categories, although there is inevitably some overlap among them: (1) relationship variables such as genuineness, empathy, and warmth; (2) other personal qualities related to the favorableness of the therapist-client relationship (e.g., affection, discomfort, identification); and (3) therapist self-disclosure. Under each category, I have highlighted instruments used to investigate leadership, summarized relevant research, and suggested guidelines for clinical practice.

Relationship Variables

Seventeen studies bear directly on the importance of relationship variables. A variety of self-report (Table 1: 2, 17, 20), client rating (Table 2: 19, 20, 21, 25, 28, 47, 48), and observer rating (Table 3: 1, 3, 12, 36) methods have been employed across a wide spectrum of treatment settings. The preferred method of assessing the quality of relationship variables has been through ratings provided by group members. A variety of relationship scales have been devised which differ in length, but generally incorporate the dimensions of genuineness, empathy, and warmth. The scales are quite adaptable to clinical practice, even for the busiest of practitioners who wish to evaluate this facet of their leadership style and perhaps also the quality of relationship established among group members. Although leader and observer rating procedures have been explored, they fail to tap the crucial aspect of the relationship — the patient's perception of the therapist's interpersonal skills.

The results of the various studies generally demonstrate that *the qual-*

ity of the therapist-client relationship is important for group process and therapeutic outcome (e.g., Bolman, 1971; Cooper, 1977; Danish, 1971). In a recent review of this literature, however, Gurman and Gustafson (1976) indicate that leader genuineness, empathy, and warmth represent only a part of the necessary attributes of the successful group leader. Although these characteristics may be essential for effective group treatment in many settings, the research contradicts the Rogerian assumption that they are "sufficient" (cf. Rogers, 1957). Undoubtedly, many of the group psychotherapists who served in the research projects reported in this review were performing at least at moderate levels of interpersonal functioning. The failure to find differential effects in some studies may thus be due to the fact that therapists were meeting minimum standards on these important attributes and that other treatment variables were therefore more important. A number of investigators (e.g., C. V. Abramowitz, Abramowitz, Roback, and Jackson, 1974; DiLoreto, 1971; Jessell and Bush, 1973) have shown that client ratings of relationship variables are not different across dissimilar types of group structure, even though therapeutic outcome is influenced by the variations in group format. Thus, relationship variables and other aspects of therapist style may be independent. An active, structured approach to group leadership may not differ from a less active, nonstructured approach in terms of the levels of leader empathy, warmth, and genuineness experienced by group members.

The research findings suggest a number of reasonably clear conclusions about relationship variables. Gurman and Gustafson (1976) conclude that the consistent link between relationship variables and therapeutic outcome in individual treatment does not receive the same level of support in group treatment. They offer several possible interpretations of this diminished effect. First, the therapeutic technique may systematically deemphasize the role of the leader and accentuate the relationships among group members. Frankiel (1971), for example, found that the number of mutually therapeutic relationships established among co-members related significantly to group outcome. Along these lines, several writers have attempted to show that the relative influence of the group therapist has been exaggerated. Lundgren (1977) reports that over 90% of the discussion within his groups centered on the members or intermember interaction, while less than 10% concerned the leader or leader-member interaction. Luke (1972) instructed group members to rate the degree to which each participant and the leader influenced the development and maintenance of group norms, while P. B. Smith (1976) had members evaluate the major sources of influence on their own learn-ing within the group. Both authors found that co-members were credited with the major proportion of the influence. Donovan, Bennett, and McElroy (1979) asked members of outpatient, crisis-oriented groups to indicate several reasons their group had been beneficial. Their reasons fell into the following categories: 47% group support; 44% knowledge that others had similar problems; 42% opportunity to ventilate feelings; 19% insight; with only 7% mentioning that the therapist was helpful. The authors indicate: "At 1-year follow-up 42% felt that the group mem-bers and not the therapist had been helpful, and 28% responded that both had been of aid. Only 5% stated that the therapist alone was a major contributor to change" (p. 908).

Compared with other individuals within the group, the leader is typically perceived as the most influential, but there is consensus that group composition is at least as powerful, and probably more so (Lieber-man, Yalom, and Miles, 1973; Smith, 1976). Lundgren (1979) concludes that leaders play a significant role in facilitating an open and supportive atmosphere within the group, but that it is the interaction among group members that is the most direct mechanism of change in the therapeutic process. A recent review of the literature on curative factors in group psychotherapy (Butler and Fuhriman, in press) shows that five factors are regarded as central to therapeutic change for most clients: interper-sonal input (feedback), catharsis, group cohesiveness, self-understand-ing, and interpersonal output (socializing skills). These factors highlight interpersonal processes unique to group treatments which do not neces-sarily involve direct client-therapist relationships. According to Yalom (1975), "to a very large extent, *it is the group which is the agent of change*. This makes for a crucial difference in the basic role of the individual therapist and the group therapist. In the individual format the therapist functions as the solely designated direct agent of change; in the group therapeutic format he functions far more indirectly" (p. 107).

In the second reason Gurman and Gustafson (1976) offer to account for the reduced effect of the therapist-client relationship, they state that even though therapists may intend to emphasize their relationship with group members, participants may choose to deemphasize the leader. Several studies note that members vary in their perceptions of leadership along relationship dimensions as a function of their own personal styles. The work of Abramowitz et al. (1974), who explored psychological-mindedness; Freedman and Hurley (1979), who looked at self-accep-tance; Lundgren (1971, 1973), who evaluated member status within the group; and Seldman, McBrearty, and Seldman (1974), who examined members' dependency, demonstrates that the centrality of the leader is related to the client's own needs or position within the group.

Closely related to this point is Gurman and Gustafson's third suggestion, that certain patients require more from the group therapist (and group members) than a warm, genuine, and empathic relationship. To illustrate, studies conducted by Truax (e.g., 1971b; Truax, Wargo, and Volksdorf, 1970) show clear differences related to the patient's level of psychopathology. Whereas relationship variables correlated with outcome in an outpatient setting, there was no association with an inpatient schizophrenic group. Results from several studies demonstrate that *as the patient population becomes more psychologically impaired, relationship variables are less likely to be "sufficient" as moderators of therapeutic outcome. Thus, with more disturbed patients technical aspects of leadership (e.g., active structuring) assume greater saliency* (Roback and Strassberg, 1975; Vitalo, 1971).

Clearly, the therapist's interpersonal skills, genuineness, empathy, and warmth, are important for effective group treatment. Nevertheless, there is no guarantee that group psychotherapists with these attributes will be successful. The quality of relationships established among group members is more fundamental to therapeutic change. It is therefore incumbent on group leaders to devote considerable attention to cultivating helpful interpersonal norms. For many patients, especially those with deficient interpersonal skills, more active interventions by the group leader are essential to foster the kind of group climate necessary for therapeutic growth. I shall have more to say about the nature of these interventions in subsequent sections.

Favorableness of the Relationship

A number of investigators have been concerned with aspects of the therapist-client interaction not covered under the rubric of traditional relationship variables. A total of 17 studies, using 45 different measures, evaluate such variables as therapist's liking of group members, client's experience of tension in relation to the group leader, identification with the therapist, intensity of confrontation, and valence of the interactions between the therapist and group members. An inspection of the numerous measures listed in the tables in this chapter might lead one to conclude that researchers have been competing to see how many different ways they can ask the same question, i.e., "How well do the client and therapist like each other?" Undoubtedly, the client's perception of the favorableness of the relationship is important to consider. Practitioners and researchers who wish to evaluate this aspect of the client-therapist relationship have the option of using measures that have been refined statistically (e.g., Table 2: 16) or approaches that are more adaptable to one's own group therapy situation. For example, group psychotherapists can easily administer a set of bipolar adjectives (Table 2: 36) at the end of their session and ask group members to evaluate virtually any aspect of leadership, e.g., friendly-unfriendly, trusting-distrusting, and helpful-nonhelpful (Dies, 1973b). One should, however, be mindful of the caveat offered earlier about "floating reference points" in assessing leadership.

Although a review of the findings based on the scattered self-report, client rating, and observer-based evaluations seems a little like comparing the proverbial "apples and oranges," reasonable coherence can be introduced by organizing the results along a positive to negative continuum. The study that best represents both extremes on that continuum is the landmark investigation of leadership styles conducted by Lieberman et al. (1973). Through a variety of comparatively intricate instruments and careful methodological controls, these authors demonstrated that leadership style was systematically linked to therapeutic outcome, i.e., certain types of leadership behaviors were clearly associated with therapeutic gain while other behaviors were implicated in therapeutic decline.

Using this study as a starting point, it is possible to evaluate the clinical implications of leadership behaviors along a valence continuum. On the positive end of the scale, Lieberman and his colleagues found that high levels of leader caring were essential for therapeutic improvement. On the basis of their findings, they concluded that group leaders should attempt to maximize the levels of acceptance, encouragement, and concern they express to their group members. Obviously, these generalizations are quite compatible with the relationship findings outlined in the previous section.

A wide range of findings from other studies corroborate the basic conclusion that *a positive relationship between the therapist and group members plays a significant role in the development of constructive group norms and in facilitating therapeutic change.* Babad and Amir (1978) and Babad and Melnick (1976), for instance, established a correlation between therapist liking of group members and the leader's reinforcement of active, positive member roles. Participants who experienced greater positive feelings from their leaders reported more therapeutic benefit. Similarly, Bolman (1971, 1973) found that leader affection was related to members' fondness of the group leader and that identification contributed to learning. Peters (1973) demonstrated that as group members came to construe their self-concepts as closer to their perceptions of the group leader, they valued their subsequent learning more. Hurley and Rosenthal (1978a, 1978b) showed that therapists who were viewed by group members as high on self-acceptance and acceptance of others were more likely to produce favorable change. Rosenzweig and Folman (1974) linked positive therapist feelings about clients to the likelihood that clients would remain in treatment. In terms of group process, Harrow, Astrachan, Tucker, Klein, and Miller (1971) discovered that ratings of group leaders influenced the evaluations of other group members, while Hurst, Stein, Korchin, and Soskin (1978) established that leader caring and levels of group cohesiveness were correlated. Finally, Flowers (1978; Flowers and Booraem, 1976) documented a strong correspondence between the frequency of positive therapist interventions and similar interactions among group members.

Overall, then, there is substantial support for the importance of a positive therapist-client relationship. The findings of Lieberman and his colleagues (1973) suggest that as the therapist-client relationship becomes less favorable, the amount of group tension increases and the potential for therapeutic gain diminishes. In fact, as the relationship becomes more and more negative, the likelihood of deleterious group outcomes increases. Lieberman et al. found that leaders with an "impersonal" or "laissez-faire" style did not produce many constructive outcomes and had a slightly better chance of precipitating adverse reactions to the group experience. Several studies have contrasted leaders who attempt to remain relatively aloof or distant in their interactions with group members to those who are oriented toward more open and positive relationships. In investigating the differences in perceptions of T-group leaders versus Tavistock study group leaders, Harrow et al. (1971) noted that the former were viewed as less distant and more satisfying, pleasant, and friendly, whereas the latter were depicted as rigid, authoritarian, unemotional, and guarded. Similarly, T. L. Morrison and Thomas (1976) found that leaders of communications groups were much more favorably evaluated than leaders of the Tavistock study group. Lundgren (1971, 1973) reported that an inactive leadership role produced a high degree of covert strain between participants and group leaders. The members felt that the leader had been aloof, unclear, and neither supportive nor accepting, and that sessions were disorganized and confusing.

Bolman (1971, 1973) showed that leaders who were perceived as more judgmental produced greater discomfort for individual group members and more overall group tension. Similarly, Flowers (1978; Flowers and

Booraem, 1976) discovered that as higher-intensity negative statements by therapists increased, members became less satisfied with group sessions. Group members were more inclined to imitate their therapists' positive statements than their negative remarks. Interestingly, Flowers and Booraem found that the correlation between the average number of negative statements given by the therapist and the average number of positive statements received by the therapist from group members was inversely associated. The authors concluded that group members did not reward punitive group leaders.

Clearly, group members experience greater tension and feel more negative toward leaders who are viewed as aloof, distant, and judgmental. These leadership styles can certainly stimulate confrontations around issues of authority and may perhaps even facilitate the working through of problems in this area. However, a critical question is the potential risk of these more "negatively oriented" leadership styles in short-term group treatment. So far we can see that there is increased tension within the group and more dissatisfaction with the leader. But Morrison and Thomas (1976) also indicate that the unpleasant learning environment generated by such leadership styles may cause group members to experience a loss of self-esteem. Cooper (1977) demonstrated that closed-incongruent and introverted-withdrawn leaders most often contributed to clients' negative group outcomes. Other research findings indicate that as therapists become more extreme in their negative orientation to group leadership, the risks of harmful group effects escalates. Lieberman et al. (1973) found that group members who were damaged by their group experience cited "attack" or rejection by the group leader (or group members) as a principal factor in the negative outcome. These individuals regarded their leaders as intrusive, overly challenging, and as making severe demands on group members. Other contratherapeutic group outcomes were attributed to aloof, distant, and nonsupportive leaders, who seemed blatantly unaware of the potential impact of hostile exchanges among group members. Moreover, Lieberman et al. reported that many of their group dropouts cited concern about attack, anger, or rejection from their co-members or leader. Reviews of the negative outcome literature in group psychotherapy consistently cite forcefully confronting therapists as the highest-risk type of leadership style (Dies and Teleska, in press; Hartley, Roback and Abramowitz, 1976).

It is not possible to debate the relative merits of different theoretical approaches to group leadership in this chapter. Understandably, some degree of confrontation and tension-inducing challenge by the group leader is essential for client change (Frankiel, 1971; Lieberman et al., 1973). Smith (1976) has shown, for example, that group members evaluated their leaders as more influential when they experienced some tension in their interactions with them. Truax (1971a) even found that with juvenile delinquents the degree of "negative transference" with the therapist may relate to positive therapeutic outcome. Yalom (1975) has stated: "There will be times when the therapist challenges the patient, shows anger and frustration, suggests that if the patient is not going to work he consider leaving the group. But these efforts (which in the right circumstances may have therapeutic clout) are never effective unless they are experienced against a horizon of an accepting, concernful therapist-patient relationship" (pp. 105–106). Melnick and Woods (1976) have proposed a model of group composition which is highly compatible with these observations. They argue for a support-plus-confrontation model, i.e., "moderate diversity in group composition, recognizing that if either support or confrontation dominates the group culture, learning will not be facilitated. Too much ease or comfort in the group engenders complacency, while low cohesiveness coupled with high conflict engenders physical or psychological termination" (p. 507).

The clearest generalization to be made from the accumulated research findings is that *group members favor and seem to benefit more from a positive style of intervention, and that as leaders become more actively negative, they increase the probability that participants will not only be dissatisfied but also potentially harmed by the group experience.* Group leaders should convey an active and positive involvement in their group process, and intervene to moderate the intensity of confrontative exchanges among group members. Thus, group therapists should not tacitly sanction counterproductive norms by remaining aloof and detached in their therapeutic style. Nor should they engage in highly challenging interventions in their relationships with group members, especially in the absence of a solid foundation of interpersonal trust within the group. Since it takes time to establish a supportive group atmosphere, confrontative therapist-client and client-client interactions should be limited until later in the group's development. There will be more to say on this issue as we lay the empirical groundwork for a model of short-term group leadership.

Therapist Self-Disclosure

The question of whether or not there is a relationship between therapist self-disclosure and therapeutic outcome cannot be answered simply.

The findings from the 13 studies covered in this review indicate that the issue is quite complex. A variety of self-report (Table 1: 11), client rating (Table 2: 7, 8, 11, 12, 13, 23, 43, 47), and observer rating (Table 3: 7, 10, 30) systems have been devised, and the diversity of these measures indicates that self-disclosure is multidimensional. Practitioners and researchers who wish to explore the implications of therapists' behavior in this area are well advised to go beyond simple rating schemes and to adopt more multifaceted scaling procedures (e.g., Dies et al., 1979; Moss and Harren, 1978).

In a recent review of this body of literature (Dies, 1977a), I concluded that the various dimensions of self-disclosure (valence, focus, depth, breadth, and frequency) and the numerous qualifiers of content (such as credibility, perceived intent, timing, and context) have not been sufficiently explored through empirical work. The research literature on therapist self-disclosure is inconclusive in demonstrating uniform effects of "transparency." Some investigators offer positive conclusions (e.g., Dies et al., 1979; Hurley and Force, 1973), others report that therapist self-disclosure is unimportant (e.g., Bolman, 1971, 1973), while still others find that self-disclosure may even be detrimental (e.g., Lieberman et al., 1973). In the final analysis perhaps all of these researchers are correct; the effect of therapist self-disclosure depends more precisely on such variables as the type of group, stage of group development, and the content of the disclosure itself.

I have already proposed that the nature of the group experience and the participants' expectations regarding its purpose represent important situational modifiers which affect the perceived appropriateness of transparency by a group leader (Dies, 1977a). T-group and encounter group members, for example, are more inclined to view themselves as normal people attempting to function more effectively than as distressed individuals seeking symptomatic relief. Accordingly, the leader is viewed more as a leader-member interested in mutual exploration and growth than as a leader-therapist whose goal is client change. Thus, self-disclosure by the encounter group leader would be experienced as role-consistent whereas transparency on the part of the group psychotherapist would be experienced as role-incongruent. Research has shown that encounter group participants are indeed more favorable toward leader openness than members of treatment groups (Dies and Cohen, 1976), and that experienced group practitioners hold parallel attitudes toward the appropriateness of leader self-disclosure in the different group settings (Dies, 1973a). Weigel, Dinges, Dyer, and Straumfjord (1972) found that self-disclosure by the therapist may "evoke negative evaluations of his mental health or even lead some clients to feel that he is guilty of unprofessional conduct by not being 'cooly professional'" (p. 51). Similarly, I found that although self-revealing therapists were judged more positively along several likeability dimensions, they were also viewed as less relaxed, less stable, and less sensitive (Dies, 1973b). In contrast, May and Thompson (1973) discovered positive relationships among ratings of leader self-disclosure, mental health, and helpfulness. These authors, however, were studying encounter group participants, so they testified that leader self-disclosure is more suitable in that context than in the treatment setting. Although it is not possible at this point to offer a firm conclusion about the relationship between therapist self-disclosure and type of group, it appears that *as the client population becomes more psychologically impaired, group therapist self-disclosure becomes increasingly less appropriate.* This generalization is compatible with the aforementioned conclusion correlating relationship variables and client psychopathology.

A few studies have suggested a relationship between therapist self-disclosure and phase of group development. For instance, I have demonstrated that client perceptions of therapist openness may vary as a function of length of time in treatment (Dies, 1973b). Counseling center clients who had been in group therapy for a greater number of sessions expressed a preference for leader transparency while inexperienced clients favored a less disclosing leadership style. In another study group therapists' self-disclosures were evaluated as increasingly more helpful as the group matured (Dies and Cohen, 1976). Disclosures judged as harmful in early phases of the group were later viewed not only as appropriate but also quite facilitative. For example, early in treatment group members objected to therapists who shared such information as "feelings they have trouble expressing," "aspects of their personality they dislike," and "what it takes to make them anxious." Later, however, these same disclosures were seen as desirable. In my opinion (Dies, 1973b) it seems reasonable to assume that *most clients will expect the group therapist to convey a certain amount of competence and confidence and to provide some initial structuring of the treatment situation, and that clients will neither anticipate nor desire the therapist to be too revealing of her or his own feelings, experiences, or conflicts early in therapy.* *

* *Editors' Note:* This chapter has much in common with later ones in this monograph which deal with such group level concepts as developmental stages, social roles, normative expectations, and change mechanisms. Indeed, a number of findings from the leadership literature take on added meaning in light of these ideas. For example, devel-

In one of the few investigations of the content of therapist self-disclosure, Cohen and I found considerable consensus among group members (Dies and Cohen, 1976). Content analyses showed that group members preferred therapists who were confident in their leadership abilities and in their own emotional stability and who were willing to share positive strivings (personal and professional goals) and normal emotional experiences (e.g., loneliness, sadness, anxiety). In contrast, group members expressed reservations about the appropriateness of therapists' confronting individual members with such negative feelings as distrust, anger, and disdain, and criticizing the group experience by admitting feelings of frustration, boredom, or isolation. These findings are consistent with the range of results outlined above, under the heading of "Favorableness of the Relationship," in particular the findings from the Lieberman et al. (1973) study showing that one of the principal reasons people drop out of groups is their fear of attack or confrontation by the group leader. The most harmful leaders in this study were described as extremely revealing of their feelings, not only in terms of challenging group members through personal confrontation, but also through an emphasis on "intrusive modeling, and use of self" (p. 237). Similarly, it was found that group leaders who were very open, but who modeled conflict and disagreement within the co-therapy relationship, produced unfavorable group outcomes, in contrast to open co-leaders who shared more positive attitudes toward each other (Dies et al., 1979).

Thus, self-disclosure by the group therapist may have either a constructive or a detrimental effect on group process and outcome as a function of such factors as type of group, phase of group development, and content of the disclosure. Therapists who are willing to be open with their group members are more likely to facilitate the development of the positive interpersonal relationships emphasized in the two preceding sections. Self-disclosure is only one of many possible interventions available to the group leader, however, and like most other interventions, its effectiveness will undoubtedly depend on the extent to which it is systematically integrated into a more comprehensive model of group leadership. Therapist transparency can encourage corresponding behavior among group members, yet we also know that even without sharing feelings and experiences, therapists can generate self-revelation within the group. For example, therapists can reinforce personal expression among

opmental stage concepts give greater coherence to data suggesting that the therapist should not be overly self-disclosing in a new group and that confrontation is destructive without an established positive atmosphere for support.

group members, and rely on other participants to serve as role models for interpersonal openness (Dies, 1977a). These techniques will receive further consideration in subsequent sections of this chapter.

Throughout the present review of personal aspects of leadership, it has been implicit that the influence of a group therapist's personal style is moderated by more technical aspects of the therapist role. Reddy and Lippert (1980), for instance, have proposed that the group therapist's levels of affection and activity interact to produce different outcomes. Affectionate, active therapists presumably produce strong positive change; affectionate, inactive therapists generate mild positive change; unaffectionate, inactive leaders, mild negative change; and unaffectionate, active leaders, strong negative change. It is time to turn our attention to some of the more technical aspects of leadership to see if, in fact, they do interact with the group therapist's personal qualities.

TECHNICAL DIMENSIONS OF LEADERSHIP

This section on the technical aspects of leadership covers three general categories: (1) structured versus nonstructured groups, (2) cognitive input by the group leader, and (3) therapist reinforcement and modeling. These areas have received considerable attention in the literature, and there is a growing consensus supporting certain generalizations about their contribution to group outcome. In choosing to focus on these three topics, however, I have eliminated many studies which address a range of variations bearing importantly on the issue of therapeutic structure. In a prior review of research on group psychotherapy leadership (Dies, 1977a), I noted that a variety of verbal and nonverbal techniques have been investigated, but that the evidence on any one of these methods is inconclusive, in spite of the fact that a majority of the studies underscore the potentially influential role of leadership in groups.

Structured versus Nonstructured Groups

A majority of the 20 studies in this area have not incorporated formal measures of leadership into their research designs (e.g., Berlin and Dies, 1974; Levin and Kurtz, 1974; J. K. Morrison, Libow, Smith, and Becker, 1978; W. Wright, Morris, and Felting, 1974). Instead, investigators have simply varied the degree of structure introduced into their group treatments and then evaluated the impact of this variation on group process and/or outcome. Only a few researchers have actually verified the efficacy of their experimental manipulation of leadership style, despite the obvious importance of this methodological safeguard (e.g., Abramowitz et al., 1974; Kinder and Kilmann, 1976). When studies have employed instruments to assess technical aspects of leadership relevant to the issue of structure/nonstructure, they have relied primarily on client ratings (Table 2: 32, 45) and observer ratings (Table 3: 15, 18, 32, 39). Investigators have rarely defined exactly what they mean by structured and nonstructured treatments. Clearly, structure can be introduced through a variety of approaches, including role-play, process commentary, questioning, reflection, interpretation, and so forth. For the most part, the studies covered in this section evaluate varying amounts of therapist directiveness or structure in a global sense, i.e., without furnishing detailed accounts of the types of structure used to guide the group process. Nevertheless, these studies are sufficiently similar to be grouped within the same general category.

Research projects comparing structured and nonstructured groups have been conducted within a broad spectrum of clinical settings, although 60% of the studies used nonpatient groups, ranging from undergraduates participating in encounter or growth group experiences (e.g., Barrilleaux and Bauer, 1976; Jessell and Bush, 1973; Kilmann and Sotile, 1976), to graduate students enrolled in a group counseling practicum (Levin and Kurtz, 1974), to participants in T-group training laboratories (Luke, 1972; Lundgren, 1971, 1973). The results of these diverse investigations with nonpatient populations fail to reveal any clear-cut superiority of either structured or nonstructured group procedures.

When we turn to the studies using patient populations, however, the various findings converge to reveal definite advantages to structured treatments, particularly with more psychologically impaired inpatient groups. Goldstein (1971), for example, introduced a psychodrama technique called "doubling" to elicit verbal behavior from severely withdrawn schizophrenics. She found that this method for increasing group structure was highly successful in improving the patients' level of participation during the group sessions. Gruen (1977) established that leader control in treatment promoted therapeutic movement and working through. He comments: "low visibility of the leader, long exchanges between patients without any intervention from him, and general absence of focusing, interpreting, or summarizing remarks, slows down the group movement," and "anxiety builds up when issues or forces are not examined by the leader from time to time" (p. 149). On the other hand, Jensen and McGrew (1974) found that their schizophrenic patients experienced more anxiety in structured group sessions than in sessions with nondirective leaders. The increased anxiety was attributed to the therapists instructing patients to interact more actively during treatment. The authors observed that members of the nonstructured groups were more inclined to act out (e.g., withdraw from verbal participation, insist on leaving the group situation, hallucinate) and to use more defenses against anxiety than members of the structured groups.

The investigators in these three inpatient studies conclude that structured groups are unquestionably superior for patients with more severe psychopathology. This generalization receives further substantiation from a review of the literature on leaderless groups by Desmond and Seligman (1977). In surveying 28 studies, they found that 18 of these projects reported positive results for leaderless groups. However, a majority of these investigations used college students as subjects. Most of the studies that failed to affirm the efficacy of leaderless groups were conducted with institutionalized patients; Desmond and Seligman therefore argued against the use of leaderless and nonstructured group approaches with patients whose problems were serious enough to warrant hospitalization. Again, the conclusion offered in the "Relationship Variables" section of this chapter has considerable merit: with more disturbed patients, the technical aspects of leadership (e.g., active structuring) assume greater salience over factors such as the quality of the therapist-client relationship.

Additional studies with inpatient groups have demonstrated that the potential value of structure depends on the nature of the intervention. Thus, Anderson, Harrow, Schwartz, and Kupfer (1972) and Schwartz, Harrow, Anderson, Feinstein, and Schwartz (1970) failed to corroborate the correlation between therapist activity and directiveness and group members' satisfaction with treatment. Only when the patients felt that task-oriented or therapeutic events had occurred did they report satisfaction with the sessions. Similarly, Wogan, Getter, Amdur, Nichols, and Okman (1977) concluded from their study of counseling center groups that "it is not leader activity per se which is effective in promoting fruitful group interaction. Once the leader's activity has reached a certain minimum level, the content of his interventions probably becomes increasingly more important in influencing the course of group discussion than the mere fact that he is intervening" (p. 44). With Teleska, I have concluded from a review of negative outcomes in group psychotherapy that high therapist activity, in and of itself, is neither helpful nor harmful: *the type of structure or therapist activity that seems to be most beneficial in the group set-*

ting is that which adds meaning and significance to the group therapeutic enterprise (Dies and Teleska, in press). For example, Lieberman and his colleagues (1973) found that structure offered by leaders in terms of "meaning attribution" (providing concepts for how to understand a person's behavior or events within the group) was highly conducive to positive group outcome. On the other hand, structure in terms of the "executive function" (setting limits, suggesting rules, managing time) was curvilinearly related to outcome; either too much or too little structure was counterproductive. Both inactive, laissez-faire leaders and overactive, "movie director" types were far less effective than leaders who assumed a more moderate stance.

Kinder and Kilmann (1976) have documented the importance of sequencing structure. Their findings reveal that groups are more productive when they begin with a structured format and then shift to a relatively unstructured approach. Leadership that reverses this sequence, and groups following only structured or nonstructured approaches, are not as effective. Similarly, Bednar, Melnick, and Kaul (1974) present a developmental model for initiating group psychotherapy, based on their review of the literature. They argue that "lack of structure in early sessions not only fails to facilitate early group development but actually feeds client distortions, interpersonal fears, and subjective distress, which interferes with group development and contributes to premature client dropouts" (p. 31). Conversely, *when therapeutic goals are clear, appropriate client behaviors are identified, and the therapeutic process is structured to provide a framework for change, clients tend to engage in therapeutic work more quickly.* I have elsewhere (Dies, 1977b) generalized from a survey that leadership behaviors which are important at one stage of group development may not be suitable at another: "whereas a leader-centered approach may be more efficacious early in a group's development, a group-centered style seems most appropriate during later phases" (p. 235). A large number of empirical findings corroborate these conclusions about structure as it relates to group development (e.g., DiLoreto, 1971; Lundgren, 1971, 1973, 1977; Lundgren and Knight, 1978; Lundgren and Schaeffer, 1976; Silbergeld, Manderscheid, and Koenig, 1977). Results also suggest the importance of an initial group structure that builds supportive group norms and highlights positive intermember interactions. *Too rapid an excursion into confrontative interactions before a climate of trust has been established may be counterproductive* (Dies and Cohen, 1976; A. Jacobs, 1974b; Lieberman et al., 1973).

Research findings illustrate that therapeutic structure must be

carefully monitored *throughout* group treatment. Regrettably, the literature is replete with studies using post-test-only designs to understand
leadership effects. This practice must be suspended if we are to advance
our knowledge of leadership with any degree of sophistication. Clinicians and researchers who wish to evaluate the influence of the therapist's
efforts to structure the group experience should be prepared to incorporate periodic assessment of leadership into their practice. Approaches
using the "leader's contribution to group norms," bipolar adjectives, critical incidents, and post-meeting checklists represent a few of the possibilities (Table 2: 32, 36, 37, and 45, respectively).

A final set of studies relevant to our discussion of structured versus
nonstructured treatments shows that the potential value of therapeutic
structure depends on the client's personality or behavioral style within
the group. Thus, several of the studies that failed to establish overall
differences between treatment variations were successful at identifying
interaction effects relating to such factors as client gender (F. Wright,
1976), psychological-mindedness (S. I. Abramowitz and Abramowitz,
1974), dependency (Seldman et al., 1974), and compatibility with the
therapist in terms of interpersonal needs (Lundgren, 1975; Lundgren
and Knight, 1974). The greatest consensus comes from those studies
linking client needs for structure with directive leadership styles. Four
studies have reported that group members with a generalized expectation of external control actually experienced greater benefit from structured approaches to treatment (Abramowitz et al., 1974; Kilmann, 1974;
Kilmann, Albert, and Sotile, 1975; Kilmann and Sotile, 1976); on the
other hand, internally oriented individuals, who express a preference for
self-control, generally experienced greater satisfaction and gain from
nondirective group psychotherapy. Closely related to these findings are
those of McLachlan (1972, 1974), with patients low on conceptual level
(i.e., more dependent on authority), and Gilstein, Wright, and Stone
(1977), with conservative group members. These studies show that these
clients also favored directive or structured group therapy. Finally, Lundgren (1973) found that high-status group members preferred inactive
leaders, and tended to react most negatively when an active leadership
style was used, apparently as a result of their sense of competition with
those leaders. Overall, then, the findings suggest that clients with external orientations and those with dependent, conservative, or authority-
oriented personality styles prefer structured group psychotherapy. In
contrast, high-status group members and internally oriented, nonde-
pendent members favor less structured treatments.

This brings us to the end of our examination of the general issue of structured versus nonstructured approaches to leadership. Our review has illustrated that an "either-or" perspective on this topic is untenable. Structure must be more precisely delineated, beyond the global structured/nonstructured dichotomy. Nevertheless, we can see that structured approaches to group treatment are generally preferred for patients whose psychopathology restricts their capacity to interact in socially competent ways. For these more disturbed patients, nonstructured group treatment, even with interpersonally skilled therapists, will be of limited value. We have also seen that clients whose personality styles are more dependent and externally oriented will favor and perhaps even benefit more from structured group formats. The dilemma for the group leader, of course, is that group composition is usually heterogeneous, with a mix of personality styles, so that some of the participants will be more receptive to therapeutic structure and others less receptive. Group therapists must be sensitive to these differences and adjust structure accordingly. A flexible approach to therapeutic structure and moderation in its implementation will be most effective. For the most part, extremes in therapeutic directiveness should be avoided. Therapists must also recognize the need for structure that matches the developmental hurdles of the group. Structure is most appropriate early in the treatment process, as patients struggle to define therapeutic goals, and this initial structure is most valuable when it stresses positive and supportive group interactions and norms. Finally, therapeutic structure that furnishes a coherent framework for understanding individual experiences and group processes will be of greatest value.

Cognitive Input

In the preceding section it was suggested that initial group structure that provides clients with a conceptual framework for viewing group development may contribute to overall therapeutic benefit (Bednar et al., 1974). The implication is that cognitive input by the group leader serves to clarify the task for group members, thereby facilitating the learning process. It was also proposed that structure in terms of "meaning attribution" is conducive to positive group outcome. The purpose of the present section is to explore further the potential value of cognitive input by the group psychotherapist. Fifteen studies conducted between 1970 and 1979 were identified as pertinent to this topic.

Lieberman et al. (1973) reported that approximately 30% of the events cited by group members as important to their personal growth contained some reference to cognitive learning. The client reports were split about equally between references to insight and to acquisition of information. Furthermore, the authors found that "Of the fourteen mechanisms participants ranked in terms of importance to their own learning... *understanding,* 'understanding why I think and feel the way I do; discovering previously unknown or unacceptable parts of myself,' was ranked fifth" (p. 365). A review of curative factors in group psychotherapy by Butler and Fuhriman (in press) generally supports the significance of insight in therapeutic change. Interventions "providing concepts for how to understand, explaining, clarifying, interpreting, and providing frameworks for how to change" (Lieberman et al., 1973, p. 238) have been shown to produce significantly greater levels of client improvement. Schwartz et al. (1970) found greater satisfaction among hospitalized patients when they felt they had achieved insight during group sessions. The findings revealed that patients and therapists often differed in their views of insight, but the important consideration was the patient's own perspective. Gruen (1977) found that the depth of therapists' interpretations as well as their ability to anticipate group themes related to group cohesiveness and therapeutic movement. According to Gruen, leaders' interventions that accurately anticipated group themes fostered an atmosphere that encouraged group members to work more effectively on resolving their conflicts. This movement toward more constructive problem solving was enhanced by the therapists' ability to offer interpretations that served to integrate complex personal and group-related events. Similarly, P. B. Smith (1971) reported that when his group leaders were data-oriented (clarifying, analyzing), group outcome was more productive.

Nonetheless, findings from several studies suggest that highly abstract analyses by the group psychotherapist are not as valuable as interpretations more closely tied to the experiences of group members within the sessions. Thus, Bolman (1971) failed to find a significant link between "conceptual input" by the group leader and several process and outcome criteria. His operational definition of conceptual input, however, was anchored by such items as leaders' contributions that include a "considerable amount of conceptual and theoretical content" and give "a theoretical explanation of why it occurred" (p. 315). Lieberman et al. (1973) reported that cognitive input in terms of advice and interpersonal understanding were ranked much higher by group members than genetic insight (insight into causes and childhood foundations for current problems). S. I. Abramowitz and Jackson (1974) compared the effective-

ness of "there-and-then" versus "here-and-now" therapist interpretations
in group psychotherapy and discovered that neither approach taken
separately was as effective as treatment combining the two interpretive
perspectives, or group therapy that was simply problem-focused. Analo-
gously, Roback (1972) contrasted the efficacy of interaction, insight, and
insight plus interaction groups and showed that the latter was slightly
more helpful with his inpatient sample. Nichols and Taylor (1975) concluded from their study that "clarifications and interpretation may turn
out to be the group therapist's most productive intervention, but perhaps
not until after group cohesiveness is developed in early sessions" (p. 729).

   *The accumulated evidence, then, strongly supports the value of interpretation
as a vehicle for therapeutic change.* It should be kept in mind that these
studies were all conducted with short-term groups, and that this fact may
have influenced the particular nature of interpretations experienced as
helpful by group members. Whether or not patients come to value
genetic insights in long-term group treatment remains an empirical
question. At this point, however, findings from several studies suggest
that the cognitive input is valued more if it promotes generalizability to
current interpersonal problems. Both Abramowitz and Jackson (1974)
and Roback (1972) have indicated that group treatment emphasizing the
integration of group process interpretations and the understanding of
outside personal experiences is more effective. Similarly, Lieberman et
al. (1973) discovered that their encounter groups were more constructive
when norms favored open boundaries and the discussion of external personal material within the context of a generally here-and-now oriented
model. Moreover, the individuals who showed the most long-term benefit from these group experiences were those who experimented and used
active insight outside the group sessions to build on the interpersonal experiences acquired within the group.

   On the basis of a careful analysis of their group outcomes, Lieberman et al. conclude: "The expression of anger, of rage, the experience of
profound emotions, the receipt of feedback, self-disclosures in and of
themselves, appeared not to differentiate markedly those who learned
and those who remained unchanged. It was only when cognitive events
modified these experiences that statistically significant differences obtained among the learners and those who remained unchanged" (p.
375). This generalization also demonstrates that cognitive events should
not be examined as independent of other important experiences within
group treatment. The effective group leaders in the Lieberman et al.
study were not only high on cognitive input but also high on caring. On

two other basic dimensions, "emotional stimulation" (e.g., challenging, confronting, revealing feelings) and the "executive function" (setting limits, managing time), effective leaders were found to be moderate. Hurst et al. (1978) have investigated the same four dimensions in their study of adolescent groups, and have found that caring and emotional stimulation contribute significantly to group cohesiveness. They speculate that their younger clients probably placed less emphasis on the leader's capacity to clarify or explain the experience so that meaning attribution did not show up as important. Other researchers, however, have commented that meaning attribution is especially effective when combined with high levels of caring on the part of the leader. Thus, Hurley and Pinches (1978) conclude that their T-group results strongly support the value of leader behaviors which are cognitively guiding in addition to accepting. Smith (1971) has reported better outcomes with data-oriented (clarifying, analyzing) and people-oriented (showing close friendship, discussing personal details) group leaders.

At the very least, the various findings suggest that leadership attributes are multifaceted and are best explored through multidimensional techniques. For example, Bolman's (1971, 1973) leadership measure (Table 2: 47) is a carefully devised and statistically refined instrument including seven behavioral dimensions. Intercorrelations among the various scales have identified complex associations with process and outcome measures. The questionnaire used by Nichols and Taylor (1975; Table 3: 22) covers a range of technical and personal dimensions, such as facilitation, clarification, interpretation, reassurance, and therapist disclosure. DiLoreto's (1971; Table 1: 28) measure is a self-report inventory tapping multiple dimensions of leadership style. Clinicians and researchers who plan to incorporate leadership instruments into their group treatments are well advised to consider one of these measures, or other instruments listed in the combined Personal/Technical Dimensions of Tables 1, 2, or 3. Regrettably, all too many of the instruments summarized in these tables are either unidimensional, or if they are multidimensional, they have had very restricted use; most of the instruments have not been replicated in follow-up research.

So far we have discussed cognitive input as a form of therapeutic interpretation without specifically defining the parameters of the intervention. It may have been assumed that what is meant is a sophisticated integration of complex psychological material. Yet the findings from various studies imply that what the clients want is much more pragmatic. Some group members have even taken the heretical position that they

value advice and simple understanding of interpersonal events above
genetic insight (Lieberman et al., 1973). We should not overlook the fact
that advice and feedback are also forms of cognitive input available to the
group psychotherapist. Flowers (1979) has argued that the use of advice
in psychotherapy has received only scant attention in the literature
because it is presumed that such an intervention is minimally effective
and seldom employed. His own findings, however, clearly show that *advice can indeed be an effective therapeutic ploy if its potential impact is properly
understood.* Flowers compared the effects of simple advice (statements
about what the client should do without explaining how to do it), alternatives (statements of two or more possibilities for handling a situation),
and instruction (statements of a single piece of advice explained in a step-
by-step manner). He found that therapeutic outcome was significantly
enhanced by the judicious use of advice. Patients were rated as "more
improved" on goals transmitted by alternatives and instructions than by
simple advice. Vitalo (1971) has also shown that direct instructional
methods can be effective. Working with hospitalized patients, his group
leaders gave direct suggestions, offered advice, and reinforced behavioral practice. A wide range of behaviorally-oriented studies have been
conducted to document the value of direct advice and therapeutic
instruction. A discussion of this research, however, is reserved for the
next section.

Feedback as cognitive input by the group psychotherapist (i.e., providing information about one's perceptions of client behavior) has also
received very little empirical attention. Jacobs (1974b) has reviewed this
body of literature and shown that research has not focused specifically on
feedback delivered by the group leader. One exception is a study by
Robinson (1970), who notes that group outcome may be improved when
feedback from the leader is made more specific. In summarizing the
results from many projects, Jacobs (1974b) reports that *positive feedback is
almost invariably rated as more desirable, having greater impact, and leading to
greater intention to change than negative feedback. Descriptive or behaviorally
oriented feedback appears to be more effective than emotional feedback.* However,
"emotional feedback delivered publicly seems to have a potentiating
effect, which can be used to increase the believability of behavioral feedback with which it is associated. Finally, positive feedback, particularly if
emotional, seems to be highly related to group cohesiveness" (p. 445).

These conclusions are consistent with my earlier generalization
about the value of a positive therapist-client relationship and my observation that personal (e.g., caring) and technical (e.g., interpretation)
aspects of leadership interact to facilitate treatment. Moreover, cognitive

aspects of leadership interact to facilitate treatment. Moreover, cognitive input as a form of therapeutic structuring enhances the potential of group treatment by clarifying therapeutic goals. In short-term group therapy, clients benefit most from interpretations that foster generalization from interactions within the group sessions to personal experiences outside the treatment context and vice versa. Advice, instructions, and specific feedback can augment that learning process. Thus, the various results favor an active leadership style which provides a conceptual framework for therapeutic change and attempts to help group members to appreciate the relevance of interactions within the group to their interpersonal conflicts outside the treatment sessions.

Therapist Reinforcement and Modeling

In a prior review (Dies, 1977b), I outlined findings on therapist reinforcement to show that the leader is capable of conditioning a variety of behaviors in group settings, including rate of interaction, direction of verbalization, sequence of speakers, group cohesiveness, and hostility toward the therapist. Through the differential use of such positive qualities as empathy and warmth, group therapists have been able to effect predictable changes in patients' in-therapy and extra-therapy behavior. A. Jacobs (1974a) has summarized other learning-oriented approaches to group intervention to illustrate that shaping, modeling, instructions, sets, and prompts have all been demonstrated to influence the behavior of group members. The present survey examines 17 studies that evaluated the role of both reinforcement and modeling in therapeutic change.

As one might expect, a majority of these investigations relied on behaviorally oriented measures to assess the influence of therapeutic style. In most cases, ratings were made by independent observers who listened to tape recordings of the group interactions. These judgments were quite objective and required comparatively little inference, so that with only minimal training high levels of interscorer reliability were obtained. Table 3 highlights the approaches that have been explored: for example, number of positive and negative statements given and received (9); advice ratings (14); frequency of therapist-patient interaction (21); reinforcement-prompt code (29); and time spent in conversation and silence (31). Cohen (1973) has shown that it is quite feasible for group psychotherapists to analyze recordings of their own sessions to understand the influence of leadership style. Understandably, clinicians may not have the time to engage in this form of "self-supervision." They may also find it impractical to have colleagues serve as group observers or listen to recordings of sessions to evaluate the group interaction. For this reason, clinicians who wish to assess this aspect of their therapeutic style may have to rely on client reports. These ratings from group members will be much more global, analogous to the relationship and favorableness of therapist-client interaction measures discussed above.

Several investigators have used token reinforcements to effect changes in group process. Hauserman, Zweback, and Plotkin (1972), for instance, distributed tokens to facilitate verbal initiation in group therapy with hospitalized adolescents. They found that the reinforcements had a substantial effect. Adolescents who were typically non-verbal and considered poor candidates for group psychotherapy were able to participate in the group sessions. Moreover, once the initiations increased, social reinforcements through peer pressure brought about a decrease in inappropriate, off-topic verbalization and a subsequent increase in initiations which were more relevant to the therapeutic goals. Flowers, Booraem, Brown, and Harris (1974) also found that tokens could be used to encourage patients to interact more effectively. Of even greater importance, however, was the finding that differential reinforcement could produce greater behavioral improvement. Outpatients exposed to token reinforcement group therapy showed significant progress in employment and educational objectives, and improved social interaction outside the treatment setting (Flowers and Booraem, 1976).

Other investigators have used more natural reinforcements, such as the therapist's attention, approval, and interest, to influence group process and outcome. Liberman (1970a, 1970b, 1971) studied two matched outpatient therapy groups over a period of nine months. In both groups the leaders attempted to maximize the therapeutic potential of patient interactions, but one group therapist was specifically trained to use prompts (statements directed to elicit verbal responses from the patient) and social reinforcement to facilitate the development of intermember cohesiveness. Liberman found that the behavioral techniques were extremely effective in shaping group norms and improving therapeutic outcome. Patients in the "experimental" group showed significantly more cohesiveness, greater personality change, and earlier symptomatic improvement than those in the "comparison" group.

Liberman established that his therapists had a strong influence on group behavior even when they were not aware of the contingencies of their responsiveness. He urges that it is "crucial for all group therapists to understand and systematically use their influence in directing group members toward behavior that will be of therapeutic value" (1970a, p. 172). In his opinion (1971), *therapists can maximize their impact by (1) reinforcing appropriate patient behaviors as soon as they occur, (2) speaking directly to the patients rather than talking indirectly about them, (3) using acknowledgments or reinforcements more frequently than prompts, (4) keeping interventions as unidimensional and uncomplicated as possible, and (5) avoiding excessive emphasis on a single content area within any session.* *

Despite the significant influence of the therapist, however, Liberman also found that the group leader does not serve as the exclusive determiner of group interaction, since group members also prompt and reinforce each other's behavior. As the group develops, "the group members take over from the therapist some of his influence in shaping behavior. While the therapist initially is important in establishing a group culture, later some of his influence is mediated by the group members themselves" (1970a, p. 172). Overall, Liberman's findings are highly consistent with my earlier generalizations regarding the importance of a positive therapist-client relationship and the value of structure, particularly early in treatment, in establishing the therapeutic potential of the group. His results also place the therapist's role in proper perspective by documenting the significance of client-client relationships in facilitating therapeutic gain.

DiLoreto (1971) demonstrated that his group leaders were more active in the early phases of group development and that they used behavior shaping (approval and disapproval) and modeling to encourage group members to become more responsible for the content of the sessions. Other investigators have also shown the importance of therapist reinforcement and modeling, especially during initial group meetings (Luke, 1972; Roback, 1972; Vitalo, 1971). Silbergeld and his colleagues (1977, 1979) explored content and work styles in group treatment and discovered that the therapeutic quality of interactions improved over time. They interpreted the growing isomorphism or similarity between therapists and clients as reflecting the significance of modeling and reinforcement. In his behavioral investigation of modeling, Flowers (1978) found that when group leaders expressed 86% positive therapist-client statements, the participants made 79% positive client-client comments. When the level of positive therapist-client remarks dropped to 23%, the

**Editors' Note:* Clearly, the therapist has at hand powerful nonspecific tools of reinforcement and modeling with which to shape group events. The therapist is never just a person (although that is important), but also a knowledgeable and deliberate social engineer. The therapist must translate theoretical understanding of group events into appropriate behavior, but theory is often revealed in action more than in words.

group members' level fell to 59% for positive intermember statements, ostensibly reflecting the influence of modeling. Flowers suggests that increasing the proportion of client-client interactions over therapist-client interactions serves to increase group members' trust, level and rate of disclosure, and risk-taking. Exemplifying the impact of therapist modeling is Kangas's (1971) analysis of tape recordings of group sessions, which shows that "to a considerable degree self-disclosure begets self-disclosure in small group settings. This holds true whether it is a group member or the group leader who first discloses" (p. 69).

Several studies support the conclusion that therapists may intervene to establish group members as effective role models within treatment sessions. Babad and Melnick (1976) found that leaders' differential liking for group members correlated with levels of participation and involvement, which in turn were associated with quantity and quality of feedback received by these members. Sampson (1972) demonstrated that leaders who were oriented toward the group members most liked by the group were more effective, in terms of members' satisfaction and achievement of group goals, than were leaders who were oriented toward the least-liked members of their group. Sampson reasoned that well-liked group members are more likely to represent the values and norms of the group. Consequently, "the leader who is oriented toward such persons is oriented toward 'gatekeepers' in [the group's] network of liking and influence relationships" (p. 573). Such leaders presumably seem more in tune with the groups' norms and values and are better "able to facilitate the group by reinforcing the desired rather than the undesired aims of the group" (p. 573).

Warner and Hansen (1970) demonstrated the merits of both verbal reinforcement and model reinforcement in therapeutic outcome. Verbal reinforcement takes place when a positive reward following a desired behavior serves to increase the reoccurrence of that behavior. Model reinforcement adds the aspect of vicarious learning, based on the idea that a group member who observes another participant receive a reward will imitate that behavior in order to receive a comparable reward. Warner and Hansen found that both approaches were effective in reducing clients' feelings of alienation. Thus, therapists can reinforce client behavior *directly* by working with specific group members, or *indirectly* by having other participants benefit through observational learning. Most of the reinforcement and modeling experiences, however, will still relate most directly to patient-patient interactions.

The findings summarized in this section highlight the importance of social reinforcement and modeling. Liberman (1970a) has noted that group therapists may not be fully aware of the potential value of these powerful learning processes, and it is clear that more attention should be turned toward training. Several authors have shown that even experienced group leaders can benefit from specific training in the application of learning principles to group psychotherapy (Flowers, 1979; Liberman, 1970a, 1970b, 1971; Pattinson, Rardin, and Lindberg, 1977). Throughout this review, it has also been suggested that practitioners can enhance their understanding of leadership through the selective use of research measures. Elsewhere (Dies, 1980), I have shown how instruments can be incorporated into various aspects of training to improve therapeutic practice.

CO-THERAPY

A majority of group psychotherapists prefer to conduct their groups with a co-leader. The priority given to co-therapy has been attributed to therapist security, to increased efficacy of treatment, and to the unique opportunities for personal and professional growth available to the therapists (Dies et al., 1979). Although the group treatment literature is replete with articles on co-leadership, only a handful of the published reports cite empirical findings. In the present survey I have been able to identify only five investigations of co-leadership during the entire decade of research. This is in spite of the fact that nearly half of the 95 studies used co-led groups. Results from the five studies indicate that we should not be too casual in our assumption that co-therapy is always beneficial.

Frankiel (1971) hypothesized that the number of mutually perceived therapeutic relationships among group members would correlate meaningfully with ratings of group outcome. His predictions were confirmed for groups with only one leader, but not for those with two. Frankiel argued that the presence of a second group leader affects the quality of member-member relationships. He inferred that in solo-led groups the leader is a primary model for mutually therapeutic relationships (supportive, accepting, caring) and confrontation, especially early in the group's development. In contrast, co-leader teams seem less likely to play this role. Although co-leaders may very well have complex and rich relationships with each other, they rarely share this with group members and consequently "deprive members of an opportunity to witness or model such a relationship" (p. 462). Thus, Frankiel found that solo-led groups had certain advantages over groups with co-leaders.

Hurley and Rosenthal (1978a) also suggested that single-led groups may be more effective, particularly when the co-leaders have not had a previous opportunity to work together in a group. They proposed that even highly competent group therapists may have difficulty in performing as a skillful team without prior familiarity with each other's style. Implicit in both Frankiel's and Hurley and Rosenthal's investigations is the notion that the relationship established between co-leaders *within* the group sessions is critical in determining their influence on therapeutic process and outcome. Unfortunately, neither investigation examined the quality of the relationship between co-leaders directly. The three remaining studies are more pertinent to this issue.

Hurst et al. (1978) identified two dimensions of leadership that contributed to group cohesiveness — caring and self-expressiveness. They reasoned that a trusting and supportive atmosphere must precede and accompany an emotionally stimulating, expressive style: "Emotional prodding or sharing without warmth and support (e.g., high-Self-Expressive, low-Caring) is likely to be ineffective" (p. 275). Interestingly, they demonstrated that both co-leaders must separately evidence appropriate levels on the two leadership dimensions. Leader pairs in which either partner is low on one or both of the variables were generally found to have less cohesive groups. Thus, leader pair similarity was important.

In contrast, Piper, Doan, Edwards, and Jones (1979) argued that dissimilarity of co-leaders is not counterproductive as long as the differences are complementary. In fact, dissimilar co-therapists provide a wider variety of interventions for patients to work with and may thereby actually enhance therapeutic outcome. The critical consideration in resolving the discrepancy between the reports of Hurst and Piper and their colleagues appears to be the idea of balance in the relationship, i.e., differences that are not divisive but rather complementary. Piper et al. demonstrated that a more central factor was consistency in the co-leadership team. Their findings revealed significant associations between consistent co-therapy behavior and higher percentages of patient work and reports of greater improvement. The researchers stated that patients from inconsistent co-leader teams were probably more confused about what each therapist wanted to pursue, and that the competition for leadership may have unduly complicated the therapeutic process.

Additional light is shed on the importance of the co-therapy relationship in the final study (Dies et al., 1979). My colleagues and I explored self-disclosure within co-leader teams and found important differences between their more and less effective groups. Four categories of leader self-disclosure were identified: (1) *relationship* — openness about their relationship within the sessions; (2) *leader/member* — personal reactions to individual group members; (3) *self/group* — personal feelings, reactions, or experiences related to here-and-now events; and (4) *self/external* — content focused on issues unrelated to the group process. In general, we found that effective co-leader teams were more self-disclosing about relationships (both with their co-leader and with group members); less effective co-leaders concentrated more on "self" issues. One exception to this pattern was a pair of leaders who were very open about their relationship, but whose group was not especially productive. However, their relationship openness reflected conflict and disagreement. We generalized that openness between co-leaders within group sessions is appropriate and may enhance the therapeutic value of a group, but only when such openness does not reflect unresolved tension.

Overall, the findings from these five studies suggest that the co-leadership model may complicate the group therapeutic process and actually precipitate problems that are not evident in groups with only one leader. This difficulty seems most likely to occur when therapists have not worked through differences in their leadership styles, and consequently expose their conflicts within the group setting. *Compatibility despite dissimilarity appears to be the key consideration in establishing co-therapist teams, and the capacity to model an open and positive relationship within the sessions seems to be the critical dimension in maintaining an effective team.* Surprisingly, in spite of the popularity of male and female co-leader teams, researchers have not explored issues related to co-therapist gender until very recently (Greene, Morrison, and Tischler, 1981).

Without question, the various findings on co-therapy stress the value of open communication between the co-leaders. The nature of their relationship should be understood before they agree to work together as a team, and they should establish consistent guidelines for maintaining mutually compatible interactions throughout treatment. This requires ongoing communication within and after the sessions. Co-leaders may occasionally seek an outside consultant to facilitate their understanding of the relationship, or they may use instrumentation to serve this end. Thus, group members may be asked to rate various dimensions of the co-therapy relationship (e.g., Table 2: 11, 12, 13, 20, 30, 46). Co-leaders can also use self-report measures and then compare each other's perceptions on these scales (e.g., Table 1: 4, 17, 20, 26, 27, 28).

CONCLUSIONS

Throughout this chapter we have examined the implications of research for the practice of group psychotherapy. I shall now sketch the broad outlines of a model for leadership in short-term group treatment based on these empirical foundations. It is impossible, however, to offer a comprehensive model of leadership on the basis of the research conducted thus far; the range of findings is just too limited. Still, some general prescriptions for therapeutic practice can be recommended.

First and foremost, it should be recognized that group psychotherapy offers a powerful and unique form of treatment which requires specialized knowledge and skills of the group psychotherapist. The intervention strategies practiced in individual therapy are not readily transferable to the group situation, and may, in fact, be counterproductive in that setting. As I have shown elsewhere (Dies, 1980), one of the most common limitations of group psychotherapists is their failure to understand group process and how to use group dynamics to effect individual change. Successful group psychotherapy is not based on one-to-one relationships between the leader and group members, nor is it a function of the insights or feedback given to individual clients by the group therapist. One-to-one work with individual group members may actually inhibit the learning potential inherent in the group process. The important learning mechanisms in groups relate most directly to the interactions among co-members. The group is the primary vehicle of therapeutic change. The leader serves mainly to facilitate the development of a group culture that is conducive to therapeutic growth. In the roles of "model-setting participant" and "technical expert" (Yalom, 1975, p. 110), the group psychotherapist provides therapeutic *structure* and guides the development of a *meaningful* and *positive* learning environment, which can then be used to bring about change in the individual participants.

The following outline highlights the recommendations for group leaders:

I. *Providing Therapeutic Structure*
   A. Setting up the group:
      1. Select clients in terms of interpersonal compatibility to fit the particular group instead of using traditional, individually oriented criteria.
         a. Screen clients carefully to achieve a reasonable balance of interpersonal styles (e.g., expressed and wanted needs for inclusion, control, affection).
         b. Screen clients to establish comparable levels of psychopathology.
      2. Compose groups with moderately diverse clients to provide optimal opportunities for support and confrontation. Avoid potential scapegoats or "misfits."

3. Orient group members toward constructive interpersonal behaviors in pre-group interviews or training sessions. Inform clients about the unique properties of group psychotherapy and about "curative factors" such as interpersonal output (socializing skills), interpersonal input (feedback), catharsis, group cohesiveness, and self-understanding.

B. Maintaining the task focus:

1. Introduce more structure earlier in treatment, until the therapeutic potential of the group is developed sufficiently. Less directive leadership is appropriate later in the group.

2. Generally avoid extremes in therapeutic directiveness. Introduce moderate structure in terms of time management, limit setting, suggesting rules, and emotional stimulation (e.g., confrontation, revealing feelings).

3. Use more structured interventions with patients whose psychopathology restricts their capacity to interact in socially competent ways.

4. Be active but not monopolistic. Interventions should be frequent but focused, brief, and designed to encourage members to assume more responsibility for the content of the sessions.

5. Keep therapeutic goals clear by monitoring the number of issues "on the agenda" at any given time in the group (i.e., keep the therapeutic task reasonably simple and focused).

6. Use acknowledgments and reinforcements more frequently than questions.

7. Avoid excessive emphasis on a single content area within any one session.

8. Speak directly to clients instead of talking indirectly about them.

9. Shift from a group-centered to a more individualized *content* focus as clients acquire skills in interacting effectively. Continue to focus on *process* issues throughout treatment.

II. *Developing a Meaningful Learning Environment*

A. Structure initial sessions to provide a coherent framework for understanding individual experiences and events within the group.

B. Throughout the group, maximize interventions that provide concepts for how to understand behavior and events within the sessions:

1. Minimize highly abstract interpretations and those stressing "genetic insights," especially with time-limited

groups (e.g., 15 or fewer sessions). As the number of sessions increases (e.g., 30 to 40), exploration and interpretation of clients' earlier experiences may be fruitful.

2. Focus mainly on pragmatic interpretations emphasizing the understanding of interpersonal events.

   a. Try to give advice in the form of alternatives (not "you ought to . . .") or simple instructions.

   b. Provide feedback that is descriptive and behaviorally-oriented, and encourage members to do the same.

   c. Keep interventions as unidimensional and uncomplicated as possible.

3. Reinforce group members' efforts to offer helpful advice, feedback, and understanding.

C. Highlight interpretations that foster generalizability to current problems.

1. Actively work to encourage direct translation of here-and-now experiences in terms of outside relationships, and vice versa.

2. Encourage experimentation between sessions to build on interpersonal experiences acquired within the group sessions.

III. *Building a Supportive Learning Environment*

A. Personal style of the group psychotherapist:

1. Convey an active and positive involvement in the group process through genuine, empathic, and caring interactions with group members. Avoid impersonal, detached, and judgmental leadership styles.

2. Maintain a reasonably open therapeutic style, with a willingness to share "normal" feelings, reactions, and emotional experiences, particularly as they relate to events and relationships within the group.

   a. Do not be too revealing, but gauge disclosures according to the level of group development. Initially show confidence in leadership ability and stress the potential of the group.

   b. Avoid intrusive and highly personalized disclosures.

   c. Remember that with clients who are more psychologically impaired, group therapist self-disclosure and relationship variables are comparatively less influential than technical qualities of leadership.

3. Although some degree of challenge of clients is essential, avoid intrusive and overly critical confrontations. Limit critical challenges until a foundation of trust has been established.

4. Avoid hostile therapist-client exchanges.

B. Relationship focus:

1. Continue to stress the importance of positive therapist-client relationships, but increasingly emphasize the value of supportive client-client relationships.

2. Intervene to establish group members as effective role models within the sessions, especially those clients who demonstrate desirable behavior and reflect the goals of the group.

   a. Reinforce appropriate client behavior directly and as soon as it occurs.

   b. *Provide opportunities for all group members to participate actively and constructively in the group process.*

3. Intervene to moderate the intensity of confrontative exchanges among group members, especially if they occur before a climate of trust has been established within the group. Prevent hostile and destructive interactions.

4. With co-leader teams, model openness and support within the co-leader relationship during the group sessions.

   a. Maintain a compatible and consistent co-therapy relationship by continuing to communicate within and after the sessions.

   b. Avoid showing unresolved tension and conflict within the sessions.

C. Group focus:

1. Introduce initial structure to build supportive group norms and to highlight positive interactions.

2. Structure the group early to emphasize sharing personal feelings and experiences more than exchange of feedback.

3. Attend to obstacles within the group which may impede the development of a constructive learning environment.

   a. Highlight the importance of understanding group process and interpersonal events within the group.

   b. Maintain a proactive rather than a reactive therapeutic style by anticipating potential difficulties and intervening to short-circuit their potentially destructive effects.

4. Help clients to understand the value of openness and support, and the risks of negative exchanges, by providing a clear rationale for the therapeutic interventions.

TABLE 1

Self-Report Measures of Leadership

Instruments	Focus	Investigators
Personal Dimensions		
1. Acceptance versus Rejection of Others	Bipolar adjectives (e.g., warm-cold, involved-detached)	Hurley and Rosenthal (1978a, 1978b)
2. Affective Sensitivity Scale	Ability to understand affective communication	Danish (1971)
3. Attitude Scales	Attitudes toward general topics (e.g., need for laws)	Beutler (1971); Beutler et al. (1974)
4. Bipolar Adjectives	Evaluative scales (e.g., fair-unfair, helpful-unhelpful)	Lundgren (1974)
5. Cattell 16PF	General personality factors	Cooper (1977); Shapiro and Klein (1975)
6. Conceptual Level	Developmental level (predependent to inter-dependent)	McLachlan (1972, 1974)
7. Ease of Empathy	Ease of empathy with client	Rohrbaugh and Bartels (1975)
8. Edwards Personal Preference Schedule	General personality variables	DiLoreto (1971)
9. FIRO-B	Reported behavior toward others in areas of inclusion, control, affection	Lundgren (1975); Lundgren and Knight (1974, 1977)
10. FIRO-F	Feeling level of FIRO-B	O'Day (1976)
11. Group Therapist Orientation Scale	Leader self-disclosure	Dies (1973a)
12. Interpersonal Checklist	Dominance-submission and love-hate dimensions	DiLoreto (1971); Liberman (1970a, 1970b, 1971)
13. Liking of Members	Liking of members	Babad and Amir (1978); Babad and Melnick (1976); Rosenzweig and Folman (1974)
14. Myers-Briggs Type Indicator	Introversion-extroversion	DiLoreto (1971)
15. Patient's Ability to Form a Therapeutic Relationship	Judgment about relationship potential of client	Rosenzweig and Folman (1974)

TABLE 1 (*Continued*)
Self-Report Measures of Leadership

Instruments	Focus	Investigators
16. Personal Anticipations Questionnaire	Expectations about value of group experience	Bugen (1978); Lieberman et al. (1973); Peteroy (1979)
17. Relationship Inventory	Genuineness, empathy, regard	Frankiel (1971)
18. Satisfaction with Group	Group satisfaction	Rohrbaugh and Bartels (1975); Schwartz et al. (1970)
19. Self-Acceptance versus Rejection	Bipolar adjectives (e.g., shows feelings — hides feelings)	Hurley and Rosenthal (1978a, 1978b)
20. Therapist Self-Ratings	Therapist interest, pleasure, understanding, etc.	Anderson et al. (1972)
21. Total Impression Made by Patient	Favorableness of first impression	Rosenzweig and Folman (1974)
22. Trainer's Attitude toward Group Members	Positive or angry feelings toward members	Lundgren (1971, 1973)
Technical Dimensions		
23. Degree of Member Confrontation by Trainer	Perceived confrontation by members	Lundgren (1971, 1973)
24. Orientation to High- or Low-Preference Member	Leader's focus on least- or most-preferred group members	Sampson (1972)
25. Trainer Activity	Degree of activity, structure	Lundgren (1971, 1973)
Personal/Technical Dimensions		
26. Post-Meeting Reaction Form	Attitude toward trainer style	Lundgren (1971, 1973)
27. Self-Perception	Perception of role behavior during sessions	Jenkins et. al. (1971)
28. Therapist Orientation Sheet	Preferred therapist interventions	DiLoreto (1971)
29. Therapist Personal Data Sheet	Theoretical orientation	DiLoreto (1971)

TABLE 2

Client Ratings of Leadership

Instruments	Focus	Investigators
Personal Dimensions		
1. Acceptance versus Rejection of Others	Bipolar adjectives (e.g., warm-cold, involved-detached)	Hurley and Rosenthal (1978a, 1978b)
2. Attitude Scales	Attitudes toward general topics (e.g., need for laws)	Beutler (1971); Beutler et al. (1974)
3. Attractiveness	Interpersonal attractiveness	Lieberman et al. (1973)
4. Bipolar Adjectives	Variable focus (e.g., friendly-unfriendly, trusting-distrusting)	Dies (1973b); Dies et al. (1979); Lundgren (1971, 1973, 1974, 1975); Peters (1973)
5. Cattell 16PF	General personality factors	Shapiro and Klein (1975)
6. Desired Similarity with Trainer	Ideal self versus leader description	Peters (1973)
7. Focus of Self-Disclosure	Leader/member/group focus	Dies et al. (1979)
8. Group Therapist Orientation Scale	Leadership self-disclosure	Dies (1973b)
9. Identification with Trainer	Perceived similarity	Peters (1973)
10. Interpersonal Checklist	Dominance-submission and love-hate dimensions	Lieberman (1970a, 1970b, 1971)
11. Leader Openness (Examples)	Members furnish examples of leader self-disclosure	Dies et al. (1979)
12. Leader Openness (Ranking)	Leader's relative standing within the group	Dies et al. (1979)
13. Leader Openness (Rating)	Rating of leader self-disclosure	Dies et al. (1979)
14. Like/Dislike of Leader	Liking of leader by members	Hurley and Rosenthal (1978a, 1978b); Weigel et al. (1972)
15. Liking by Leader	Leader's feelings toward members	Babad and Amir (1978); Smith (1976)
16. Member Reaction to Trainer	Discomfort, identification, liking	Bolman (1971, 1973)
17. Mental Health Rating	Perception of leader's adjustment	May and Thompson (1973); Weigel et al. (1972)

TABLE 2 (*Continued*)
Client Ratings of Leadership

Instruments	Focus	Investigators
18. Peer Nomination Rating Form	Nominations of members regarding who has been open and sensitive	Seldman et al. (1974)
19. Ratings of Therapist Behavior	Therapist interest, pleasure, understanding, etc.	Anderson et al. (1972)
20. Relationship Inventory	Genuineness, empathy, warmth	Abramowitz et al. (1974); Abramowitz and Abramowitz (1974); Abramowitz and Jackson (1974); DiLoreto (1971); Frankiel (1971); Roback (1972); Roback and Strassberg (1975); Strassberg et al. (1975)
21. Scales of Facilitative Interpersonal Functioning	Genuineness, empathy, regard	Seldman et al. (1974)
22. Self-Acceptance versus Rejection	Bipolar adjectives (e.g., shows feelings–hides feelings)	Hurley and Rosenthal (1978a, 1978b)
23. Self-Disclosure	Rating of leader openness	Hurley and Force (1973); May and Thompson (1973); Weigel et al. (1972)
24. Sociometric Liking of Therapist	Liking of therapist	Liberman (1970a, 1970b, 1971)
25. Truax Relationship Inventory	Genuineness, empathy, warmth	Jessell and Bush (1973); Truax (1971b)
26. Trust	Trust	Flowers (1978); Smith (1976)
27. Who Behaves to Make You Tense	Degree of tension experienced	Smith (1976)
28. Wisconsin Relationship Orientation Scale	Willingness to disclose to leader	Danish (1971)
Technical Dimensions		
29. Amount of Influence	Perceived influence	Peters (1973); Smith (1976)
30. Bipolar Adjectives	Variable focus (e.g., competitive-cooperative)	Dies et al. (1979)

TABLE 2 (*Continued*)
Client Ratings of Leadership

Instruments	Focus	Investigators
31. Confrontation	Experienced tension in relation to leader	Frankiel (1971)
32. Contribution to Group Norms	Degree of influence on norms specifically delineated	Luke (1972)
33. Effectiveness	Perceived helpfulness	Hurley and Force (1973); Hurley and Pinches (1978); Smith and Miller (1979)
34. Feedback-Seeking	Willingness to solicit feedback	Hurley and Force (1973)
35. Helpfulness	Helpfulness	May and Thompson (1973)
Personal/Technical Dimensions		
36. Bipolar Adjectives	Variable focus (e.g., close-distant, strong-weak)	Harrow et al. (1971); Kilmann and Sotile (1976); Morrison and Thomas (1976); O'Day (1973); Seldman et al. (1974); Wright (1976)
37. Critical Incidents	Report of helpful experiences	Lieberman et al. (1973)
38. Curative Factors	Perception of leader's contribution	Dashef et al. (1974); Freedman and Hurley (1979)
39. Helpfulness	Perception of what helped group members during sessions	Donovan et al. (1979)
40. Interpersonal Reaction Form	Perceptions of group, self, leader	Lundgren and Knight (1974, 1977)
41. Leader Evaluation Form	Leader's ability to facilitate group	Jacobs et al. (1973)
42. Leadership Questionnaire	Leadership style on personal and technical dimensions	Lieberman et al. (1973)
43. Leadership Styles Scale	Self-expressive, caring, controlling, interpreting	Hurst et al. (1978)
44. Perception of Therapist	Perception of role behavior	Jenkins et al. (1971)
45. Post-Meeting Checklist	Attitude toward trainer style	Lundgren (1971, 1973)

TABLE 2 (*Continued*)
Client Ratings of Leadership

Instruments	Focus	Investigators
46. Recommendations about Group or Leader	Written comments about group and leader	Dies et al. (1979)
47. Trainer Behavior Scale	Conceptual input, conditionality, dominance, openness, etc.	Bolman (1971, 1973)
48. Trainer Style Questionnaire	Task competence, congruence, authority profile, etc.	Cooper (1977)

TABLE 3

Observer Ratings of Leadership

Instruments	Focus	Investigators
1. Accurate Empathy	Judgment of empathy from taped interactions	Trotzer (1971); Truax (1971b); Truax et al (1970, 1971); Vitalo (1971)
2. Attractiveness	Interpersonal attractiveness	Lieberman et al. (1973)
3. Congruence	Judgment of genuineness from taped interactions	Trotzer (1971); Truax (1971b); Truax et al. (1970, 1971); Vitalo (1971)
4. Intensity of Negative Statements	Rating of negativity of leader's comments	Flowers (1978)
5. Interaction Process Analysis	Frequency and valence of acts	Liberman (1970a, 1970b, 1971)
6. Interpersonal Checklist	Dominance-submission and love-hate dimensions	Liberman (1970a, 1970b, 1971)
7. Moss Behavioral Rating of Self-Disclosure	Quality dimensions of leader disclosure	Moss and Harren (1978)
8. Negative Transference	Judgment of negative transference	Truax (1971a)
9. Number of Positive and Negative Statements Given and Received	Frequency count	Flowers (1978); Flowers and Booraem (1976)
10. Self-Disclosure	Categories of self-disclosure	Kangas (1971)
11. Sign Process Analysis	Positive interactions with group members	Liberman (1970a, 1970b, 1971)
12. Unconditional Positive Regard	Judgment from taped interactions	Trotzer (1971); Truax (1971b); Truax et al. (1970, 1971); Vitalo (1971)
13. Valuation Analysis	Value-laden comments	Shawver and Lubach (1977); Shawver and Pines (1978)
Technical Dimensions		
14. Advice Ratings	Simple advice, alternatives, instruction, process advice	Flowers (1979)
15. Amount of Control Exerted	Amount of guidance evident	Gruen (1977)
16. Confrontation of Trainer	Degree of confrontation of trainer	Lundgren (1971, 1973)

TABLE 3 (*Continued*)
Observer Ratings of Leadership

Instruments	Focus	Investigators
17. Depth of Interpretation	Reflection to deep interpretation	Gruen (1977)
18. Directive/Nondirective Leadership	Structuring of therapist's role	Abramowitz et al. (1974); Gilstein et al. (1977); Kinder and Kilmann (1976); McLachlan (1972, 1974)
19. Feedback Given	Various feedback dimensions	Lundgren and Schaeffer (1976); Robinson (1970); Robinson and Jacobs (1970)
20. Frequency of Statements Received	Frequency count	Flowers and Booraem (1976)
21. Frequency of Therapist-Patient Interactions	Frequency count	Flowers et al. (1974)
22. Group Therapist Interventions Scale	Focus of interventions, degree of challenge	Nichols (1977); Nichols and Taylor (1975)
23. Hill Interaction Matrix–Group	Work style and content focus of interactions	Lewis and Mider (1973); Pattinson et al. (1977); Piper et al. (1979); Silbergeld et al. (1977, 1979)
24. Insight/Noninsight-Oriented	Degree therapist fosters past and here-and-now interpretations	Abramowitz and Abramowitz (1974)
25. Leader Anticipation of Group Themes	Awareness of developing themes	Gruen (1977)
26. Leader-Initiated Comments	Frequency count	Abramowitz et al. (1974)
27. Number of Therapist Interventions	Frequency count	Cohen (1973); Flowers (1979)
28. Persuasive Potency	Judged social influence ability	Truax and Lister (1970)
29. Reinforcement-Prompt Code	Prompting and reinforcement of group interactions	Liberman (1970a, 1970b, 1971)

TABLE 3 *(Continued)*
Observer Ratings of Leadership

Instruments	Focus	Investigators
30. Self-Reference Content Analysis	Self-references or self-disclosures	Pino and Cohen (1971)
31. Time Spent in Conversation and Silence	Frequency count	DiLoreto (1971)
32. Trainer Activity	Degree of activity or structure	Lundgren (1971, 1973)
Personal/Technical Dimensions		
33. Frequency of Use of Specific Techniques	Tabulation of frequency of various intervention strategies	DiLoreto (1971)
34. Group Interaction Profile	Personal-impersonal and group-related/unrelated	Wogan et al. (1977)
35. Group Process Categories	Coding of speaker, receiver, type, and valence of communication	Lundgren (1977); Lundgren and Knight (1978)
36. Group Rating Schedule	Process variables that contribute to learning	Cooper (1977)
37. Interaction Process Analysis	Instrumental-adaptive and social-emotional behavior	Pino and Cohen (1971)
38. Leader Style Categories	Type of therapeutic intervention	Lieberman et al. (1973)
39. Post-Meeting Reactions	Attitude toward trainer style	Lundgren (1971, 1973)
40. Process Analysis Scoring System	Affective and thematic categories of group process	Gibbard and Hartman (1973)
41. Training Style Scoring System	Definitional, behavioral, and emotional components of style	O'Day (1973, 1974, 1976)
42. Verbalization Instrument for Group Observation and Rating	Therapeutic role behavior	Angell and DeSau (1974)

REFERENCES

Abramowitz, C. V., Abramowitz, S. I., Roback, H. B., & Jackson, C. (1974), Differential effectiveness of directive and nondirective group therapies as a function of client internal-external control. *J. Consult. Clin. Psychol.,* 42:849–853.

Abramowitz, S. I., & Abramowitz, C. V. (1974), Psychological-mindedness and benefit from insight-oriented group therapy. *Arch. Gen. Psychiat.,* 30:610–615.

———— & Jackson, C. (1974), Comparative effectiveness of there-and-then versus here-and-now therapist interpretations in group psychotherapy. *J. Counsel. Psychol.,* 21:288–293.

Anderson, C. M., Harrow, M., Schwartz, A. H., & Kupfer, D. J. (1972), Impact of therapist on patient satisfaction in group psychotherapy. *Comprehen. Psychiat.,* 13:33–40.

Angell, D. L., & DeSau, G. T. (1974), Rare and discordant verbal roles and the development of group problem-solving conditions. *Small Group Behav.,* 5:45–55.

Babad, E. Y., & Amir, L. (1978), Trainers' liking, Bion's emotional modalities, and T-group effect. *J. Applied Behav. Sci.,* 14:511–522.

———— & Melnick, I. (1976), Effects of a T-group as a function of trainers' liking and members' participation, involvement, quantity, and quality of received feedback. *J. Applied Behav. Sci.,* 12:543–562.

Barrilleaux, S. P., & Bauer, R. H. (1976), The effects of Gestalt awareness training on experiencing levels. *Int. J. Group Psychother.,* 26:431–440.

Bednar, R. L., & Kaul, T. J. (1978), Experiential group research: Current perspectives. In: *Handbook of Psychotherapy and Behavior Change: An Empirical Analysis,* ed. S. L. Garfield & A. E. Bergin. New York: Wiley.

————, Melnick, J., & Kaul, T. J. (1974), Risk, responsibility, and structure: A conceptual framework for initiating group counseling and psychotherapy. *J. Counsel. Psychol.,* 21:31–37.

Berlin, J. S., & Dies, R. R. (1974), Differential group structure: The effects on socially isolated college students. *Small Group Behav.,* 5:462–472.

Beutler, L. E. (1971), Predicting outcomes of psychotherapy: A comparison of predictions from two attitude theories. *J. Consult. Clin. Psychol.,* 37:411–416.

————, Jobe, A. M., & Elkins, D. (1974), Outcomes in group psychotherapy: Using persuasion theory to increase treatment efficiency. *J. Consult. Clin. Psychol.,* 42:547–553.

Bolman, L. (1971), Some effects of trainers on their T groups. *J. Applied Behav. Sci.,* 7:309–325.

———— (1973), Some effects of trainers on their groups: A partial replication. *J. Applied Behav. Sci.,* 9:534–539.

Bugen, L. A. (1978), Expectation profiles: Members expect more than they get while leaders give more than they expect. *Small Group Behav.,* 9:115–123.

Butler, T., & Fuhriman, A. (in press), Curative factors in group therapy: A review of the recent literature. *Small Group Behav.*

Cohen, A. I. (1973), Group therapy: An effective method of self-supervision. *Small Group Behav.,* 4:69–80.

Cooper, C. L. (1977), Adverse and growthful effects of experiential learning groups: The role of the trainer, participant, and group characteristics. *Human Rel.,* 30:1103–1129.

Danish, S. J. (1971), Factors influencing changes in empathy following a group experience. *J. Counsel. Psychol.,* 18:262–267.

Dashef, S. S., Espey, W. M., & Lazarus, J. A. (1974), Time-limited sensitivity groups for medical students. *Amer. J. Psychiat.,* 131:287–292.

Desmond, R. E., & Seligman, M. (1977), A review of research on leaderless groups. *Small Group Behav.*, 8:3–24.

Diamond, M. J., & Shapiro, J. L. (1975), Method and paradigm in encounter group research. *J. Humanist. Psychol.*, 15:59–70.

Dies, R. R. (1973a), Group therapist self-disclosure: Development and validation of a scale. *J. Consult. Clin. Psychol.*, 41:97–103.

_____ (1973b), Group therapist self-disclosure: An evaluation by clients. *J. Counsel. Psychol.*, 20:344–348.

_____ (1977a), Group therapist transparency: A critique of theory and research. *Int. J. Group Psychother.*, 27:177–200.

_____ (1977b), Pragmatics of leadership in psychotherapy and encounter group research. *Small Group Behav.*, 8:229–248.

_____ (1978), The human factor in group psychotherapy research. In: *Group Therapy 1978: An Overview*, ed. L. R. Wolberg, M. L. Aronson, & A. R. Wolberg. New York: Stratton Intercontinental Medical Book Corp.

_____ (1979), Group psychotherapy: Reflections on three decades of research. *J. Applied Behav. Sci.*, 15:361–373.

_____ (1980), Group psychotherapy: Training and supervision. In: *Psychotherapy Supervision*, ed. A. K. Hess. New York: Wiley.

_____ & Cohen, L. (1976), Content considerations in group therapist self-disclosure. *Int. J. Group Psychother.*, 26:71–88.

_____, Mallet, J., & Johnson, F. (1979), Openness in the coleader relationship: Its effect on group process and outcome. *Small Group Behav.*, 10:523–546.

_____ & Teleska, P. A. (in press), Negative outcome in group psychotherapy. In: *Above All Do Not Harm: Negative Outcome in Psychotherapy and What to Do about It*, ed. D. T. Mays & C. M. Franks. New York: Springer.

DiLoreto, A. O. (1971), *Comparative Psychotherapy: An Experimental Analysis*. Chicago: Aldine-Atherton.

Donovan, J. M., Bennett, M. J., & McElroy, C. M. (1979), The crisis group—an outcome study. *Amer. J. Psychiat.*, 136:906–910.

Flowers, J. V. (1978), The effect of therapist support and encounter on the percentage of client-client interactions in group therapy. *J. Commun. Psychol.*, 6:69–73.

_____ (1979), The differential outcome effects of simple advice, alternatives and instructions in group psychotherapy. *Int. J. Group Psychother.*, 29:305–316.

_____ & Booraem, C. D. (1976), The use of tokens to facilitate outcome and monitor process in group psychotherapy. *Int. J. Group Psychother.*, 26:191–201.

_____, Booraem, C. D., Brown, T. R., & Harris, D. E. (1974), An investigation of a technique for facilitating patient to patient therapeutic interactions in group therapy. *J. Commun. Psychol.*, 2:39–42.

Frankiel, H. H. (1971), Mutually perceived therapeutic relationships in T groups: The co-trainer puzzle. *J. Applied Behav. Sci.*, 7:449–465.

Freedman, S. M., & Hurley, J. R. (1979), Maslow's needs: Individual perceptions of helpful factors in growth groups. *Small Group Behav.*, 10:335–367.

Gibbard, G. S., & Hartman, J. J. (1973), The oedipal paradigm in group development: A clinical and empirical study. *Small Group Behav.*, 4:305–354.

Gilstein, K. W., Wright, E. W., & Stone, D. R. (1977), The effects of leadership style on group interactions in differing socio-political subcultures. *Small Group Behav.*, 8:313–331.

Goldstein, J. A. (1971), Investigation of doubling as a technique for involving severely withdrawn patients in group psychotherapy. *J. Consult. Clin. Psychol.*, 37:155–162.

Greene, L. R., Morrison, T. L., & Tischler, N. G. (1981), Gender and authority:

Effects on perceptions of small group co-leaders. *Small Group Behav.*, 12:401–413.
Gruen, W. (1977), The effects of executive and cognitive control of the therapist on the work climate in group therapy. *Int. J. Group Psychother.*, 27:139–152.
Gurman, A. S., & Gustafson, J. P. (1976), Patients' perceptions of the therapeutic relationship and group therapy outcome. *Amer. J. Psychiat.*, 133:1290–1294.
Harrow, M., Astrachan, B. M., Tucker, G. J., Klein, E. B., & Miller, J. C. (1971), The T-group and study group laboratory experiences. *J. Soc. Psychol.*, 85:225–237.
Hartley, D., Roback, H. B., & Abramowitz, S. I. (1976), Deterioration effects in encounter groups. *Amer. Psychologist*, 31:247–255.
Hauserman, N., Zweback, S., & Plotkin, A. (1972), Use of concrete reinforcement to facilitate verbal initiations in adolescent group therapy. *J. Consult. Clin. Psychol.*, 38:90–96.
Hurley, J. R. & Force, E. J. (1973), T-group gains in acceptance of self and others. *Int. J. Group Psychother.*, 23:166–176.
_____ & Pinches, S. K. (1978), Interpersonal behavior and effectiveness of T-group leaders. *Small Group Behav.*, 9:529–539.
_____ & Rosenthal, M. (1978a), Interpersonal perceptions within AGPA's annual institute groups. *Group*, 2:220–238.
_____ _____ (1978b), Interpersonal rating shifts during and after AGPA's institute groups. *Int. J. Group Psychother.*, 28:115–121.
Hurst, A. G., Stein, K. B., Korchin, S. J., & Soskin, W. F. (1978), Leadership style determinants of cohesiveness in adolescent groups. *Int. J. Group Psychother.*, 28:263–277.
Jacobs, A. (1974a), Learning-oriented and training-oriented approaches to the modification of emotional behavior in groups. In: *The Group as Agent of Change*, ed. A. Jacobs & W. Spradlin. New York: Behavioral Publications.
_____ (1974b), The use of feedback in groups. In: *The Group as Agent of Change*, ed. A. Jacobs & W. Spradlin. New York: Behavioral Publications.
Jacobs, M., Jacobs, A., Gatz, M., & Schaible, T. (1973), Credibility and desirability of positive and negative structured feedback in groups. *J. Consult. Clin. Psychol.*, 40:244–252.
Jenkins, J. L., Keefe, T., & Rosato, L. W. (1971), Therapists' awareness of how group therapy patients perceive them. *Correct. Psychiat. J. Soc. Ther.*, 17:17–24.
Jensen, J. L., & McGrew, W. L. (1974), Leadership techniques in group therapy with chronic schizophrenic patients. *Nursing Res.*, 23:416–420.
Jessell, J. C., & Bush, J. F. (1973), Effects of principal actor time structuring on goal attainment in group counseling. *Counsel. Ed. Supervision*, 12:105–110.
Kangas, J. A. (1971), Group members' self-disclosure: A function of preceding self-disclosure by leader or other group member. *Compar. Group Studies*, 2:65–70.
Kilmann, P. R. (1974), Direct and nondirect marathon group therapy and internal-external control. *J. Counsel. Psychol.*, 21:380–384.
_____, Albert, B. M., & Sotile, W. M. (1975), Relationship between locus of control, structure of therapy, and outcome. *J. Consult. Clin. Psychol.*, 43:588.
_____ Sotile, W. M. (1976), The effects of structured and unstructured leader roles on internal and external group participants. *J. Clin. Psychol.*, 32:848–856.
Kinder, B. N., & Kilmann, P. R. (1976), The impact of differential shifts in leader structure on the outcome of internal and external group participants. *J. Clin. Psychol.*, 32:857–863.
Levin, E. M., & Kurtz, R. R. (1974), Structured and nonstructured human relations training. *J. Counsel. Psychol.*, 21:526–531.

Lewis, J., & Mider, P. A. (1973), Effects of leadership style on content and work styles of short-term therapy groups. *J. Counsel. Psychol.*, 20:137–141.

Liberman, R. (1970a), A behavioral approach to group dynamics. I. Reinforcement and prompting of cohesiveness in group therapy. *Behav. Ther.*, 1:141–175.

——— (1970b), A behavioral approach to group dynamics. II. Reinforcing and prompting hostility-to-the-therapist in group therapy. *Behav. Ther.*, 1:312–327.

——— (1971), Reinforcement of cohesiveness in group therapy: Behavioral and personality changes. *Arch. Gen. Psychiat.*, 25:168–177.

Lieberman, M. A. (1975), Some limits to research on T-groups. *J. Applied Behav. Sci.*, 11:241–249.

——— (1976), Change induction in small groups. *Ann. Rev. Psychol.*, 27:217–250.

———, Yalom, I. D., & Miles, M. B. (1973), *Encounter Groups: First Facts*. New York: Basic Books.

Luke, R. A. (1972), The internal normative structure of sensitivity training groups. *J. Applied Behav. Sci.*, 8:421–437.

Lundgren, D. C. (1971), Trainer style and patterns of group development. *J. Applied Behav. Sci.*, 7:689–709.

——— (1973), Attitudinal and behavioral correlates of emergent status in training groups. *J. Soc. Psychol.*, 90:141–153.

——— (1974), Trainer-member influence in T groups: One-way or two-way? *Human Rel.*, 27:755–766.

——— (1975), Interpersonal needs and member attitudes toward trainer and group. *Small Group Behav.*, 6:371–388.

——— (1977), Developmental trends in the emergence of interpersonal issues in T groups. *Small Group Behav.*, 8:179–200.

——— (1979), Authority and group formation. *J. Applied Behav. Sci.*, 15:330–345.

——— & Knight, D. J. (1974), Leadership styles and membership attitudes in T groups. *Pers. Soc. Psychol. Bull.*, 1:263–266.

——— ——— (1977), Trainer style and member attitudes toward trainer and group in T-groups. *Small Group Behav.*, 8:47–64.

——— ——— (1978), Sequential stages of development in sensitivity training groups. *J. Applied Behav. Sci.*, 14:204–222.

——— & Schaeffer, C. (1976), Feedback processes in sensitivity training groups. *Human Rel.*, 29:763–782.

May, O. P., & Thompson, C. L. (1973), Perceived levels of self-disclosure, mental health, and helpfulness of group leaders. *J. Counsel. Psychol.*, 20:349–352.

McLachlan, J. F. C. (1972), Benefit from group therapy as a function of patient-therapist match on conceptual level. *Psychother.: Theory, Res., Prac.*, 9:317–323.

——— (1974), Therapy strategies, personality orientation and recovery from alcoholism. *Can. Psychiat. Assn. J.*, 19:25–30.

Melnick, J., & Woods, M. (1976), Analysis of group composition research and theory for psychotherapeutic and growth-oriented groups. *J. Applied Behav. Sci.*, 12:493–512.

Morrison, J. K., Libow, J. A., Smith, F. J., and Becker, R. R. (1978), Comparative effectiveness of directive vs. nondirective group therapist style on client problem resolution. *J. Clin. Psychol.*, 34:186–187.

Morrison, T. L., & Thomas, M. D. (1976), Participants' perceptions of themselves and leaders in two kinds of group experience. *J. Soc. Psychol.*, 98:103–110.

Moss, C. J., & Harren, V. A. (1978), Member disclosure in personal growth groups: Effects of leader disclosure. *Small Group Behav.*, 9:64–79.

Nichols, M. P. (1977), The delayed impact of group therapists' interventions. *J. Clin.*

Psychol., 33:258-262.

_____ & Taylor, T. Y. (1975), Impact of therapist interventions on early sessions of group therapy. *J. Clin. Psychol.,* 31:726-729.

O'Day, R. (1973), Training style: A content-analytic assessment. *Human Rel.,* 26:599-637.

_____ (1974), The T-group trainer: A study of conflict in the exercise of authority. In: *Analysis of Groups,* ed. G. S. Gibbard, J. J. Hartman, & R. D. Mann. San Francisco: Jossey-Bass, 1974.

_____ (1976), Individual training styles: An empirically derived typology. *Small Group Behav.,* 7:147-182.

Parloff, M. B., & Dies, R. R. (1978), Group therapy outcome instrument: Guidelines for conducting research. *Small Group Behav.,* 9:243-285.

Pattinson, P. R., Rardin, M. W., & Lindberg, F. H. (1977), Effects of immediate feedback on the therapeutic content of group leaders' statements. *Small Group Behav.,* 8:303-311.

Peteroy, E. T. (1979), Effects of member and leader expectations on group outcome. *J. Counsel. Psychol.,* 26:534-537.

Peters, D. R. (1973), Identification and personal learning in T-groups. *Human Rel.,* 26:1-21.

Pino, C. J., & Cohen, M. (1971), Trainer style and trainee self-disclosure. *Int. J. Group Psychother.,* 21:202-213.

Piper, W. E., Doan, B. D., Edwards, E. M., & Jones, B. D. (1979), Cotherapy behavior, group therapy process, and treatment outcome. *J. Consult. Clin. Psychol.,* 47:1081-1089.

Reddy, W. B., & Lippert, K. M. (1980), Studies of the processes and dynamics within experiential groups. In: *Small Groups and Personal Change,* ed. P. Smith. London: Methuen.

Roback, H. B. (1972), Experimental comparison of outcomes in insight-and non-insight-oriented therapy groups. *J. Consult. Clin. Psychol.,* 38:411-417.

_____ & Strassberg, D. S. (1975), Relationship between perceived therapist-offered conditions and therapeutic movement in group psychotherapy. *Small Group Behav.,* 6:345-352.

Robinson, M. B. (1970), A study of the effects of focused video-tape feedback in group counseling. *Compar. Group Studies,* 1:47-75.

_____ & Jacobs, A. (1970), Focused video-tape feedback and behavior change in group psychotherapy. *Psychother.: Theory, Res., Prac.,* 7:169-172.

Rogers, C. R. (1957), The necessary and sufficient conditions of therapeutic personality change. *J. Consult. Psychol.,* 21:95-103.

Rohrbaugh, M., & Bartels, B. D. (1975), Participants' perceptions of "curative factors" in therapy and growth groups. *Small Group Behav.,* 6:430-456.

Rosenzweig, S. P., & Folman, R. (1974), Patient and therapist variables affecting premature termination in group psychotherapy. *Psychother.: Theory, Res., Prac.,* 11:76-79.

Sampson, E. E. (1972), Leader orientation and T-group effectiveness. *J. Applied Behav. Sci.,* 8:564-575.

Schwartz, A. H., Harrow, M., Anderson, C., Feinstein, A. E., & Schwartz, C. C. (1970), Influence of therapeutic task orientation on patient and therapist satisfaction in group psychotherapy. *Int. J. Group Psychother.,* 20:460-469.

Seldman, M. L., McBrearty, J. F., & Seldman, S. L. (1974), Deification of marathon encounter group leaders. *Small Group Behav.,* 5:80-91.

Shapiro, R. J., & Klein, R. H. (1975), Perceptions of the leaders in an encounter group. *Small Group Behav.,* 6:238–248.

Shawver, L., & Lubach, J. (1977), Value attribution in group psychotherapy. *J. Consult. Clin. Psychol.,* 45:228–236.

———— & Pines, A. (1978), Value attribution in encounter groups. *Small Group Behav.,* 9:14–22.

Silbergeld, S., Manderscheid, R. W., & Koenig, G. R. (1977), Evaluation of brief intervention models by the Hill interaction matrix. *Small Group Behav.,* 8:281–302.

————, Thune, E. S., & Manderscheid, R. W. (1979), The group therapist leadership role: Assessment in adolescent coping courses. *Small Group Behav.,* 10:176–199.

Smith, D., & Miller, R. (1979), Personal growth groups: A comparison of the experiences of Anglo and Mexican Americans. *Small Group Behav.,* 10:263–270.

Smith, P. B. (1971), Correlations among some tests of T-group learning. *J. Applied Behav. Sci.,* 7:508–511.

———— (1976), Sources of influence in the sensitivity training laboratory. *Small Group Behav.,* 7:331–348.

Strassberg, D. S., Roback, H. B., Anchor, K. N., and Abramowitz, S. I. (1975), Self-disclosure in group therapy with schizophrenics. *Arch. Gen. Psychiat.,* 32:1259–1261.

Trotzer, J. P. (1971), Process comparison of encounter groups and discussion groups using videotaped excerpts. *J. Counsel. Psychol.,* 18:358–361.

Truax, C. B. (1971a), Degree of negative transference occurring in group psychotherapy and client outcome in juvenile delinquents. *J. Clin. Psychol.,* 27:123–126.

———— (1971b), Perceived therapeutic conditions and client outcome. *Compar. Group Studies,* 2:301–310.

———— & Lister, J. L. (1970), Effects of therapist persuasive potency in group psychotherapy. *J. Clin. Psychol.,* 26:396–397.

————, Wargo, D. G., & Volksdorf, N. R. (1970), Antecedents to outcome in group counseling with institutionalized juvenile delinquents: Effects of therapeutic conditions, patient self-exploration, alternate sessions, and vicarious therapy pretraining. *J. Abnorm. Psychol.,* 76:235–242.

————, Wittmer, J., & Wargo, D. G. (1971), Effects of the therapeutic conditions of accurate empathy, non-possessive warmth, and genuineness on hospitalized mental patients during group therapy. *J. Clin. Psychol.,* 27:137–142.

Vitalo, R. L. (1971), Teaching improved interpersonal functioning as a preferred mode of treatment. *J. Clin. Psychol.,* 27:166–171.

Warner, R. W., & Hansen, J. C. (1970), Verbal-reinforcement and model-reinforcement group counseling with alienated students. *J. Counsel. Psychol.,* 17:168–172.

Weigel, R. G., Dinges, N., Dyer, R., & Straumfjord, A. A. (1972), Perceived self-disclosure, mental health, and who is liked in group treatment. *J. Counsel. Psychol.,* 19:47–52.

Wogan, M., Getter, H., Amdur, M. J., Nichols, M. F., & Okman, G. (1977), Influencing interaction and outcomes in group psychotherapy. *Small Group Behav.,* 8:25–46.

Wright, F. (1976), The effects of style and sex of consultants and sex of members in self-study groups. *Small Group Behav.,* 7:433–456.

Wright, W., Morris, K. T., & Felting, D. (1974), Comparative effects of social skill development. *Small Group Behav.,* 5:211–221.

Yalom, I. D. (1975), *The Theory and Practice of Group Psychotherapy,* 2nd Ed. New York: Basic Books.

3

Change Measures and Clinical Practice in Group Psychotherapy

ERICH COCHÉ, Ph.D.

SOME INTRODUCTORY CONSIDERATIONS

The need to build an element of formal evaluation into the practice of group psychotherapy has been emphasized (e.g., Glatzer, 1976). Many clinicians would agree that the systematic assessment of therapy outcome may provide additional information on a patient's progress in treatment so as to augment the therapist's clinical impression, perhaps supported by the group, that the patient is ready to leave therapy. Furthermore, assessments of outcome may enhance a therapist's self-esteem, respectability, and credibility as a scientist-practitioner. Such evaluations, especially if combined with process data, can also provide valuable feedback on aspects of one's practice which may need modification or improvement.

Nevertheless, the clinician with all good intentions to add an outcome measure to the standard operating procedures of a therapy group may be foiled in the attempt by a variety of factors—not the least of which is the confusing multitude of available instruments. In addition, as Hartman (1979) and Dies and I (Coché and Dies, 1981) have described, there may be an attitudinal gulf between researchers and clinicians, based on the stereotyped views each has of the other (see Chapter

Thanks are extended to the hospital administration of Friends Hospital in Philadelphia for the generous support afforded the projects mentioned in this chapter. Thanks are also due to Joan Cooper and Joseph Sillitti for their faithful data-gathering efforts, and to Virginia Brabender, the leader of the groups under study.

1 by Dies). Thus, in providing guidelines for the selection of adequate outcome measures, I shall try to avoid discouraging clinicians by making excessive research demands while also cautioning against wasting time through the use of inadequate measures.

Selection of Outcome Criteria

Outcome assessment, if it is to be meaningful, entails more than merely administering a test before and after treatment. The tests need to relate logically to the goals of the group and to the needs of the patient in treatment. Thus, one of the first questions to be answered is whether the group is homogeneous, with highly similar problems (e.g., a group of depressives), or heterogeneous, with a diversity of presenting complaints (e.g., adult neurotic outpatients). In the latter case, broad-spectrum inventories such as the Minnesota Multiphasic Personality Inventory (MMPI) or the Self-Report Symptom Inventory (Derogatis, 1977) are more desirable tools, while in the former situation a specific measure such as the Beck Depression Inventory (Beck, Ward, Mendelson, Mock, and Erbaugh, 1961) is much more economical and to the point. Basically, the clinician has to grapple with the question: "How will I know that these patients have improved?"* Clinically appropriate criteria have to be established first, after which the search for proper tests is more straightforward, often requiring little more than a creative perusal of Buros's handbooks (1975, 1978) or the change-measures manual edited by Waskow and Parloff (1975).

Individual versus Group-Oriented Instruments

Group therapy differs from individual therapy; the processes leading to improvement are unique, despite some overlap. Therefore, it may at

---

*Editors' Note: The measurement of change in psychotherapy is a complex task, and there is considerable divergence of opinion on this issue. The principal controversy centers on the question of whether change should be assessed by overt behavioral measures or whether it is more sensitively evaluated by looking at internal psychological dimensions. Those adopting the former approach claim to represent the real world, where results of internal change must be manifest. Those taking the latter position suggest that the task of psychotherapy is to deal with internal conflicts and misperceptions so that change measures should deal directly with such phenomena. For a further discussion of these issues, the reader is directed to Waskow and Parloff's book (1975) and MacKenzie and Dies's monograph (1982). Both of these publications review measures that cover a breadth of viewpoints while remaining concise enough for regular use in a clinical setting. In Chapter 9, Lieberman also addresses this question of subjective versus objective change measures.

first appear that the outcome measures, too, should be different and oriented to the group treatment modality. The patient who enters treatment, however, comes because of a problem which requires amelioration. While an effective and cohesive group may be necessary to bring about the desired change, the ultimate test of success is whether the patient has improved. Individual group members, who have invested considerable amounts of time and money in their treatment, are in the end most concerned with their own personal symptoms, sufferings, and treatment goals, regardless of the overall quality of the group to which they belonged. As Kaul and Bednar (1978) have stated, "many of the dependent variables in group research can and should be posed in terms of individual outcomes (though, of course these can be amalgamated and the group can be treated as the unit of data)" (p. 178). Thus, the prospective group therapy evaluator may make full use of the instruments already available to the investigator of individual therapy.

Divergent Points of View

Clinicians are familiar with patients who report great strides in therapy but remain essentially unchanged in behavior and symptomatology. Similarly, others, who presumably change as a result of treatment, fail to report a sense of improvement. Often such discrepancies may be due to a difference in viewpoint between the therapist and the patient.

Strupp and Hadley (1977) assert that psychotherapy outcome can be viewed from any one of three vantage points, each of which implies a different genus of outcome criteria: (1) the patient, who is usually most interested in a subjective sense of well-being; (2) society (the patient's family, employers, authorities, etc.), with its focus on behavioral adjustment; and (3) the therapist, who concentrates on theoretical constructs such as ego strength or soundness of personality structure. While in many cases all three sources may agree that the patient is better, quite often there are degrees of difference. The researcher, interested in a smooth, valid, and unified measure of therapy success, may curse this discrepancy. The practitioner, on the other hand, will be cognizant of the inevitable inconsistencies, and structure outcome measures accordingly, seeing the discrepancies as a source of valuable information and insights into the complexity of change.

When faced with low correlations between two outcome measures, many investigators have tended to blame the instruments, suspecting low reliability or validity and considering the divergences an artifact of the assessment procedures. Clinical experience, however, shows that such divergent opinions about the success of therapy are perfectly under-standable. Strupp and Hadley (1977) give several examples in which the patient and therapist disagree about progress, although each has a valid assessment from a particular point of view.

THE CORE BATTERY

In focusing on psychotherapy outcome measures which may be of use to group psychotherapists, I would like to begin with the CORE Battery (MacKenzie and Dies, 1982). The CORE Battery was developed between 1977 and 1981 by members of the Research Committee of the American Group Psychotherapy Association as a self-assessment kit to be used by practicing group psychotherapists. The kit contains helpful hints on how to use the CORE Battery in clinical practice and instruc-tions for the proper scoring of the measures, together with some back-ground data on the tests.

From the outset, the plan was to include a broad spectrum of tools to make the kit useful to a wide variety of groups and clients. Mindful of the advice given by Strupp and Hadley (1977), the CORE Battery incor-porates patient self-report instruments, therapist reports, and, whenever feasible, some techniques involving "significant others."

Self-Report Symptom Inventory (SCL-90-R)

This test, developed by Derogatis (1977) and his co-workers, is the successor to the Hopkins Symptom Checklist. A 90-item questionnaire, it yields scores on nine symptom dimensions (e.g., *depression, somatiza-tion, psychoticism*) and three summary scores, including a global severity index (see Table 1, p. 86). The SCL-90-R takes about 20 minutes for clients to complete. Scoring is relatively straightforward. The items are simply written, and appear on an easy-to-read form; thus, the SCL-90-R requires a lower level of reading ability, vocabulary, and intelligence than the MMPI or the Social Adjustment Scale (see below).

Social Adjustment Scale (SAS)

This test, developed by Weissman and Bothwell (1976), takes about 20 minutes to administer. Scoring requires a little more practice than the SCL-90-R, but is still quite easy. The main advantages of the SAS are that even though it is a self-report instrument it focuses specifically on adjustment to the social surroundings (e.g., work, leisure, family), and its items are well anchored behaviorally.

Emotions Profile Index (EPI)

The EPI, created by Plutchik (1980), is a collection of self-descriptive adjectives in a format which requires the subject to choose between any two such adjectives in all possible combinations. It takes about 15 minutes to administer and is easy to read, although a few subjects may complain about the format (occasionally they feel that neither item describes them very well, and they may resent having to choose). The test results consist of scores on eight personality dimensions (see Table 1) and a social desirability score. The scores can be presented in numerical or graphic form.

Whereas the SCL-90-R is most definitely symptom- and pathology-oriented, the EPI is oriented toward the normal personality. With certain client populations, this turns out to be the greatest advantage of the EPI, because it lends itself to direct feedback to the clients. Furthermore, the scale dimensions have direct relevance for interpersonal styles and thus to behavior in a small group setting. Findings from the EPI can be linked to a person's group participation, making it a highly desirable tool when a combined process and outcome study is planned.

Target Goals (Patient)

Objective tests, such as the SCL-90-R or the MMPI, when used as outcome measures, usually require the additional assumption that change is always desirable in one direction only, i.e., away from the "pathological." Unhappy with that assumption, several authors have recently worked on tools more specifically tailored to the individual patient. Kiresuk and Sherman's (1968) Goal Attainment Scaling and the Target Goals Procedure of Battle, Imber, Hoehn-Saric, Stone, Nash, and Frank (1966) represent two examples.

In these techniques, which are not "tests" in the usual sense of the word, the subject is asked to make a list of the three most important goals he or she would like to work on during therapy. The patient is encouraged to keep these goals in behavioral terms. After the treatment group is over, the patient is asked to rate goal achievements on a seven-point scale from "worse" to "total improvement." Thus, in this effort to construct an individualized outcome measure, effectiveness of treatment is measured solely by the degree to which individual, behaviorally phrased, predetermined goals have ultimately been reached.

Global Assessment Scale (GAS)

The GAS, as presented by Luborsky (1962), is one of the two measures based on therapist-supplied data. It consists of a 100-point continuum anchored by personality descriptions given for every ten-point range. For example, the anchor statement for 71–80 reads: "No more than slight impairment in functioning, varying degrees of 'everyday' worries and problems that get out of hand. Minimal symptoms may or may not be present." All that is required from the therapist is to assign the patient a simple numerical rating at the point of entering therapy and again at the end of the experience. Because of its simplicity, the completion time required for the GAS, after some initial practice, is about one minute.

Target Goals (Therapist)

In principle, this part of the CORE Battery is analogous to the member-administered Target Goals Procedure. Three behavioral goals, this time chosen by the therapist after evaluating the patient, are to be listed; goal attainment is rated at the end of therapy. In addition, the therapist is asked to rate his or her expectations for this client and to make a personal assessment of how effective the therapist believes he or she is with the type of problems listed. Finally, there is a Global Improvement Rating Scale to complete. All these scales take very little time after brief training; the total therapist rating involvement is no more than five minutes. The therapist is also encouraged to record data on the group, its composition, the therapist's demographics and theoretical orientation, as well as demographic and diagnostic information on individual clients.

Measures of "Significant Others"

The framers of the CORE Battery did not include any specific tests to be given to "significant others" as the third source of information regarding client improvement. Instead, they suggested the Social Adjustment Scale, Emotions Profile Index, and Target Goals Procedure as possible instruments. Consistent with the thoughts presented by Strupp and Hadley (1977), it is probably wisest to administer the SAS to a relative or friend of the client. Both other instruments seem somewhat unlikely as worthwhile tools for this endeavor.

If the "significant other" is a mental health professional (e.g., the unit nurse in a psychiatric hospital), the GAS is a valuable approach. Its time requirements are minimal and it can be given to several persons on the staff, making it possible to evaluate interrater reliability and to pool ratings. My own experiences with this approach so far have been quite rewarding.

The CORE Battery also includes a data summary sheet, scoring forms, advice on determining the clinical significance of change, helpful hints to overcome patient resistance to research, a consent form, and a bibliography on significant group psychotherapy research and reviews.

EXPERIENCES WITH THE CORE BATTERY

A Preliminary Study

In the fall of 1980, the Group Psychotherapy Research Staff at Friends Hospital began experimenting with the CORE Battery in an investigation designed essentially to gather experiences with this new set of tests. Some data from this study will be presented to illustrate the use of the CORE Battery.

The participants in the study were patients who completed the brief group psychotherapy program at Friends Hospital, a short-term psychiatric institution. The groups, led by one experienced group psychotherapist and a therapist in training, were closed and lasted for eight one-and-a-half-hour sessions, distributed over a two-week period. Usually, at the conclusion of group treatment, approximately half of the patients are discharged from the hospital. The remaining group members are transferred to an open-ended, ongoing group, in which they may stay for several additional weeks.

When we began experimenting with the CORE Battery, we elected to use the full battery, with the exception of the Social Adjustment Scale, which did not seem appropriate for an in-hospital group. Instead, we decided to use the Global Assessment Scale as a measure to be administered by a person other than the patient or therapist. The remaining measures were administered to the patients and therapists by the research staff, as planned.

Results

Table 1 outlines the results from this initial investigation. It shows that on the SCL-90-R, there was a general, smooth improvement on all of the scales. The SCL-90-R comes with a manual which gives the therapist-researcher a choice of using norms developed from either a normal or a clinical population. Using the clinical set, we found that our hospitalized patients were approximately three to four points above the clinical average for severity of illness at the time of their admission to the group. Two weeks later, at the time of their discharge from the group (which was not always the same as their discharge from the hospital),

TABLE 1

CORE Battery Means for 34 Hospitalized Patients
(12 Males, 22 Females)

Instrument	X̄ Pre	X̄ Post	X̄ Change[a]
Emotions Profile Index (EPI)			
Trustful	43.4	55.7	12.3
Dyscontrol	26.2	31.3	4.9
Timid	56.0	60.8	4.8
Depressed	71.4	57.5	13.9
Distrustful	49.9	46.7	3.2
Control	43.5	53.6	10.1
Aggressive	61.1	43.1	18.0
Gregarious	44.9	61.0	16.1
Bias	35.2	49.8	14.6
Self-Report Symptom Inventory (SCL-90-R)			
Somatization	55.9	48.8	7.1
Obsessive-Compulsive	53.4	48.3	5.1
Interpersonal Sensitivity	52.1	48.2	3.9
Depression	52.6	47.2	5.4
Anxiety	54.7	47.9	6.8
Hostility	50.9	46.1	4.8
Phobic Anxiety	53.4	50.3	3.1
Paranoid Ideation	53.2	48.6	4.6
Psychoticism	55.7	47.2	8.5
Global Severity Index	54.5	47.5	7.0
Positive Symptom Index	54.5	48.7	5.8
Positive Symptom Distress Index	53.2	45.4	7.8
Global Assessment Scale (GAS)	57.3	63.1	5.8
General Improvement Rating	—	—	4.5
Target Goals (Patient)			
Expectation	3.3	—	—
Attainment	—	—	3.5
Target Goals (Therapist)			
Expectation	2.2	—	—
Attainment	—	—	1.9

[a]Plus or minus signs have purposely been omitted. All changes are in the desirable direction.

they had improved to a point at which they were below the clinical mean for severity of illness in all SCL-90-R categories except *phobic anxiety.* Here the difference from the clinical norm was minuscule. The average improvement was about two-thirds of a standard deviation, which is noteworthy but not statistically significant overall. In individual cases, however, significant improvement, or lack thereof, was demonstrable.

The picture on the EPI was not as smooth. Here the hospitalized patients scored anywhere from 0 to 24 points away from the population mean (50), depending on the scale under study. At the time of post-testing, all of the scales reflected some degree of change, yet the direction and magnitude of change were not uniform (see Table 1).

On the GAS filled out by unit personnel, our patients showed a pretreatment level of 57.3, which improved to a level of 63.1. The overall improvement was of a magnitude similar to that in most other tests (about half the standard deviation), but the individual degree of change was remarkably variable. While the mean change was 5.8, the standard deviation of the *change* attained by our group members was as much as 15 points.

On the Target Goals Procedure, group members rated themselves 3.5 in improvement, which is halfway between "some" and "quite a bit" in response to the question: "To what degree have you attained this goal?" It is worth noting that the patients' expectations (3.3) were actually somewhat rosier than the ultimate outcome, due to the slightly different wording of the scales (3.3 resides between "quite a bit" and "a great deal"). It is also of interest that the patients' expectations and attainment of their goals had a correlation of 0.28, which just barely attains statistical significance at the 0.05 level.

Our therapists gave the patients an overall improvement rating of 4.5, halfway between "some" and "quite a bit." In achievement of the therapeutic goals, the patients did not do quite so well. Their average attainment (1.9) is closest to the marking for "very little." Therapists also were quite consistent in their expectations and their final achievement ratings. The correlation between their expectations and attainment ratings turned out to be 0.44, which is statistically significant.

Relationships among the CORE Battery Instruments

In assessing the correlations among the various scales, we found that they essentially yielded two major sets of data: one cluster of SCL-90-R data and a second factor dominated by EPI scores. These results were somewhat disappointing, showing that the two major contributors to our data were essentially unrelated to each other, although generally consistent within themselves. Nevertheless, we were pleased to find that the EPI "Depression" Scale and the SCL-90-R "Depression" Scale, which are after all supposed to measure the same thing, had a correlation of 0.45, which is again quite statistically significant. Similarly, improvement on the GAS (filled out by the nurses) had a correlation of 0.49 with the therapists' ratings on the Target Goals Procedure. The patients' attainment ratings on Target Goals did not fare quite as well, correlating only weakly with the therapists' and the nurses' ratings.

Use of CORE Data in Answering General Questions

The data from our first experiment allowed us to tackle some institutional questions about our short-term group therapy approach.* Overall, we were able to show that in the short span of two weeks the combined treatment of hospital regimen and group psychotherapy could effect significant changes in the majority of our patients. These changes were most noteworthy in the reduction of psychoticism, anxiety, and depression. We were also able to see that the patients were more positive about their improvement than was the staff.

Use of CORE Data for Individual Assessment

The more rewarding use of the CORE Battery, however, was not in answering questions posed by the institution, but in analyzing individual gains and losses. Within a few hours after the last group session, we were able to obtain each patient's individual profile of pre, post, and change scores. The group therapists could then view their own ratings of improvement in the light of the patient's personal assessment. Data could also be reported back to the attending psychiatrist, to aid in mak-

---

* *Editors' Note:* Data regarding the changes made by patients going through a particular program may be quite useful in helping program staff to determine those areas in which they are most effective, so that there can be an objective refinement of the goals of a program and selection of patients most suited for it. It is important, however, that results obtained on instruments such as those presented in this chapter are used as only one source of data and are not assumed to be the most accurate representation of individual change. Results reflecting divergent opinions between the patient and the staff, or between staff members themselves, can be the source of fruitful clinical discussion. It is a fact of clinical life that divergent viewpoints exist, and the use of routine instruments can help to bring those differences to the fore so that they can be discussed and understood. Data can similarly be used as an alerting process for individual patients, who not infrequently are willing to commit to paper issues they are reluctant to put into words. Finally, the use of standard measures adds greatly to a better understanding of clinical research reports by providing a common language.

ing discharge decisions, and to the therapist of the ongoing group, if the patient was transferred to that group. Occasionally serious discrepancies between therapist and patient ratings became "grist for the therapeutic mill," i.e., both parties were able to compare and discuss their perceptions of therapeutic progress.

Table 2 presents an example of an actual case from the Friends Hospital study. This 25-year-old white single woman, to whom we gave the pseudonym "Linda Smith," was diagnosed as "borderline personality" with depressive features and a history of drug abuse.

In the pre-testing, Linda presented herself as a somewhat overcontrolled, depressed person, whose general level of pathology was in the mid-to-lower range for our sample. Her expectations for improvement were quite high; the goals she listed were all interpersonal in nature. During the next two weeks, group therapy became the major modality of treatment, though Linda did participate in other activities, took some medication, and had regular brief visits from her psychiatrist. Within the group, Linda was extremely active, occasionally monopolizing the group, reaching out for others in egocentric and ambivalent ways. The group in turn confronted her on her behavior, and helped her to develop a real awareness of her egocentrism. At the end, the group members felt that she was ready to leave the hospital and form a functioning alliance with her outpatient therapist.

The change data show that Linda was very happy with the changes she made, to the point of exaggerating her wellness (Bias score on EPI). While she saw herself as "a great deal" improved on her target goals, the therapists were much less sanguine, seeing her goal attainment as "very little." Two "outside observers" (unit nurses) saw her as somewhat better (GAS) but still in the "moderate symptoms" range.

Linda left the hospital a few days later with the intention of continuing to work on her problems. Outpatient group therapy was recommended to her.

Cooperation among Study Participants

In many cases like the one above, the group therapists, attending psychiatrists, and unit personnel were interested in comparing their assessments with those of the patient and of other staff members, and venturing hypotheses to explain discrepancies when they occurred. Sharing the information gained through the CORE Battery greatly aided in maintaining the mental health team's enthusiasm for the project. Resistance from professionals was generally minimal because they were

TABLE 2

Sample Case of Patient "Linda Smith"

Instrument	Pre	Post	Change[a]
Emotions Profile Index (EPI)			
Trustful	70	79	9
Dyscontrol	12	29	17
Timid	65	78	13
Depressed	78	19	59
Distrustful	45	37	8
Control	47	83	36
Aggressive	38	5	33
Gregarious	60	98	38
Bias	47	95	48
Self-Report Symptom Inventory (SCL-90-R)			
Somatization	50	31	19
Obsessive-Compulsive	47	33	14
Interpersonal Sensitivity	55	38	17
Depression	58	36	22
Anxiety	47	34	13
Hostility	50	41	9
Phobic Anxiety	52	39	13
Paranoid Ideation	50	41	9
Psychoticism	55	37	18
Global Severity Index	48	33	15
Positive Symptom Total	45	32	13
Positive Symptom Distress Index	53	34	19
Global Assessment Scale (GAS)	52	57	5
General Improvement Rating	—	—	5
Target Goals (Patient)			
Expectation	3.67	—	—
Attainment	—	—	5.33
Target Goals (Therapist)			
Expectation	2.67	—	—
Attainment	—	—	2.00

[a]Plus or minus signs have purposely been omitted. Whether something constitutes a gain or a loss has to be evaluated from the context.

able to see the benefits with little investment of time on their part.

The patients, too, were generally quite cooperative since they had been informed that the research project was aimed at assessing outcome in order to ultimately improve service. Only a few participants grumbled about the requirements of testing; the complaints were usually more pronounced if the patient was scheduled for discharge from the hospital but the post-testing had yet to be completed. All patients had been informed that participation was voluntary and that they could still be a group member even if they chose not to do the tests. In this study no one took this option.

ADDITIONAL TESTS

It would be too extensive an undertaking to list all the other tests that could be used as outcome measures. Instead, the reader is referred again to the works by Waskow and Parloff (1975) and Buros (1975, 1978). At this point I shall mention only a few additional techniques which we have used in the past few years with varying degrees of success.*

Minnesota Multiphasic Personality Inventory (MMPI)

The MMPI is probably the most frequently used outcome measure in psychotherapy research. The impressive body of research on this instrument and the easy availability of high-quality scoring services make it well-suited for outcome evaluation purposes. However, it does have some drawbacks. Foremost among these is its length: many patients will complain about having to answer 566 true-false questions. Although short forms of the MMPI are available, they do not encompass the full range of scales. Thus, an abbreviated MMPI approach, as reviewed by Hoffman and Butcher (1975), can in many ways resolve certain of the problems posed by the entire MMPI, but valuable information may be sacrificed. If an instrument of moderate length is desired in which a patient can show symptomatic improvement, or deterioration, the SCL-90-R is preferable to an abbreviated MMPI. A full MMPI is probably quite appropriate when the patient population is moderately to severely disturbed and has been in therapy for a considerable length of time.

Editors' Note: A number of instruments are in wide use and the selection of a particular one reflects personal opinion as much as sound psychometric arguments. Measures chosen should have a direct connection with the treatment being employed so that a continuous theme can be discerned from entry assessment, through treatment technique, to clinical outcome.

With a client population of mild neurotics, however, the pathology orientation of the MMPI may be more of a hindrance than a help. Nor is the MMPI recommended for short-duration therapies, as most of its scales are oriented toward enduring personality traits rather than those aspects of a person which are more amenable to change.

Adjective Checklist

This instrument, originally developed by Gough and Heilbrun (1965), has had a varied history. As an instrument of personality assessment, it received negative reviews in early editions of Buros's handbooks. As an outcome measure in psychotherapy research, however, the Adjective Checklist has proved to be quite useful. In our own studies (Blumberg and Coché, 1980; Coché and Douglas, 1977; Coché, Polikoff, and Cooper, 1980), we have used the Adjective Checklist repeatedly and have been pleased with it.

The instrument consists of 200 alphabetically ordered adjectives which are later scored on 24 scales. Patients simply mark those adjectives they consider self-descriptive. In psychotherapy studies this instrument has shown clinically meaningful changes which were in concordance with other available data. Because of the ease of administrating and scoring it, the Adjective Checklist offers a worthwhile alternative to group therapists who may not be satisfied with the instruments offered in the CORE Battery.

Projective Techniques

Projective techniques, especially the Rorschach Test, while widely used in personality assessment, have never become very popular with psychotherapy outcome researchers. This is partially due to the statistical properties of instruments such as the Rorschach, which are indeed very cumbersome to the researcher. Only recently has the Comprehensive Rorschach System developed by Exner (1974, 1978) demonstrated adequate reliability and statistical properties to make it useful for outcome studies. To my knowledge, it has already been used in some individual psychotherapy research but not as yet with groups.

The Thematic Apperception Test (TAT) shows a similar history. Although a considerable amount has been written on the TAT over the years, its use in psychotherapy outcome research has been minimal. Encouraged by the favorable review by Endicott and Endicott (1975), the group therapy research staff at Friends Hospital has launched a series of studies aimed at developing a reliable scoring system for the TAT, which would permit its use in therapy outcome research. So far, this scoring system has been shown to be a helpful and valid indicator of depression and, as such, can be applied to group therapy outcome research with depressed patients (Coché and Sillitti, in press).

Behavioral Observation Techniques

Certain patients come to the attention of therapists because a specific behavior is causing distress, not necessarily primarily for the patient but perhaps more so for family, friends, and others. In these cases, as well as in those in which a reliable informant cannot be found, an *in vivo* observation technique may be the ideal approach. One widely used technique is the Ward Behavior Inventory (Burdock and Hardesty, 1960). In situations where the outcome of an in-hospital group is being investigated, the Ward Behavior Inventory is a particularly useful instrument. However, a serious cautionary note is necessary. In a psychiatric hospital with an average length of stay of 30 days or less, the Ward Behavior Inventory is not advisable. It has been our experience that a pathological behavior (e.g., "talks to self") may not be scored at first on the Ward Behavior Inventory because the nurse-observer did not see this behavior during the patient's first three days on the unit (see Wondolowski, 1978). Thus, it is not scored "present" in the pre-testing. Over the next three weeks, however, the nurse may see the pathological behavior and score it as present on the post-testing. Thus, patients may be rated as more disturbed in such instances when, in fact, they merely remained the same. This artifact, if it occurs frequently, can destroy an otherwise well-thought-out research project.

Other Behavioral Indices

Finally, it should be mentioned that for certain groups, simple and direct behavioral indices may be the best outcome measures. If six to eight patients form a weight control group, for instance, the amount of weight lost is indeed the most desirable outcome measure. Similar behavioral indices apply to "stop smoking" groups, sex offender groups, and other groups of patients with homogeneous behavioral symptomatology. These indices can be made part of the Target Goals Procedure and thus part of the CORE Battery, if a more comprehensive assessment is desired.

Occasionally hospital outcome researchers use readmission or relapse rates to assess the value of group therapy. Erickson (1975), however, argues that such indicators as relapse rates are rather unfortunate, largely because they imply a "snakepit attitude," i.e., an underlying assumption that being out of the hospital is always good, and that being in the hospital is always bad. It is known that some persons who manage to stay out of hospitals — frequently in their homes, in "one-person chronic wards" managed by their families — may in fact be much more disturbed than others who come back to the hospital for an occasional relapse in between long periods of productive living.

APPLICATIONS

Evaluations of Group Therapy Efficacy

Eysenck's (1952) original, startling statement that psychotherapy is ineffective set in motion an extensive research effort at many centers, in various countries, aimed at proving that psychotherapy is effective after all. Twenty years later, the question was essentially settled, and the original simple question "Does psychotherapy work?" was replaced by more sophisticated questions such as: "Which kind of therapy works under which circumstances for which type of patient?" Developments in group psychotherapy outcome research have been basically quite similar. Early reviews of the research literature in the 1960s were noncommittal or cautiously positive at best. This trend changed during the 1970s, when research reviewers became more confident in their conclusions that group psychotherapy is indeed beneficial (Dies, 1979). At the same time there was a growing desire to develop greater specificity in the kinds of evaluative statements which could be made. Although there is no further need for studies to prove that group psychotherapy "works," there is still a great need to learn more about the value of group psychotherapy in different settings.

Evaluations in Clinics

Clinics and community health centers so far have furnished the bulk of group therapy outcome studies. The large numbers of patients seen in these settings, the availability of a variety of therapists, and the possibility of creating groups out of the large pool of persons in need of therapy have made clinics and mental health centers a fertile ground for group therapy research. Unfortunately, the recent budget cutbacks at most mental health centers have forced many of these facilities to place research very low on their list of priorities. Therefore, it is likely that there will be fewer studies in these settings in the coming years. The general reduction of research funding on a national level is further exacerbating this problem.

Research in Medical Hospitals

Group therapy for medical patients is receiving increasing attention (e.g., Cooper-Lonergan, 1980; Coven, 1981). Medical patients are placed in groups which can help them to improve self-esteem, increase their willingness to cooperate with the medical regimen, and provide mutual support among people in similar life circumstances. Although descriptions of the efficacy of group treatment with medical patients are very encouraging, research on outcome is still in its rudimentary stage. Yet the ground for such research is fertile. In groups with medical patients, outcome measures such as those contained in the CORE Battery can be combined with behavioral indicators like drug compliance or frequency of medical emergencies.

Research in Psychiatric Hospitals

Researchers in hospitals for the mentally ill have been among the major contributors to the group therapy literature. For many years, the main question in these settings was whether the addition of group psychotherapy contributed a valuable new element to the patient's normal treatment regimen. Most of the studies have been very positive, but, as Erickson (1975) points out, one cannot help but have the impression from some of these studies that any type of group activity which pulled the patient out of the boredom of a chronic ward would show beneficial effects. Thus, more sophisticated designs, including not only "no-therapy controls" but also parallel activity groups, are needed. When such methodological safeguards have been introduced, some noteworthy supportive findings on group psychotherapy in psychiatric hospitals have indeed been obtained (e.g., Olsen and Greenberg, 1972).

Research in Private Practice

It is a peculiar phenomenon that while a large percentage of the American population receives psychotherapy from private practitioners, there is hardly any research on this form of service delivery. Thus, we know a fair amount about therapy effectiveness in clinics and mental health centers, but little about the generalizability of these results to the private practice setting (Orlinsky, 1981). Most practitioners shy away from making research an integral part of their practice for a variety of reasons (Coché and Coché, 1978).

To begin with, practitioners who eschew the institutional setting tend to see themselves as clinicians first, and they often harbor a rather negative attitude toward research (Coché and Dies, 1981). The systematic gathering of data simply does not fit their self-image. Furthermore, many practitioners feel that to ask their clients to fill our paper-and-pencil tests for research purposes is an unwarranted intrusion into the interpersonal activity of psychotherapy. Although one could look on such data gathering as an integral part of psychotherapy, which may in fact make it more meaningful, very few practitioners take this view. Finally, there is the fact that time spent on gathering and processing psychotherapy research data is, in monetary terms, "unproductive time." If a research assistant is employed to do some of the work, it only adds to the cost, and outside funding is difficult or even impossible for the individual practitioner to obtain.

The introduction of the CORE Battery, however, has reduced the power of the above reasons. This easily administered set of instruments does not intrude into the therapeutic relationship; instead, the data generated can be incorporated into treatment (e.g., the Target Goals Procedure can provide a focus for the group). The cost involved is also minimal, and it does not require high-level research skills to administer or score the tests.

Given the dearth of information, it is important that we gather more data on the conduct and efficacy of group psychotherapy in the private practice setting. With mounting pressure from legislators and insurance carriers to document the value of our efforts, it becomes increasingly untenable to blithely assume that results obtained in other settings also apply to independent practice.

Contributions to Research Knowledge

As I have already indicated, there is little additional need for studies showing that group psychotherapy "works," but there is still a great need for more differentiated statements about what aspects of group treatment contribute to therapeutic change. The traditional division of therapy research into process and outcome helps us to classify studies and tools in a meaningful way. Yet this division may become counterproductive if we conduct only studies that investigate one without the other. We need more studies that systematically investigate the effects of variations in the conduct of group psychotherapy on the success of the treatment.

Variations in treatment can be evaluated in several ways. Planned changes can be made in leadership styles, for instance. Specifically, the intervention foci described by Borriello (1979) — group as a whole, interpersonal, and individual — might be systematically alternated by one and the same therapist or by a planned rotation of therapists, and the effect of this variation on group outcome could be studied by means of the instruments described in this chapter. From a different angle, one might look at the phases in group development described by Beck and her associates (Chapter 6) and by MacKenzie and Livesley (Chapter 4), and relate these phases to group outcome. Can a group still be effective if it does not work through the developmental task of a certain phase? What is the outcome of a group that completely skips one or two phases? These and other questions are of more than academic interest.

On a final note, I would like to suggest the study of group composition in relation to outcome (Melnick and Woods, 1976). The literature is replete with dialogue on the advisability of homogeneous versus heterogeneous groups. Yet empirical documentation in this area is still largely nonexistent.

CONCLUSION

Throughout this chapter, I have tried to show that evaluating the outcome of one's therapy groups is not only desirable but also quite feasible. The task need not be overwhelming, intrusive, or expensive. Assessment can be done quite economically. Most of all, gathering data on groups may deepen one's understanding of the effects and limitations of group treatment, thus adding meaning to the group psychotherapeutic enterprise for the client, the therapist, and other professionals interested in advancing the field of group psychotherapy.

REFERENCES

Battle, C., Imber, S., Hoehn-Saric, R., Stone, A., Nash, E., & Frank, J. (1966), Target complaints as criteria of improvement. *Amer. J. Psychother.*, 20:184–192.

Beck, A. T., Ward, C. H., Mendelson, N., Mock, J., & Erbaugh, J. (1961), An inventory for measuring depression. *Arch. Gen. Psychiat.*, 4:561–571.

Blumberg, S., & Coché, E. (1980), The use of movement in a psychotherapy group. *Amer. J. Dance Ther.*, 3:56–64.

Borriello, J. F. (1979), Intervention foci in group psychotherapy. In: *Group Psychotherapy 1979*, ed. L. R. Wolberg & M. L. Aronson. New York: Stratton Intercontinental.

Burdock, E., & Hardesty, A. (1960), *WBI: Ward Behavior Inventory Manual.* New York: Springer.

Buros, O. K. (1975), *Personality Tests and Reviews, II.* Highland Park, N.J.: Gryphon Press.

98 *Erich Coché*

_____ (1978), *The Eighth Mental Measurements Yearbook.* Highland Park, N.J.: Gryphon Press.

Coché, E., & Coché, J. M. (1978), The private practice psychologist as researcher: Ethical and professional considerations. Presented at the 19th International Congress of Applied Psychology, Munich.

_____ & Dies, R. R. (1981), Integrating research findings into the practice of group psychotherapy. *Psychother.: Theory, Res., Prac.,* 18:410–416.

_____ & Douglas, A. (1977), Therapeutic effects of problem-solving training and play-reading groups. *J. Clin. Psychol.,* 33:820–827.

_____, Polikoff, B., & Cooper, J. (1980), Participant self-disclosure in group. *Group,* 4:28–35.

_____ & Sillitti, J. (in press), The Thematic Apperception Test as an outcome measure in psychotherapy research. *Psychother.: Theory, Res., Prac.*

Cooper-Lonergan, E. (1980), Group for medical patients: A treatment for damaged self-esteem. *Group,* 4:36–45.

Coven, C. R. (1981), Ongoing group treatment with severely disturbed medical outpatients: The group formation process. *Int. J. Group Psychother.,* 31:99–116.

Derogatis, L. R. (1977), *The SCL-90-R: Administration, Scoring and Procedures Manual, I.* Baltimore: Clinical Psychometric Research.

Dies, R. R. (1979), Group psychotherapy: Reflections on three decades of research. *J. Applied Behav. Sci.,* 15:361–373.

Endicott, N. A., and Endicott, J. (1975), Assessment of outcome by projective tests. In: *Psychotherapy Change Measures,* ed. J. E. Waskow & M. B. Parloff, Eds. Washington, D.C.: NIMH, U.S. Government Printing Office, Stock Number 1724-00397.

Erickson, R. C. (1975), Outcome studies in mental hospitals: a review. *Psychol. Bull.,* 82:519–540.

Exner, J. E. (1974), *The Rorschach: A Comprehensive System,* Vol. I. New York: Wiley.

_____ (1978), *The Rorschach: A Comprehensive System,* Vol. II. New York: Wiley.

Eysenck, J. J. (1952), The effects of psychotherapy: an evaluation. *J. Consult. Psychol.,* 16:319–324.

Glatzer, H. (1976), Presidential address: Service to patients—the ultimate priority. *Int. J. Group Psychother.,* 26:267–280.

Gough, H. G., & Heilbrun, A. B., Jr. (1965), *The Adjective Checklist Manual.* Palo Alto: Consulting Psychologists Press.

Hartman, J. J. (1979), Small group methods of personal change. *Ann. Rev. Psychol.,* 30:453–476.

Hoffman, N. G., & Butcher, J. N. (1975), Clinical limitations of three MMPI short forms. *J. Clin. Consult. Psychol.,* 43:32–39.

Kaul, T. J., & Bednar, R. L. (1978), Conceptualizing group research: A preliminary analysis. *Small Group Behav.,* 9:173–191.

Kiresuk, T. J., & Sherman, R. E. (1968), Goal Attainment Scaling: A general method for evaluating comprehensive community mental programs. *Commun. Ment. Health J.,* 4:443–453.

Luborsky, L. (1962), Clinicians' judgments of mental health. *Arch. Gen. Psychiat.,* 7:407–417.

MacKenzie, K. R., & Dies, R. R. (1982), *The CORE Battery.* New York: American Group Psychotherapy Association.

Melnick, J., & Woods, M. (1976), Analysis of group composition research and theory for psychotherapeutic and growth-oriented groups. *J. Applied Behav. Sci.,* 12:493–512.

Olsen, R. P., & Greenberg, D. J. (1972), Effects of contingency contracting and decision making groups with chronic mental patients. *J. Consult. Clin. Psychol.,* 38:376–383.

Orlinsky, D. (1981), Research on dropouts and failures in psychotherapy: Do our definitions determine the facts? Presented at Ninth Annual Friends Hospital Clinical Conference, Philadelphia.

Plutchik, R. (1980), *Emotions: A Psychoevolutionary Synthesis.* New York: Harper & Row.

Strupp, H. H., & Hadley, S. W. (1977), A tripartite model of mental health and therapy outcomes. *Amer. Psychologist,* 32:187–196.

Waskow, I. E., & Parloff, M. B., Eds. (1975), *Psychotherapy Change Measures.* Washington, D.C.: NIMH, U.S. Government Printing Office, Stock Number 1724–00397.

Weissman, M. M., & Bothwell, S. (1976), Assessment of social adjustment by patient self-report. *Arch. Gen. Psychiat.,* 33:1111–1115.

Wondolowski, M. (1978), Interpersonal problem solving training groups for hospitalized aged psychiatric patients. Doctoral dissertation, Temple University, Philadelphia.

Yalom, I. D. (1975), *The Theory and Practice of Group Psychotherapy,* 2nd Ed. New York: Basic Books.

4

A Developmental Model for
Brief Group Therapy

K. ROY MacKENZIE, M.D., F.R.C.P.(C), and
W. JOHN LIVESLEY, M.B., Ph.D.

There is general agreement in the research literature that groups progress through different stages of development (Bales and Strodbeck, 1951; Bennis and Shepard, 1956; Hill and Gruner, 1973; Kaplan and Roman, 1963; Lacoursiere, 1980; Mann, 1967; Saravay, 1978; Schutz, 1966). Tuckman (1965) first summarized this material, using the terms "forming," "storming," "norming," and "performing"—to which others have added "adjourning." Beck (1974) found considerable similarities in the descriptions and sequencing of developmental stages, although some differences existed in the number of stages described and the ways they were labeled. Indeed, most studies have focused on the descriptive features of each stage. This descriptive approach will be augmented in this chapter with detailed consideration of the functional importance of each stage, both for the group as a whole and for the individual member. We hope in this way to increase the usefulness of the group developmental model in a clinical setting.

The idea that groups progress through a series of stages implies the notion of the group as a living social system with its own organizational properties. A theoretical basis for understanding the way systems develop and become organized is provided by general systems theory (see Durkin, 1981). As any system develops, its organization becomes in-

This chapter is adapted from a presentation made at the Annual Conference of the American Group Psychotherapy Association, Los Angeles, 1980. The research program from which it originates is supported by operating grants from the National Institute of Mental Health (1 RO3 MH 34901-01) and the Research and Development Fund of Foothills Hospital, Calgary, Alberta, Canada.

101

creasingly complex, with differentiation of internal subsystems and specialization of their functions. Group developmental stages provide a specific example of a living system acquiring interactional complexity. Each stage is characterized by its own organization, and successive waves of organizational change are followed by consolidation and stabilization as group structure undergoes a series of transformations.

This process can be conceptualized in terms of the resolution of a series of boundary issues involving the group as a whole and its individual members. The term "boundary" is not used in a physical sense. Psychological boundaries exist when there is an awareness that two entities are different; this information about differences constitutes the boundary. For example, the experience of intensive engagement in a group, together with an awareness of how this differs from past interpersonal experiences, begins to establish the external boundary of the group. Subsequently, realization by the members that they are different from each other focuses attention on the intermember boundaries. As a group system deals with the particular challenge of each stage, the individual member is forced to confront parallel issues. This interweaving of social system development and individual events provides significant leverage for inducing change.

Clinical experience indicates that the group developmental model is particularly useful when applied to brief group therapy with a time-limited course of 30 to 40 sessions. For groups of approximately eight members, this course works out to the equivalent of one day of therapy per group member, a not unreasonable expenditure of professional resources.* Such an approach to group therapy is in keeping with the general trend in psychotherapy toward briefer treatments (Malan, 1976; Mann, 1973; Sifneos, 1972). Since the therapeutic potential of a group cannot be maximized until a mature system is established, the value of the developmental model for brief groups is that it directs the therapist's attention to events critical for the rapid establishment of such a working system.

THE DEVELOPMENTAL STAGES

Our discussion of group development will focus on five stages plus termination, although other authors, notably Beck (1974), have identi-

*Editors' Note: This comment should not be taken too literally. Each client, of course, may attend all 40 sessions, which amounts to 40–60 hours of therapy per client. Similarly, although a given client may speak and be spoken to for only 10% of a session, that does not mean that the individual only benefits 10% of the time. Considerable indirect learning occurs through modeling or observation during the entire session.

fied as many as nine stages (see also Chapter 6 by Beck and her colleagues). By the time the fifth stage is reached, the group has become a complex working system. At this point a stage approach is less useful and other descriptive dimensions are needed to account for the way the system functions.

A central developmental task will be identified for each stage. This task involves a set of interpersonal issues which come into focus during that stage and which the group must address if the group's development is to progress. The pressure to resolve this task causes each member to reveal his or her position, either verbally or nonverbally, producing a polarization of views. This dialectic tension provides a particular social context, which can be utilized for inducing therapeutic change during each stage (Beck, 1981). In addition to the task faced by the group as a whole, each stage is characterized by specific issues and challenges faced by individual members. In a sense, the functional task of the group is mirrored within each individual. This poses a greater or lesser problem for particular members, according to their characterological structure and psychopathology.

Our model conceptualizes group development as an epigenetic process in which the mature structure is attained through a series of transformations. Adequate resolution of any one stage is a prerequisite for further development. To put it simply: in relationships, as in individual growth and development, one must learn to walk before one learns to run. We believe there are consistent rules governing this process and that certain relationship tasks must be accomplished before others can be undertaken. The result is a predictable sequence through which human relationships are deepened and enriched.

Although we shall describe each stage as if it had discrete characteristics, this should not be taken to imply that the stages are discontinuous. The life of a group is a continuous process, and division into stages is to some extent arbitrary. The value of stage descriptions is that the overall process is made comprehensible by contrasting characteristics of the group at different points in time.* As Hinde (1979) points out, the danger of this approach is that it may be taken to imply the occurrence of sudden changes or transition points. In actual practice, behaviors heralding the emergence of a stage develop gradually and then appear to

---

Editors' Note: There is a danger that the idea of developmental stages may be applied in a simplistic fashion. These concepts should be viewed in the same manner as the tasks of parenting. They allow the clinician to predict in a general fashion what is likely to occur and provide some guidelines as to how to best promote and respond to stage phenomena (which will be unique in their presentation in each particular group).

crystallize into a new set of issues. Similar content themes are found in all stages but are approached differently as new structures for handling them emerge. It should also be cautioned that although the stage approach suggests that groups increase in interactive and structural complexity, this does not mean that development is consistently in a forward direction. Under stresses such as the addition of new members, or the emergence of particularly difficult themes, groups may temporarily move backward in order to consolidate earlier interactional tasks. Under some circumstances, group systems may become arrested or disintegrate.

Finally, we should note that each stage will be described in terms of characteristic group climate dimensions. The dimensions used are based on the Group Climate Questionnaire (see Chapter 7 by MacKenzie). This instrument yields three independent dimensions for describing the group: engaged, avoiding, and conflict.

Stage 1: Engagement

The fundamental task in the first stage is to resolve the issue of engagement of members. The accomplishment of this task ensures that the group has emerged as a social system and that a group identity has been established. The primary mechanism for the development of engagement is universality. This commonly takes the form of an exhilarating appreciation that others have had similar experiences to one's own — a feeling characterized by ambiguous and untested assumptions which pass unchallenged. This uncritical acceptance is a necessary phenomenon since the group does not as yet have the internal strength to withstand intermember confrontation. The functional importance of universality is that it provides a focus around which the group may coalesce and achieve cohesive interaction. Comparison between intragroup and extragroup experiences polarizes these differences and thus delineates the external boundary of the group. There is, however, the danger that the group may become entrenched in this noncritical atmosphere and fail to progress to more complex and conflictual interactional issues.

For the individual members, the task is to allow themselves to become part of a social system, as opposed to remaining isolated and detached. The fear associated with this stage is that of being found unacceptable by others. The task is initially achieved through relatively superficial self-disclosure, often of a factual nature. On a content level, members recognize similarities in their experiences and problems; at a ters in a group setting. The interweaving of these complementary mechanisms deepens the experience of universality. Even though these self-revelations are relatively superficial, the process is usually experienced as intensely arousing and threatening. Its accomplishment leads to a sense of satisfaction that contributes significantly to the development of group cohesion. The characterological dimension that is particularly important during this stage falls along the lines of sociable/withdrawn and trust/distrust. The basic issue for potential group members is whether they can accept themselves as interacting social beings.

The group climate is characterized by a sense of engagement and cohesion, which increases during this stage. Members begin to view the group as relevant to their needs and as providing an opportunity for important work. The group assumes importance in the psychological life of each member during and between sessions. Self-disclosure, interpersonal challenge, and introspective understanding are in evidence but at relatively superficial levels; they ought not to be a major focus. Conflict between members must be relatively low or group integrity will be threatened. At this stage, many important interactional issues are avoided, although members may later acknowledge awareness of them.

In boundary terminology, the external boundary of the group needs to be clearly identified. On the other hand, in a technical sense, the boundaries between the individual members need to be blurred to maintain the unchallenged assumption of universal similarity. Members focus primarily on similarities and therefore have inadequate information with which to conceptualize themselves as different, except on a relatively surface level.

The group has accomplished the first task when all members have participated to some extent in personal self-disclosure and are committed to participate. It is then ready to move into the next stage with reasonably consolidated bonds between members and with a sense of cohesion which will allow it to face the emergence of individual differences and conflicts.

Stage 2: Differentiation

The group task in this stage is to recognize that differences exist among the members. To accomplish this, the focus must shift from the external group boundary to that of the individual member. Attention to differences addresses the danger of the uncritical and comfortable environment of Stage 1 being prolonged in a way that is not conducive to change. In addition, it promotes awareness of divergent points of view so that previous assumptions of similarity are challenged, leading to an atmosphere of conflict and confrontation.

This stage is therefore characterized initially by polarization as members emphasize differences among themselves and how they personally see things. Exaggerated and stereotyped statements are made, and their unrealistic nature often goes unnoticed. The affect generated during this process results in spontaneous self-revelation, thus opening the boundaries between members, which are then closed by self-justifying and challenging statements. These complementary processes highlight intermember boundaries and result in an appreciation of genuine individual differences. One consequence of this process is the need to develop a mechanism for conflict resolution. Unless an ability to cooperate is developed, a competitive and unyielding approach may lead to group fragmentation.

The challenging and questioning of Stage 2 lead to a consolidation of explicit group norms regarding the way the group will function (MacKenzie, 1979). The role and function of the group leader will be challenged in this process. In Stage 1, expectations concerning the way the group should operate originated with the leader; in Stage 2, these are critically examined. As a result of this process, the members come to feel that they have contributed to deciding how the group should function and thus have a greater investment in it.

The group context provided by this stage forces the individual member to deal with two important issues: (1) management of hostility in self and others, and (2) acceptance and incorporation of social expectations. Members must learn to tolerate and cope with angry emotions in themselves and others, and this may enable them to begin to face aspects of themselves that others view as objectionable. There is an isomorphism between the exploration of differences among members and the individual's preliminary recognition of contradictory or isolated parts of the self—a process that will be addressed more fully later. The second dilemma faced in this stage is the extent to which one should go along with collective opinion, as opposed to challenging the system. The threat is couched in terms of either being judged to be unacceptably different or compromising oneself for the sake of the social system.

Because many people have difficulty in dealing with conflict and difference, the differentiation stage is frequently avoided and therefore never resolved. The group may also be threatened with the loss of those members who find the task too disturbing. Moreover, this stage frequently causes problems for therapists because of a misunderstanding of the task facing the group. The goal is not simply to ventilate hostility, but rather to explore differences among members and their perceptions of events, thus promoting differentiation. If this cognitive work is ignored, the affect associated with it remains either elevated and unresolved or goes underground; either way it becomes a potential threat to group integrity. As in Stage 1, a specific discussion of what it is like to express different views and to experience anger is the process work that deepens the experience.

During Stage 2, the group climate is predominantly characterized by conflict and a sense of turmoil and dissatisfaction which produces considerable anxiety. The engagement cultivated in Stage 1 is a necessary bulwark against the forces pressing for group fragmentation. Disclosure, challenge, and understanding may seem to be misused in unproductive sallies. The group exists in the ambivalent position of believing that its job is important yet not really enjoying the task. The therapist's security and confidence are important sustaining factors.

Stage 2 often begins with strong evidence of avoidance of palpable interpersonal issues, culminating in a breakthrough when these sources of tension are aired and explored. It frequently follows a course characterized by a mounting sense of frustration and lurking irritation, culminating in vigorous affective discharge. As in Stage 1, it is important that all members participate to some extent in this process. The group moves on from Stage 2 with a continuing sense of cohesion as a social entity. At the same time, it has developed a greater appreciation of the diversity of opinions and positions within its membership, as well as a mechanism for conflict resolution. This acceptance of individual uniqueness leads to the recognition that each member may play a different role in the group. The increasing complexity of the interactional milieu constitutes clear evidence of subsystem specialization at work.

Stage 3: Individuation

The task of the group in this stage is to promote individuation, allowing a deeper appreciation of the complexity of each member. The process by which this content goal is achieved is one of active interpersonal challenge in a supportive atmosphere. If the group does not pursue this therapeutic work, it may remain blocked at a "pre-work" level, oscillating between unresolved conflict and unchallenged universality. The cooperative style developed in Stage 2 is now put to productive use, creating the impression that the group is really "working." It must not be forgotten, however, that the earlier stages are necessary precursors to this.

The focus, which shifted from the external group boundary in Stage 1 to the intermember boundaries in Stage 2, now moves to the boundaries within each member. In other words, the Stage 2 emphasis on differences among members leads to a probing of different facets of each member's experience and behavior. While this is conducted through an interpersonal process, the emphasis is clearly on the individual rather than the interactional level. To use the language of the Johari window (Luft, 1970), the area "Known to Self" expands as internal conflicts are explored, leading to increasing recognition of ambivalence, contradictions, and split-off parts within the self.

For the individual, the task is to become increasingly open to psychological exploration, necessitating a challenge to characteristic defense mechanisms. During this introspective stage, the individual faces a serious threat to his or her self-esteem as previously unacknowledged parts of self are explored. This threat is somewhat mitigated by a surge of cohesion as members recognize common features, thus deepening the universality achieved in Stage 1.

While the work for the individual during this stage may be difficult and disturbing, it is generally experienced as more satisfying than Stage 2. Collaboration with other group members in the introspective process provides an important source of support. There is a danger, however, that reflective introspection may become stuck in morbid self-preoccupation. If this can be avoided, the result is greater awareness of the complexity of self. In particular, there is acceptance of those facets of the self originally considered bad or undesirable. This acceptance results in enhanced self-esteem as a more complex set of personal constructs is developed. The identification of a variety of internal states permits the individual to consider the boundaries between them and how they relate to each other. Stage 3 is generally experienced as more difficult for those having problems with dependency. The tendency to rely on others needs to be relinquished in favor of greater responsibility for self-exploration.

The climate in Stage 3 is characterized by a surge in engagement and a marked drop, sometimes very abrupt, in conflict. Working dimensions of self-disclosure, challenge, and cognitive mastery are evident, creating a sense of important psychological learning. To the members, it may seem that psychological issues are being fully explored. The observer will note, however, that while internal conflicts of individual members are indeed actively probed, the interpersonal significance of group events is downplayed or avoided altogether.

Just as the sense of group identity in Stage 1 is enriched by an awareness of individual differences in Stage 2, so Stage 3 adds further depth by revealing greater complexity within the individual. This leads to a quantum increase in the information available for group work. The third stage approaches resolution when all members have actively participated in self-revelation and demonstrated an openness to discussing important psychological topics. From this point on in the life of the group, the transition between stages becomes less acute and more overlap and blurring occurs in regard to stage-specific characteristics. In general, as living systems develop, earlier stages tend to have more rigidly defined characteristics.

Stage 4: Intimacy

The task in Stage 4 is to experience intimacy and to explore the implications of close relationships. Yet intimacy without mutual self-knowledge would be no more than a facade. Now that the members have more information available, they can understand themselves and others in more complex ways. The increased information made available in Stage 3 inevitably draws the members into closer here-and-now interaction, which can be avoided only by active withdrawal and social isolation. The growing recognition of interdependence also counteracts the danger of remaining stuck in Stage 3 introspection. The individual members (subsystems) come to have greater influence on each other as relationships within the system become deeper and more complex. The boundary most in focus during this stage is that embracing pairs of members as they mutually explore their relationship and consider the ways in which it differs from relationships with others. In the beginning, these interactions tend to be egocentric, being motivated more by individual needs than by reciprocity. As the stage progresses, this increasingly gives way to the more balanced relationships found in Stage 5.

A danger is that increasing intimacy can lead to irresponsible closeness, which may, at times, have an erotic quality. The tendency toward intense subgrouping is driven not only by individual predisposition, but also by the context of the group climate, and it may be pursued with such vigor that excessive closeness develops. Overt sexual relationships are usually catastrophic for the group since they preclude effective work for those involved. The group is a laboratory simulation of life, not the real thing. When this distinction is ignored, the potential of the group for promoting therapeutic change is lost.

The task for individual members is not merely to accept themselves, as in Stage 3, but also to accept themselves as capable of closeness and as

having relevance to someone else. This acknowledgment of the importance of relationships carries with it the threat of rejection by persons
who have become known in a complex and personal fashion. For all
members with significant interpersonal problems, experimentation with
a type of relationship that has been fearfully avoided poses a major
threat. This is particularly so for those with problems of intimacy. In addition, those with difficulties in the area of social and internal control
may respond by acting out the intimacy theme.

The group climate continues to show high engagement, with
nondefensive openness and tolerance of closeness. Conflict is low and
there may be a somewhat unrealistic euphoria reminiscent of Stage 1.
Indeed, many of the issues mentioned in Stage 1 are now reworked at a
more complex level. While interpersonal themes are explored more
fully, there is still evidence of avoidance of the deeper implications of
relationships. The transition to Stage 5 is heralded by a shift from the ex-
citement of interpersonal closeness to a dawning recognition that such
involvement, if it is to continue, must be based on a sense of interpersonal responsibility.

Stage 5: Mutuality

The task in this stage is to develop a sense of mutual responsibility
among members and to explore the meaning of closeness. This is conceptualized not as an increased sense of intimacy, but rather as an appreciation of the fundamental uniqueness of each member. The focus is
therefore on the boundary surrounding each individual in terms of both
internal autonomy and interpersonal responsibility for others. The
polarization during this stage is between unbalanced relationships based
on dependency or exploitation and those based on equality. There is
awareness that relationships cannot be unilaterally determined but must
be based on mutual agreement and cooperation. The issue of control
through dominance or submission in relationships must be resolved,
thereby addressing the danger in Stage 4 of irresponsible closeness.
Relatively little new content is introduced during this stage, although old
material may be seen in a new light as a result of the exploration of its
interactional significance.

The threat to the individual member is that of being used or aban-
doned in the context of close and meaningful interpersonal relationships.
As a counterbalance to this threat, Stage 5 may, at some points, be
characterized by a sense of unrealistic closeness. Members who have
specific difficulties in the area of trust will encounter further problems in

this stage. They may fear engulfment and loss of individuality in the face of close-binding ties within the group. The development of trust itself is an ongoing issue, from the beginning of the group. Initially, the group has to be trusted sufficiently for surface self-disclosure. As bonds between members increase, deeper levels of trust are required. In Stage 5, these issues become the prime focus. Individuals must respond to the challenge of accepting responsibility for their interactions with others.

The group climate shows a continuation of engagement and work. An increase in conflict usually occurs as members react to the system's demands for deeper commitments. Avoidance of interpersonal issues will be low.

Termination

The leaders and the individual members must now deal with the ending of this "artificial" social system. A number is not assigned to this stage because termination may occur at any point in the life of the group. It is probably fair to say, however, that significant change in individual members is unlikely to occur unless the group has progressed solidly into Stage 3. To use the language of the Hill Interactional Matrix (Hill, 1965), Stages 1 and 2 can be considered "pre-work" stages — important and necessary, but preliminary. The degree of development in any particular group by the time of termination will depend on the characteristics of the members, the skill of the therapist, and the exigencies of the service setting.

The task for the group in termination is to achieve disengagement with an incorporation of the group as a positive and constructive experience. At termination, as in Stage 1, attention is directed toward the external boundary of the group. Outside circumstances, projected objectives, and plans are compared and contrasted with group events. The history of the group and of its individual members is reviewed. Critical incidents are recalled and worked through once more. These mechanisms assist the process of incorporating the group as a personally important and lasting experience. There is a danger that this working through will be avoided, and this may prevent integration of the experience and interfere with optimum learning. Indeed, if termination is viewed in a negative fashion, earlier group progress may be undone.

For the individual member, termination is accompanied by feelings of loss and separation, but it also provides a final opportunity for trying out coping skills developed in the group. Individuals must learn to cope successfully without the group and apply the understanding they have acquired to everyday life. One danger is regression and decompensation into a demoralized, nihilistic state: "I cannot really manage without the group and so I will give up." Termination poses for each member the issue of resolving the existential problem of one's essential isolation and responsibility for oneself.

CONCLUSION

A summary of the developmental stages in brief group therapy is presented in Table 1. Our description of small group development may be seen as a set of higher-order concepts which find concrete manifestation in a wide variety of actual behaviors. The unfolding of the stages is considered to be an invariant epigenetic process if the group is to evolve toward a complex social system. The time frame for this process, however, will vary considerably according to the characterological structure of the group members, the leader's activities, and the context in which the group takes place. Groups with mature members, effective leadership, and a facilitating setting will move quickly toward advanced working stages. Other groups may become stalled or blocked at earlier stages. Some groups will fail to master even rudimentary tasks and remain structureless, with constant membership changes or actual dissolution. If a group is to evolve, it must master its organizational tasks in a sequential fashion, building an adequate foundation for more complex functioning.

The specific focus on boundary functioning provides a useful guide to understanding the stages. In addition, awareness of boundary issues provides the therapist with a set of criteria for assessing group events. The therapist may then selectively reinforce or initiate stage-appropriate behavior. Another feature of this approach is the delineation of interactional dimensions characteristic of each stage. The developing group may be viewed as a series of social contexts which have a differential impact on each member according to his or her characterological structure. This phenomenon offers a rich opportunity for process learning not available to quite the same extent in dyadic therapy.

Since boundaries consist of information about similarities and differences, an alternative way of describing stages is in terms of the informational content characteristic of each. In Stage 1, the content theme centers on similarities of problems and experiences, and differences be-

TABLE 1
Developmental Stages in Groups

Stage	Boundary Focus	Group Task	Threat to Individual	Mechanism to Resolve Threat	Individual Task—Attendant Danger	Index to Task Resolution
1. Engagement	External group	Develop group identity and cohesion	Unacceptability	Universality; preliminary self-revelation	"We're all the same" (untested universality)	Acceptance of membership; commitment to participate
2. Differentiation	Individual member	Develop mechanism of conflict resolution through cooperative exploration	Conflict	Cooperative exploration; assertion of ideas and beliefs	"I'm somewhat different" (unrealistic polarizations)	Tolerance of difference; conflict resolution
3. Individuation	Intrapsychic	Develop understanding of individual through self-revelation and reflective introspection	Loss of self-esteem	Reflective introspection; deeper self-revelation	"I'm a complex but whole person" (morbid self-preoccupation)	Acceptance of self and others; collaborative exploration
4. Intimacy	Inter-member	Develop interpersonal involvement and allow reciprocal influence	Rejection	Reciprocal influence; acknowledging importance of relationships	"I can be important to someone else" (irresponsible closeness)	Tolerance of closeness; nondefensive openness
5. Mutuality	Inter-member	Develop understanding of equality in relationships, not dependence/exploitation	Inequality	Quality in relationships; accepting implications of one's actions for others	"What I do has implications for someone else" (unrealistic closeness)	Acceptance of personal responsibility in relationships; management of dominance/control
6. Termination	External group	Allow individual autonomy and incorporate group experience	Aloneness	Incorporation of group; acknowledging loss	"I can exist even though alone" (nihilism)	Acceptance of responsibility for self; review and acknowledgment of group's importance

tween events within the group and outside. In Stage 2, it is information about differences among members that becomes important. Stage 3 is characterized by information about different aspects of self. This information is applied in Stage 4 to thematic material which compares and contrasts specific relationships both within and outside the group. In Stage 5, this informational focus is expanded to encompass broader responsibilities in relationships. Viewed in this way, the stages describe a consistent and logical expansion of the information base available for psychological consideration.

In clinical practice, the stages and their transitional zones are particularly evident from Stage 1 through Stage 3. This is especially true for groups with closed membership. These observations have important implications for the structuring of group therapy programs. The addition of new members before a group has reached reasonable consolidation in Stage 3, for instance, may seriously interfere with the creation of a working environment.

Finally, the idea of stages provides a structure for understanding the total group. The therapist can use these ideas to monitor and maintain the progress of the group. The therapist may need to elicit, reinforce, or model stage-appropriate behaviors, as well as selectively neglect or dampen material which is out-of-phase. For example, extensive revelation of sensitive personal information is inappropriate in Stage 1, and indeed correlates with premature termination. Similarly, the therapist should not expect or encourage deep introspection until the group has developed cohesion and the ability to handle conflict and challenge. It is expected that the group will need to rely on the therapist for guidance early in its life, but if this persists, individual initiative will suffer. The therapist should also use the developmental approach to ensure that each member has achieved, at least to a modest extent, stage-appropriate interactional tasks. Only then can the members share and understand a common experience. Members out-of-step with the commonality are liable to have an ineffective experience or suffer actual harm.

The concept of stages should be applied by the leader in a flexible and creative fashion. Rigid adherence to the model runs the risk of artificial manipulation rather than facilitation of a natural process. We are describing a metatheory which may become manifest in a diversity of ways. Its application is built on traditional clinical skills, and it is through these skills that the ideas presented here can be implemented.

The next chapter provides a complementary discussion of social roles — a conceptual approach that bridges between stage phenomena in groups and the contributions of the individual member.*

REFERENCES

Bales, R. F., & Strodbeck, F. L. (1951), Phases in group problem solving. *J. Abnorm. Soc. Psychol.,* 46:485–495.

Beck, A. P. (1974), Phases in the development of structure in therapy and encounter groups. In: *Innovations in Client-Centered Therapy,* ed. D. A. Wexler & L. N. Rice. New York: Wiley.

_____ (1981), Developmental characteristics of the system forming process. In: *Living Groups: Group Psychotherapy and General System Theory,* ed. J. E. Durkin. New York: Brunner/Mazel.

Bennis, W. G., & Shepard, H. A. (1956), A theory of group development. *Human Rel.,* 9:415–438.

Durkin, J. E., Ed. (1981), *Living Groups: Group Psychotherapy and General System Theory.* New York: Brunner/Mazel.

Hill, W. F. (1965), *Hill Interaction Matrix (HIM),* Rev. Ed. Los Angeles: Youth Studies Centre, University of Southern California.

_____ & Gruner, L. (1973), A study of development in open and closed groups. *Small Group Behav.,* 4:355–381.

Hinde, R. A. (1979), *Towards Understanding Relationships.* London: Academic Press.

Kaplan, S. R., & Roman, M. (1963), Phases of development in an adult therapy group. *Int. J. Group Psychother.,* 13:10–26.

Lacoursiere, R. (1980), *The Life Cycle of Groups: Group Developmental Stage Theory.* New York: Human Sciences Press.

Luft, J. (1970), *Group Processes: An Introduction to Group Dynamics.* Palo Alto: National Press Books.

MacKenzie, K. R. (1979), Group norms: Importance and measurement. *Int. J. Group Psychother.,* 29:471–480.

_____ (1981), Measurement of group climate. *Int. J. Group Psychother.,* 31:287–296.

Malan, D. H. (1976), *The Frontier of Brief Psychotherapy.* New York: Plenum Medical Book Co.

Mann, J. (1973), *Time Limited Psychotherapy.* Cambridge, Mass.: Harvard University Press.

Mann, R. D., Gibbard, G. S., and Hartman, J. J. (1967), *Interpersonal Styles and Group Development.* New York: Wiley.

Plutchik, R. (1980), *Emotion: A Psychoevolutionary Synthesis.* New York: Harper & Row.

Editors' Note: In their two chapters, MacKenzie and Livesley focus on the interactional tasks required in each stage and relate this to information processing, particularly information concerning differences across a variety of hypothetical boundaries within the group. In Chapter 6, Beck and her colleagues contribute rich observational data concerning stage characteristics, with particular interest in the contributions role leaders play in facilitating stage shift phenomena. These three chapters, then, present ideas developed from a common theoretical base but with emphasis on different features. It is hoped these complementary data will result in furthering the understanding of how groups develop in complexity over time.

Saravay, S. M. (1978), A psychoanalytic theory of group development. *Int. J. Group Psychother.*, 28:481–507.

Schutz, W. C. (1966), *The Interpersonal Underworld.* Palo Alto: Science & Behavior Books.

Sifneos, P. E. (1972), *Short-term Psychotherapy and Emotional Crisis.* Cambridge, Mass.: Harvard University Press.

Tuckman, B. W. (1965), Developmental sequence in small groups. *Psychol. Bull.*, 63: 384–399.

5

Social Roles in
Psychotherapy Groups

W. JOHN LIVESLEY, M.B., Ph.D., and
K. ROY MacKENZIE, M.D., F.R.C.P.(C)

In this chapter we shall examine the social roles characteristically found in psychotherapy groups and discuss the relationship between social role and personality. We see it as a companion chapter to the last one, in which the group was described as a social system progressing through a series of developmental stages, each with a task to be accomplished.* Since the adoption of a social role is influenced by personality dynamics, an examination of this area provides a framework for understanding the part the individual plays in group development. A descriptive model of stages and roles potentially offers a general account of group events encompassing both the group as a social system and the individual partici-

This chapter is adapted from a presentation made at the Annual Conference of the American Group Psychotherapy Association, New York City, 1982. The research program from which it originates is supported by operating grants from the National Institute of Mental Health (1 RO3 MH 34901-01) and the Research and Development Fund of Foothills Hospital, Calgary, Alberta, Canada.

Editors' Note: This chapter is also closely related to the following one by Beck et al. The concept of social role is important in integrating ideas relating to the social system of the group with those relating to personality of the individual member. Chapters 5 and 6 discuss the importance of role behavior in helping the group to develop. Of particular relevance is the constructive value given to role behavior that might generally be regarded as "negative." This is particularly true for the "divergent role" and the concept of scapegoating. As Livesley and MacKenzie note later on, role concepts also have implications for group composition since a preponderance of one kind of role behavior within the group may make it difficult for the system to address the tasks of particular stages.

pant. Within this structure, varied content themes may be enacted. Such a model may contribute a solution to the frequently expressed complaint that group psychotherapy theory, practice, and research have been hampered by the lack of a general theory (Bednar and Kaul, 1978; MacKenzie and Livesley, 1982; Parloff and Dies, 1977).

THE CONCEPT OF SOCIAL ROLE

The group as a social system may be described in terms of developmental stages, normative expectations, group climate, and interaction patterns (MacKenzie, 1981b). Group structure may also be described in terms of social positions, the roles associated with these positions, and the relationships among them (Biddle, 1979; Biddle and Thomas, 1966; Newcomb, 1950; Newcomb, Turner, and Converse, 1966; Slater, 1955). When people begin to interact in a group, each seeks to evoke satisfying responses from the others. If group membership is stable, interactions gradually fall into patterns so that each member is expected to behave in predictable ways. These expectations define social roles and become incorporated into the normative structure of the group (Hare, 1976; Parsons and Bales, 1955). Role prescriptions refer to the behaviors expected of the occupants of given positions (Sarbin, 1954). In this context, "role" refers to a cluster of behaviors of functional significance for the group system.

Beck and Peters (1981) have suggested that certain types of role behavior are required if the group is to master stage-related developmental tasks. Behaviors appropriate to stage expectations are selectively reinforced by the group members, resulting in increased frequency of occurrence. Some individuals will exhibit these behaviors more frequently than others and can therefore be considered to have taken on a particular social role. For example, in the early phase of a group, actions promoting cohesion are vital for the emergence of a sense of "groupness" and are therefore selectively reinforced, while disrupting behaviors are ignored. Consequently, those members most able to demonstrate socially engaging and trusting behaviors will figure prominently in the interaction. This cluster of behaviors is required by the system and therefore constitutes a social role. Since the behaviors constituting a role arise under the combined influence of social context and individual personality dynamics, the concept of social role provides a theoretical construct for integrating individual characteristics with the functional requisites of the group (MacKenzie, 1981a).

During the early stages of a group, role behaviors often occur in stereotyped ways, with individuals seeming to display behavior from a single role dimension. This initial role structure can be understood in terms of both systemic and individual factors. At the systemic level, the task of a new group is straightforward, involving the development of group identity and engagement of the individual (engagement stage). Following this, members begin to emerge as individuals by emphasizing their differences (differentiation stage). To achieve these objectives, the system requires relatively simple behaviors—the expression of warmth and empathy followed by the assertion of individual views. Behaviors with more complex interpersonal meaning are selectively neglected since the group mechanisms for handling them have not yet developed.

At the individual member level, the stress of joining a new social system tends to elicit coping strategies involving increased reliance on the more predominant aspects of characterological structure. The result is an exaggeration of normal interpersonal behaviors, creating the impression of rigidity and a stereotyped interpersonal style. This normal response to new social situations is magnified in patients attending group psychotherapy since they are already experiencing interpersonal dysfunction and probably utilize only a limited range of interpersonal constructs and behaviors (Ryle, 1979).

Both systemic events and individual interactive style may therefore create the impression in beginning groups that there is only one person for each role. As the informational pool available for group work increases, however, this initial perception breaks down and more complex interactional patterns emerge, facilitating the achievement of later group developmental tasks. The limited size of the group makes it necessary for individuals to learn a variety of role behaviors, which the system requires if it is to progress. This means that the individual must modify rigid, maladaptive interpersonal patterns and acquire greater role flexibility.

It should be borne in mind that the individual members are not primarily interested in the system, but rather in their own situation. Nevertheless, an isomorphism exists between the structural objectives of the developing group and the therapeutic goals of the individual. The pressure of the social system can be regarded as meeting the needs of the individual member and vice versa. Role behavior remains important throughout the group's life, but during later stages it becomes diffused throughout the membership. Individual members come to occupy a variety of social positions and exhibit an attendant breadth of interpersonal behaviors. Consequently, an important marker of individual change is the in-group demonstration of diverse role behaviors. Role flexibility provides a useful criterion of effective interpersonal functioning.

ROLE DIMENSIONS

The term "role" is used in different ways. The clinical literature recognizes a diversity of roles, each essentially offering a personality description — for example, "the help-rejecting complainer." Since such descriptions deal with the individual without reference to social system functions, they are not appropriate for defining group roles. Social psychology research has tended to deal with roles selected for a particular social context, such as the role of the consumer or the role of the health care provider. Such concepts are relevant to the formal group roles of "leader" and "member," which are of functional significance to the group system. In addition, informal social roles are described which seem particularly appropriate to understanding therapy groups. They play an important part in the therapeutic process and can be regarded as supplanting some formal leadership functions, a process Beck and Peters (1981) refer to as "distributed leadership."

Informal role structure has been extensively studied in task-oriented work groups (Bales, 1970; Bales and Slater, 1955; Benne and Sheats, 1948; Burke, 1967). Two major role functions have been emphasized: the socioemotional leader and the task leader. The socioemotional leader, usually the best-liked member of the group, is sensitive to group process and serves an important function for the group by striving to defuse tension through humor, support, or ventilation. Members occupying this role position experience difficulty dealing with negative affect, and may seek to maintain positive relationships by avoiding anger and conflict. The task leader, on the other hand, keeps the group focused on its goals and views the ultimate productivity of the system as most important. Members in this role may have significant interpersonal deficits, namely, avoidance of affect and an unremitting focus on cognitive and performance issues.

Bales (1953) suggests that as a group addresses its task, tensions arise among the members which must be defused if the group is to be productive. The group alternates between task focus and tension release, making the two leader roles mutually interdependent. Thus, a group lacking either role will be handicapped in achieving its goals.

The relationship between the task and socioemotional roles is more complex in therapy groups since it has been suggested that the same person often performs both functions (Talland, 1957). This person in essence is seen as the most influential and positive member. The convergence of these two roles may also reflect the fact that in a therapy group the task is the process. In other words, the blurring of these two classical role functions is not surprising. An important theoretical consideration, therefore, is to strive for greater clarity regarding the most appropriate role designations for therapy groups.

The "sociable role" we propose in this chapter is very similar to the classical concept of the socioemotional leader. Our description of the "structural role," however, differs somewhat from the standard "task leader" definition in that we emphasize the contribution this role makes to developing internal group structure and pay less attention to the idea of "effective leadership" for external productivity.

The clinical literature, particularly from family therapy sources, describes a third role, that of "scapegoat." This member is "assigned" the blame for family difficulties, and as in the biblical reference, it is imagined that by expulsion of that member the system will be healed. Scapegoating may be understood as a displacement phenomenon, whereby tensions within the family unit, especially within the parental subsystem, are displaced onto one of the children. This child responds to the demands of the role by demonstrating disruptive behavior, which serves to divert attention from primary problems. By addressing these problems directly, the need for a scapegoat is eliminated and the identified child may give up the provocative actions. We have chosen the term "divergent role" to emphasize the operational significance of this role in groups. The term also carries with it fewer negative value implications.

Finally, a fourth role — the "defiant member" — has been described (Beck, 1974). This person challenges the power of the group by asserting his or her individuality and provides a useful function by counterbalancing the pull of collective opinion. Members in this role may attempt to bypass the group by establishing a special relationship with the leader and thus sabotage the integrity of the group. In this chapter we emphasize a different aspect of this role. The "defiance" Beck describes seems better understood as a defensive reaction to fear of engulfment and loss of individuality. Thus, we describe this role as being fundamentally motivated by a sense of personal vulnerability, and call it the "cautionary role" — a term that also captures the significance of this role for the group system.

The following discussion is organized around these four role concepts — sociable role, structural role, cautionary role, and divergent role.

As we have indicated, our choice of these names emphasizes the functional significance of these roles for the social system.* In other words, social roles are seen in terms of the need of the developing system for particular types of behavior. The descriptions are based on theoretical dimensions. Behaviors occurring in actual groups will approximate our idealized accounts to varying degrees. We have purposely avoided the terms "leader" and "leadership" because of their implications of status and prestige. Although role functions influence the group in various ways, not all of these roles are associated with high status. Indeed, at some points in the group's life these functions, although important to the group, may be viewed negatively by the members.

SOCIABLE ROLE

Characteristic Behavior

Members enacting the sociable role are eager to establish relationships. They are gregarious and trusting, recognizing the importance of support and reassurance. They show concern that all members be included in the group and pay close attention to "home-making" details such as attendance and room arrangements. These members emphasize the importance of positive emotional tone and are concerned that everyone have a worthwhile experience. Consequently, they attend closely to interpersonal process and intervene quickly to minimize differences and reduce negative feelings.

Function for Group System

Sociable role activities promote group cohesion and facilitate engagement by helping to make the group appear less threatening. The trust characteristic of these members allows them to model self-revelation and thus encourage others to join in self-disclosure. Their emphasis

---

Editors' Note: Much empirical work remains to be done to clarify the most appropriate types of roles to consider. In this chapter Livesley and MacKenzie define the "task" or "structural" role to emphasize the organizing nature of the activities rather than the "leadership" potential. This role is distinct from that of the "designated leader," whom Beck et al. (Chapter 6) see as generally the "task leader." Livesley and MacKenzie describe role behavior in terms of dimensions of interaction available within the total potential of the group members, while Beck et al. identify roles more closely with particular members. Both approaches describe similar phenomena, but the conceptualization of roles from the standpoint of the therapist is distinctly different. Beck et al.'s orientation is compatible with the traditional literature on social roles, while Livesley and MacKenzie's approach is influenced by considerations of personality and group climate.

on similarities, in the form of common experiences and problems, allows members to identify with each other. These activities, together with the optimism these members express, provide a model of hope in the therapeutic potential of the group. The concern to incorporate others allows these members to play an important part in integrating isolated group members. During the early stages, their commitment to the group also helps to establish constructive therapeutic norms. Sociable role behavior is particularly crucial during the formative stages, although it remains an important sustaining factor throughout the group's life.

Although these role behaviors are important—indeed crucial—to the group, if they are presented too strongly or by too many members, they become a liability, impeding confrontation and challenge. The emphasis on similarities and acceptance may make it difficult for the group to recognize the value of change and to develop mechanisms for achieving it. Reluctance to recognize differences may hinder the group work so that the group becomes stalled and gradually loses its vitality and its attraction for the members.

Implications for Individual

Adoption of the sociable role brings a number of advantages. The unconditional positive approach of these members to others elicits support in return, resulting in rapid integration into the group. They are commonly viewed as the most popular members and assume a central role early in the group's life. As a result, there may be an enhancement of self-esteem (which is frequently low in individuals who adopt this role to an extreme degree). This may be accompanied by an early reduction of symptoms, which helps to foster hope in the possibility of change for all members.

If exaggerated, however, the qualities of this role may carry significant liabilities. Excessive trust may promote naiveté and gullibility. Indeed, the positive response these people elicit from others may at times be a recognition of this weakness and an acknowledgment of their vulnerability. The need to be accepted may make the assertion of opinions or rights difficult, allowing such members to be exploited—a process to which they seem remarkably susceptible. The need to be accepted may also lead to overcommitment to the group, accompanied by excessive dependency, thus creating problems at termination. These members' sensitivity to such seemingly negative dimensions as confrontation, anger, and conflict is disadvantageous. Their self-disclosure may have a superficial quality which, although constructive early in the group, may later become restrictive. A Pollyannish quality may make such members the target of group criticism.

STRUCTURAL ROLE

Characteristic Behavior

Those adopting the structural role are concerned with structuring and organizing group activity through establishing goals, and procedures for their attainment. This function is pursued in a cognitive manner, with an emphasis on verbal definitions and explanations which often has an obsessive quality. These members' concern with form and the proper way to do things has a controlling effect, which is not so much an attempt to dominate as a concern with adherence to conventional behavior. While actively promoting the structure of the group, such individuals are often quite blind to affect and actively avoid and defuse it. Often they find it difficult to empathize in an affective way and may compensate for this by adopting a compulsive advice-giving and concrete problem-solving style.

Function for Group System

Concern with form and structure provides a valuable service to the developing group, helping to establish explicit goals and norms. During the initial stages, these behaviors promote a normative climate that emphasizes the importance of psychological work. Lieberman, Yalom, and Miles (1973) have demonstrated the importance of "meaning attribution" for therapeutic change, and these members help to establish this process through their emphasis on clarity and understanding. This approach also helps to reduce the anxiety felt by all members entering a new social situation, by reducing ambiguity through cognitive structuring of the experience. Such an emphasis on the understanding of behavior and experience is an asset throughout the group's life, facilitating the incorporation of process experiences and clarifying affect. As the group approaches termination, the concern with results makes it easy for structural role members to emphasize the transfer of in-group learning to outside situations.

In conjunction with the sociable role, the structural role is essential for the development of a positive working environment. If exaggerated, however, it will give an inhibited and controlled tone to the group, which makes creative spontaneity difficult. A sterile, joyless climate may arise with the group losing its attractiveness for the members and becoming a debating forum, with little incentive for individual change.

Implications for Individual

Structural role members show a strong sense of purpose and direction. The cognitive mastery they seek has a stabilizing effect for them and serves to reduce the anxiety to which they are particularly susceptible in new social situations. The need for clarity and lack of ambiguity leads to a concerted effort to resolve issues. A comparative neglect of affect protects them from the distorting effects of intense emotions in those around them.

While those who are comfortable in adopting an organizing approach may be quite effective in task groups, they often feel helpless and lost in the lack of structure and emphasis on process characteristic of therapy groups. The avoidance of emotion may lead to a formalistic, compulsive style which makes interaction stiff and difficult. This may dampen spontaneity and the free expression of interpersonal feelings. Blindness to affect may, if carried to extremes, severely interfere with process exploration. Those who display these qualities in exaggerated form may be seen as distant and uninvolved, discouraging affiliative responses from others and leading to further isolation. Such individuals may also show obsessive rumination, which constitutes a powerful resistance to change and brings further alienation, as their fearfulness of affect may be interpreted as insensitivity.

CAUTIONARY ROLE

Characteristic Behavior

Members taking on the cautionary role behave in a circumspect, rather defensive manner. They emphasize the importance of the individual and the need for careful evaluation before commitment to a social system. This outlook makes them hesitant to reveal important feelings or ideas lest such self-disclosure make them vulnerable to group criticism or rejection. They stress responsibility for self and the value of autonomy. While these qualities may cause them to appear withdrawn and uninvolved, closer examination reveals that they are attentive to group events. Initially they may be reluctant to acknowledge this and may therefore say little. Later, however, they may more directly verbalize their reluctance to participate and their skepticism about the potential benefits of the group. Their ambivalent and distancing stance may have an angry and distrustful quality which makes it difficult for them to commit themselves to the goals of the group.

Function for Group System

The value of these members to the group lies in their emphasis on individual autonomy. They act as a brake on the overly rapid development of group consensus and so help to allay fears about being overwhelmed by the group. They model for the group self-containment and responsibility for self. In the later stages of the group, these members foster awareness of the dangers of overcommitment and excessive reliance on the social system for continued well-being, thus helping the group to prepare for termination.

If exaggerated, these cautious qualities model anti-therapeutic norms of limited self-disclosure and poor commitment. These members may disrupt group cohesion by noninvolvement and are themselves at risk of terminating prematurely. Their nonresponsiveness to the overtures of others undermines commitment to the group and belief in the possibility of change. Their unresponsiveness seems to activate and accentuate despair and hopelessness in others.

Implications for Individual

These attributes may benefit the individual by promoting autonomous functioning and therefore less reliance on others. These people can maintain greater personal stability in the face of social pressures. In a curiously contradictory fashion, their reluctance to participate often elicits strong reaction from others to include them, thus allowing them to be members of the group in a vicarious fashion.

When present to a strong degree, however, these qualities interfere with the effective use of a therapeutic group. They may lead to a rejection of help from others, which ultimately ends in withdrawal of concern from those around, leaving the person in an isolated and alienated position. These members may exhaust their social supports by their failure to reinforce the efforts of others. Indeed, they may draw the anger of the group on themselves, thereby confirming their preexisting distrust and fear of rejection.

DIVERGENT ROLE

Characteristic Behavior

Divergent role behavior is characterized by a challenging and questioning interpersonal stance, which is often seen to be deviant from the consensus. Differences rather than similarities are emphasized in ways that often appear impulsively blunt. There is usually an angry, aggressive component to this interpersonal style. These role members often seem to be actively soliciting the hostility of other group members in ways that are interpreted as insensitivity. At the same time, they are highly involved in the work of the group and are frequently recognized as important, although negative, members. While on the one hand they act as if they were insensitive to the nuances of interpersonal behavior, on the other they demonstrate an intuitive understanding of interpersonal functioning and are able to pinpoint vulnerable areas with uncanny accuracy.

Function for Group System

Behaviors associated with this role have a high profile due to their divergence from socially appropriate interactions. This may result in a tendency for those who adopt these role activities to be blamed and held responsible for lack of progress. Initially the group acts as if it cannot contain such divergent views and may seek to eject these members in order to maintain cohesion, failing to recognize the contribution this role behavior makes to the group's therapeutic development.

The exploration of differences ensures progress toward the differentiation of member identities. The function of divergent role members is particularly noticeable during the second stage of group development, which is characterized by conflict and assertion of individuality. At this point these members counterbalance the nonintrusive complacency characteristic of the universality of the early group. By seeing things differently, they polarize issues, forcing the group to develop mechanisms for cooperative collaboration in conflict resolution. In this process they actively increase the amount of information members have about each other since confrontation forces members to reveal more about themselves. In addition, these members model for the group the display and constructive use of anger and conflict. This is of value for the group as it facilitates the incorporation into group norms of the idea that anger can be tolerated and that confrontation can be positive. Throughout the group's life, divergent role members provide alternative points of view and thus prevent premature closure on important issues. Their continuous challenging of the status quo makes them sensitive to group resistance and avoidance of psychological work.

If the activity of these members is excessive, however, it may so polarize the group that resolution is impossible and group stability is seriously threatened, with a catastrophic drop in cohesion and morale. Alternatively, the absence of divergent role behavior, or expulsion of those showing it, leads to the continuation of a supportive, nonchallenging atmosphere in which important issues are evaded. The idea that the group would be better without these people may be an important form of resistance to therapeutic work, with which the therapist's countertransference may collude.

Implications for Individual

These active, challenging people are often admired and respected for their resilience and determination. They are committed to change and, by their active engagement with the forces within the social structure, bind themselves to the collectivity. They frequently have a clear idea of the need for change and demand that the system respond to this.

Yet these same qualities, if exaggerated, may become seriously disruptive, leading to isolation or even actual ejection from the group. By eliciting the anger of the group, these members may launch a self-destructive process in which they become group casualties. The rejection of consensus, if taken to an extreme, results in a sense of identity confusion since one cannot identify with others and thus obtain the support that alignment with a social system can provide.

SOCIAL ROLES AND PERSONALITY

So far we have considered social roles in terms of behaviors required for the development and maintenance of the group system. In this sense, the system can be considered to influence members to exhibit behaviors essential for its development. Some individuals, however, are better able than others to adopt these behaviors, necessitating a consideration of the relationship between personality and particular social roles.*

Systematic exploration of this relationship is hampered by the lack of a consensus on fundamental personality dimensions. Nevertheless, data from diverse sources indicate an emerging trend regarding the importance of two basic dimensions—affiliation and dominance—although

---

*Editors' Note: There is currently a major controversy over the concept of personality, particularly in regard to whether behavior is determined by the enduring characteristics of the individual or by the demands of the social context. The concept of social role offers a useful perspective on this controversy. As described in this chapter, the developing group draws forth behaviors appropriate for each stage from its membership. The therapist may reinforce this systemic tendency by encouraging individual members to try out behavior to which they are not accustomed.

they may be labeled in different ways. Analyses of personality traits point to such poles as affiliation versus hostility/dominance (Freedman, Leary, Ossorio, and Coffey, 1951), evaluative versus potency/activity (Osgood, Suci, and Tannenbaum, 1957), and affiliation versus interdependence (Benjamin, 1974). Studies of maternal and child behavior reveal similar dimensions: love/hostility versus extroversion/introversion (Schaeffer, 1961) and warmth versus control (Baumrind, 1971). An examination of management behavior identifies "concern for people" versus "concern for production" (Blake and Mouton, 1964), while studies of military and industrial groups isolate dimensions labeled love/hostility versus dominance/submission (Foa, 1961). Although these diverse studies offer quite similar pictures of the structure of interpersonal behavior, relatively little use has been made of these dimensions in either process or outcome studies of group psychotherapy (Hurley, 1980).

A two-dimensional model of interpersonal traits implies a circular or circumplex configuration. Such a model has been described by Schaeffer (1961); Lorr, Bishop, and McNair (1965); Benjamin (1974); and Wiggins (1979). These ideas are used in this chapter to explore the relationship between social roles and interpersonal dimensions. Also used is the model described by Plutchik (1980), which subdivides the two basic dimensions into eight categories (identified in the inner circle of Figure 1). Plutchik's circular arrangement has been altered in Figure 1 with regard to the position of the inhibited/impulsive categories in accord with recent studies (K. R. MacKenzie, personal communication).

Figure 1 shows the hypothetical relationship between these categories and social roles. In addition, it displays two sets of ideas regarding basic mechanisms through which role behavior influences the group. A positive interpersonal tone emphasizes similarities and collaboration so that members may work together. In contrast, a negative interpersonal tone stresses the importance of differences and challenge in producing change. The outer circle of Figure 1 focuses on interpersonal boundary maintenance. Divergent and sociable role behaviors open interpersonal boundaries, promoting interaction; while cautionary and structural role behaviors close interpersonal boundaries and deal with the need for individuals to manage their own affairs.

The concepts used to describe behavior depend on the perspective adopted. From the viewpoint of the group system, behavior can be conceptualized in terms of social roles; the same behavior, viewed from the perspective of the individual, will be seen as arising from personality dimensions. For example, supportive, caring behavior can be traced to

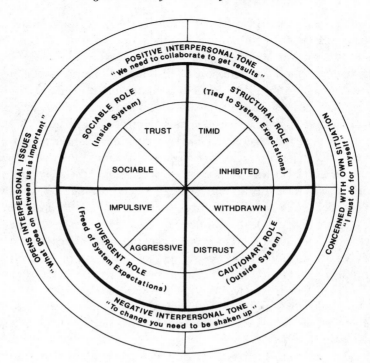

FIGURE I
PERSONALITY DIMENSIONS AND SOCIAL ROLES

the personality dimensions labeled "sociable" and "trust," or it may be viewed in terms of the social system and designated "sociable role" functioning. Figure 1 indicates similar relationships for each role. The structural role can be seen to relate to the personality dimensions of "timid" and "inhibited," underlining the distinction noted earlier that this role has been divorced from ideas of "positive leadership" and restricted to functions related to internal system structure. These individuals are interpersonally restricted and compulsively driven to meet social expectations. Still, in a general sense, the sociable and structural roles are both characterized by a positive interpersonal tone, which contributes to the development of a cohesive working climate. In contrast, the cautionary and divergent roles appear in negative interpersonal terms, and their contribution may be viewed unfavorably by group members and therapists alike. Nevertheless, they have an important function in stimulating personal responsibility and confrontation.

FURTHER CONSIDERATIONS

The ideas presented here stem from general systems theory, the base of our stage/role hypothesis. The group is conceptualized as a system, with the individual members forming parts. These structures are maintained by boundary delineations consisting of information concerning the group and its members. Role behaviors contribute to this process, so that all roles are necessary for the emergence of a functional system.

Psychological boundaries consist of information specifying differences between each side of the boundary. As more information becomes available, the boundary is clarified and there are more opportunities for transactions across it. Durkin (1981) suggests that boundaries are also identified by recurrent opening and closing — for example, a strongly felt emotional event opens interpersonal boundaries, and the attempt to understand it closes the boundary. Both processes are important in revealing the presence of a boundary. The process of therapy can be considered to involve a successive opening and closing of significant boundaries. For practical purposes, four types of boundaries need to be considered in therapy groups: the external boundary around the entire group, the boundaries around subsets of members, the boundary surrounding each individual member, and the internal boundaries delineating different aspects of psychological experience and structure.

The preceding account of social roles has emphasized the informational consequences of role behavior, which can also be viewed in terms of the effects on boundaries (J. E. Durkin, personal communication). Sociable and divergent role behaviors serve to open interpersonal and internal boundaries, leading to greater self-revelation. The former achieves this through empathic understanding, the latter through challenge and confrontation. Structural role behaviors close these boundaries by promoting efforts at understanding. Cautionary role behaviors also close the boundaries, by withdrawal and caution. Yet, in a contrary fashion, structural and cautionary role behaviors open the external group boundary — the former, by emphasizing extra-group application of learning; the latter, through concern for individual autonomy. The concern with interpersonal events in sociable and divergent role behaviors focuses on in-group phenomena and thereby closes the external boundary.

Although all of these role behaviors are important for group development, an excess of the behaviors characteristic of any one role may become a liability. Group work is endangered if one member becomes extremely dominant or if a homogeneity in group composition fosters only one interactional pattern. To use a well-known but, it is hoped, decreasingly common example: anyone who has run a group composed of depressed, middle-aged housewives will recognize the difficulty in developing a climate emphasizing confrontation and personal change.

Social roles have important implications for the formation of group norms (Bond, 1975; MacKenzie, 1979). Norms reflect the implicit goals of the group and are therefore closely related to individual expectations, particularly during the early stages. The same individual factors also have an influence on role assumption. It is important that the early group have a reasonable degree of sociable and structural role performances, for these contribute to group norms conducive to a positive working atmosphere. These role behaviors continue to be necessary to sustain an environment with adequate supports for psychological work. If the group is to progress, however, divergent and cautionary role enactments are required to encourage the development of norms that sanction confronting and individuating behaviors. It may be hypothesized that particular role behaviors are associated with the accomplishment of specific stage tasks. In this chapter we have cited some examples; Beck and her colleagues present further thoughts on this in the next chapter. The exploration of such stage and role interactions offers exciting potential for understanding the underlying systemic structure of group events.

The concept of social role is frequently used as if it were the social system equivalent of a personality trait, in that it is conceived as a cluster of behaviors characteristic of one member over time. This limits the value of the concept by tying it too closely to the individual, rather than seeing it as a functional requirement of the system, to which any member may contribute. Viewed in social system terms, the significant issue regarding social roles is not whether behaviors cluster in the individual in the ways we have suggested, but rather whether these behaviors occur at critical points in the group's development. The system needs varied roles just as the individual needs to acquire role flexibility. The danger in this confusion of social roles and personality traits is that individual behavior may be incorporated into the normative expectations of the system so that the individual may be coerced by system pressure into continuously playing the same role. The therapist may need to intervene actively to free the individual from such limiting expectations.

The ideas presented in this chapter have a number of implications for clinical practice. The idea that a diversity of behaviors is necessary for the effective development of a social system implies the need for heterogeneous membership (Woods and Melnick, 1979). The model presented here suggests that heterogeneity in regard to interpersonal style is the critical factor, that the group must have within it the potential for exhibiting all role behaviors with reasonable facility.

These ideas also have important implications for the therapist's behavior. Through an understanding of stages and roles, the therapist can facilitate stage-appropriate role behavior and thus accelerate the accomplishment of the stage's task through reinforcement of desired activities or, if necessary, through modeling them. The therapist should also be aware of the importance of ensuring that all members participate in the task of each stage so that all can progress more or less together as the group develops. In this process, the changing social context provides opportunities for the individual to try out new behaviors. Social pressures as well as in-group models assist this process. The therapist will want to ensure that during the life of the group, members have an opportunity to experience all social roles and thus move toward a broader repertoire of interpersonal behaviors and modulation of previously maladaptive interpersonal patterns.

The account of group phenomena contained in this chapter, like the preceding review of developmental stages, is descriptive, arising from clinical experience. Empirical research is needed to validate these ideas and so establish the theory on a firm foundation. The value of the present description lies in the fact that group system processes and member behavior are characterized in ways that can be quantified.

REFERENCES

Bales, R. F. (1953), The equilibrium problem in small groups. In: *Working Papers in the Theory of Action,* ed. T. Parsons, R. F. Bales, & E. A. Shils. Glencoe, Ill.: Free Press.

_____ (1970), *Personality and Interpersonal Behavior.* New York: Holt, Rinehart & Winston.

_____ & Slater, P. E. (1955), Role differentiation in small decision-making groups. In: *Family, Socialization and Interaction Process,* ed. T. Parsons & R. F. Bales. Glencoe, Ill.: Free Press.

Baumrind, D. (1971), Current patterns of parental authority. *Devel. Psychol. Monogr.,* 4:1 (Part 2).

Beck, A. P. (1974), Phases in the development of structure in therapy and encounter groups. In: *Innovations in Client-Centered Therapy,* ed. D. A. Wexler & L. N. Rice. New York: Wiley.

_____ & Peters, L. N. (1981), The research evidence for distributed leadership in therapy groups. *Int. J. Group Psychother.,* 31:43–710.

Bednar, R. L., & Kaul, T. J. (1978), Experiential group research: Current perspectives. In: *Handbook of Psychotherapy and Behavior Change: An Empirical Analysis,* ed. S.

L. Garfield & A. E. Bergin. New York: Wiley.

Benjamin, L. S. (1974), Structural analysis of social behavior. *Psychol. Rev.,* 81:392–425.

Benne, K. D. & Sheats, P. (1948), Functional roles of group members. *J. Soc. Issues,* 4(2):41–49.

Biddle, B. J. (1979), *Role Theory: Expectations, Identities and Behaviors.* New York: Academic Press.

———— & Thomas, E. J. (1966), *Role Theory: Concepts and Research.* New York: Wiley.

Blake, R., & Mouton, J. S. (1964), *The Managerial Grid.* Houston: Gulf.

Bond, G. R. (1975), Norm formation in therapy groups. Unpublished doctoral dissertation, University of Chicago.

Burke, P. J. (1967), The development of task and social-emotional role differentiation. *Sociometry,* 30(4):379–392.

Durkin, J. E., Ed. (1981), *Living Groups: Group Psychotherapy and General System Theory.* New York: Brunner/Mazel.

Foa, U. G. (1961), Convergences in the analysis of the structure of interpersonal behavior. *Psychol. Rev.,* 68:341–353.

Freedman, M. B., Leary, T. F., Ossorio, A. G., & Coffey, H. S. (1951), The interpersonal dimension of personality. *J. Pers.,* 20:143–161.

Hare, A. P. (1976), *Handbook of Group Research,* 2nd Ed. New York: Free Press.

Hurley, J. R. (1980), Two interpersonal dimensions relevant to group and family therapy. In: *Group and Family Therapy 1980: An Overview,* ed. L. R. Wolberg & M. L. Aronson. New York: Brunner/Mazel.

Lieberman, M. A., Yalom, I. D., & Miles, M. B. (1973), *Encounter Groups: First Facts.* New York: Basic Books.

Lorr, M., Bishop, P. F., & McNair, D. M. (1965), Interpersonal types among psychiatric patients. *J. Abnorm. Psychol.,* 70:468–472.

MacKenzie, K. R. (1979), Group norms: Importance and measurement. *Int. J. Group Psychother.,* 29:471–480.

———— (1981a), The concept of role as a boundary structure in small groups. In: *Living Groups: Group Psychotherapy and General System Theory,* ed. J. E. Durkin. New York: Brunner/Mazel.

———— (1981b), Measurement of group climate. *Int. J. Group Psychother.,* 31: 287–296.

———— & Livesley, W. J. (1982), Developmental stages: An integrating theory of group psychotherapy. *Can. J. Psychiat.* (in press).

Newcomb, T. M. (1950), Role behaviors in the study of individual personality and of groups. *J. Pers.,* 18:273–289.

————, Turner, R. H., & Converse, P. E. (1966), *Social Psychology.* London: Tavistock.

Osgood, C. E., Suci, G. J., & Tannenbaum, P. H. (1957), *The Measurement of Meaning.* Urbana: University of Illinois Press.

Parloff, M. B., & Dies, R. R. (1977), Group psychotherapy outcome research, 1966–1975. *Int. J. Group Psychother.,* 27:281–319.

Parsons, T., & Bales, R. F. (1955), *Family, Socialization and Interaction Process.* Glencoe, Ill.: Free Press.

Plutchik, R. (1980), *Emotion: A Psychoevolutionary Synthesis.* New York: Harper & Row.

Ryle, A. (1979), The focus in brief interpretive psychotherapy: Dilemmas, traps and snags as target problems. *Brit. J. Psychiat.,* 134:46–54.

Sarbin, T. R. (1954), Role theory. In: *Handbook of Social Psychology,* ed. G. Lindzey. Cambridge, Mass.: Addison Wesley.

Schaeffer, E. S. (1961), Converging conceptual models for maternal behavior and for child behavior. In: *Parental Attitudes and Child Behavior,* ed. J. C. Glidewell. Springfield, Ill.: Thomas.

Slater, P. E. (1955), Role differentiation in small groups. *Amer. Sociol. Rev.,* 20: 300–310.

Talland, G. A. (1957), Role and status structure in therapy groups. *J. Clin. Psychol.,* 13:27–33.

Wiggins, J. S. (1979), A psychological taxonomy of trait descriptive terms: I. The interpersonal domain. *J. Pers. Soc. Psychol.,* 37:395–412.

Woods, M., & Melnick, J. (1979), A review of group therapy selection criteria. *Small Group Behav.,* 10:155–174.

6

The Participation of Leaders in the Structural Development of Therapy Groups

ARIADNE P. BECK, M.A., JAMES M. DUGO, Ph.D.,
ALBERT M. ENG, M.S.W., CAROL M. LEWIS, M.A.,
and LANA N. PETERS, Ph.D.

Why is it that most groups have at least one member who everyone agrees is a pain in the neck?

Why are certain periods in a group smooth, cooperative, and productive, requiring little input or guidance from the leader, while other periods are contentious, tense, and nonproductive, requiring continual input or guidance from the leader?

Why do some people drop out of a group midstream?

Why do some groups seem to be perpetually involved in competitive behavior, while in others the atmosphere changes a good deal over time?

The thesis of this chapter is that the answer to these questions is best made from a perspective on the natural developmental history of a group. That history is difficult to perceive when one is immersed in the moment-to-moment process of living in or leading a group. This chapter presents a brief overview of a program of research which is aimed at studying the developmental history of therapy groups, and the emergence and function of leadership in that context.* After a brief introduc-

*Editors' Note: Beck et al.'s use of the concept of "leadership" may be unfamiliar to some readers. They are not referring to the group psychotherapist or the designated

137

tion to the model of group development that underlies the research, some of our recent results will be presented, in conjunction with a discussion of their implications for the clinician.

Our work is based on Beck's descriptive theory of the phases of group development. This model was formulated from careful study of audio-tape-recorded, time-limited (20-session) psychotherapy groups (Beck, 1974, 1981a, 1981b; Beck and Kiel, 1967). A number of theories and observations in the literature identify phases in group development (Hare, 1976; Lacoursiere, 1980; Tuckman, 1965), but Beck's system, while covering all the phases identified by others, is the only one that includes all nine phases. A review of the literature shows a high degree of agreement on the essential characteristics of the nine phases — a view that has not been recognized generally, although people have been working on this problem for at least 30 years (Beck, in prep.).

In the research area, a handful of studies have found evidence of significant, and theoretically meaningful, differences between various "periods" in a group or set of groups. No one, however, has produced empirical evidence that delineates actual phase boundaries — i.e., beginnings and endings of phases — nor, for that matter, has a methodology been available to explore such an issue across different groups.

Since 1975 we have been attempting to develop such empirical measures of the phase development of groups and of the four emerging leaders that the theory describes (Beck, 1977, 1980b; Beck and Peters, 1981; Dugo and Beck, 1980; Eng, 1980; Eng and Beck, 1980, 1981; Lewis and Beck, 1980; Lewis, Dugo and Beck, 1981; Peters and Beck, 1982). Recently, several other colleagues have taken up various aspects of this work (Coché, Cooper, Petermann, and Sillitti, 1981; Durkin, 1981; MacKenzie, 1981). Together, we feel we are building a body of knowledge that will make therapy groups more understandable, generate a more accurate theory of group development, and lead to implications for leaders of groups and to guidelines for training leaders, as well as generating a rich set of research projects. The work to be described here has been done by the Chicago area research team, and is very much in process. It represents our current understanding, based on the parts of the research that are complete at this time and on our joint clinical observations of our own groups, the groups of people we supervise, and groups conducted in various settings where we consult with the staff.

---

leader of the group, but to members who emerge as significant sources of influence on the development of the group. "Leadership" thus refers to member roles, although, as they point out, the "task leader" is often the therapist.

OVERVIEW OF PHASES

Our model of group development applies to groups of up to ten people with stable membership. It is our observation that when membership changes, the group usually recycles, beginning again at the first phase (which of course has many implications for open-ended groups). We see nine phases in the development of group structure. Structure refers to roles in the group, the norms for functioning in the group, the limits and criteria for membership, the group organizational issues, and the group level identity. The nine phases emerge in an invariant sequence as long as the membership remains stable and the group is able to handle the group-level issues of each phase in turn. Not all groups are able to do that, and therefore many groups do not progress through all or even many of the phases. Indeed, Phases 8 and 9 probably are not even possible unless a group has a planned ending and knows about it for some time ahead.

The adjective "group-level" refers to issues or problems that are particularly relevant to the group as a whole at a particular time in its development. The major themes of the nine phases are as follows:

Phase 1: Creating a "contract" to become a working group based on an initial assessment of the members and an initial statement of goals.

Phase 2: Forging a group identity, goals, and initial norms for operation, and selecting leaders in a competitive work style which must be resolved if the group is to move on.

Phase 3: Beginning the first cooperative work phase, in which members disclose themselves and further define personal goals, and in which there is experimentation with a work style for the group.

Phase 4: Forming a positive peer bond via the exploration of closeness in the group and in relationships outside the group.

Phase 5: Exploring the implications of intimacy, particularly for dependence and independence issues.

Phase 6: Moving forward on the basis of commitment to each other, with integration of the task leader into the group.

Phase 7: Pursuing in-depth self-confrontation in a mutually supportive, interdependent context in which formal and informal roles have dissipated, replaced by flexible responses based on in-the-moment assessment of needs.

Phase 8: Dealing with an evaluation or review of what has been accomplished and learned, with a focus on the transfer of learning to the rest of one's life.

Phase 9: Coping with acknowledgment of members' significance to each other while dealing with loss, separation, and termination.

Progress through the phases requires that the members possess various levels of skill. For example, a group of schizophrenic patients may spend a great deal of time in Phase 1, learning how to represent themselves to other members. This is an important task to be performed in any group in Phase 1. It is also one of the crucial forms of learning that schizophrenic individuals can get from being in a group, since their affliction leaves them fairly limited in this skill (Dugo and Beck, 1982). The point is that there are times when using the group-level developmental issues as a vehicle to work on personal developmental issues is very appropriate and healthy. There are other times, however, when a group may get stuck in a particular phase because it is unable to resolve the group-level issues of that phase and to work on the relevant developmental issues of individuals. The nine phases describe a process of development of a group structure that enables the members to accomplish the task for which they gathered. It is a process of identifying and exploring the intrapersonal and interpersonal issues that each member finds problematic; a process of encounter, interpersonal bonding, internalization, differentiation, integration, separation, and finally loss at termination.

OVERVIEW OF LEADERSHIP ROLES

The current phase of our research has focused on the experimental design of a methodology that would lead to the empirical identification of phase boundaries, characteristic within-phase processes, and the emerging leaders. There are four leadership roles that emerge in a natural way during the group's evolution (Beck and Peters, 1981; Peters and Beck, 1982). The four leaders are called the task leader, the emotional leader, the scapegoat leader, and the defiant leader. A brief description of the roles (from Beck, 1981a) is given below:

Task Leader

Is a guide to the task of the group; facilitates members' self-exploration.

Provides support and is available to all members of the group as individuals.

Facilitates members' interpersonal interaction.

Through style characteristics strongly influences:
1. openness and ease with which norms are defined;
2. clarification of goals and subgoals for the group and for individuals;
3. style of communication in the group;

4. level of participation of members;
5. depth of emotional issues addressed.

Participates in defining certain norms and certain goals.

Accurately perceives and verbally represents what goes on in the group, at a group level and on individual member levels.

Emotional Leader

Is interested in and focuses on emotional issues. Expresses concern for others and involvement in the group. Is well liked by others and serves as a positive focus.

Is eager for support from others and ready to make use of it for personal growth. Is open to being affected, although vulnerable.

Models the change process. (In a therapy group, the emotional leader usually enters ready for a developmental change and is most ready to engage in the task of the group.

Works hard on accurately perceiving and representing his or her own reality to self and to others (i.e., is self-aware and assertive).

Works hard on accurately perceiving and representing verbally what goes on in the group. May act as spokesman for the group when this is needed.

Scapegoat Leader

Is generally oriented to working on clarifying his or her perceptions and the representation of his or her own reality to other members.

Is perceived by other members as significantly different or deviant on some important dimension or criterion for membership. (It must be emphasized, however, that the content focused on by the group may be a real issue or may be a projective fantasy on their part.)

Is generally one step behind the group in understanding nonverbal messages — often asking for these messages to be made more explicit.

In early phases of group may be object of negative or hostile feelings in context of discussions of normative issues and leadership selection. (In contrast to the emotional leader, who is self-aware and assertive, the scapegoat leader appears to be assertive but not self-aware.)

In contrast to the way group perceives the scapegoat leader, is actually open, willing to be self-disclosing, and willing to engage in the give-and-take of the structure-forming process.

Makes a strong contribution to resolving group-level issues and a strong commitment to participation in the group. Is strong enough to withstand negative perceptions of himself or herself.

In later phases, is integrated into the group with greater openness; members' perceptions of him or her usually change markedly, in a more positive direction.

Defiant Leader

(The term "defiant" comes from this leader's emotional stance in the group, particularly in relation to dependency on the task leader and to cohesiveness in the group.)

Expresses ambivalence regarding participation in the group from the start.

Is likely to miss sessions, requiring others to then summarize, integrate, and define the significance of what was accomplished.

Is oriented toward helping others in the group and to representing verbally what is going on in the group. In some ways shares with task leader a somewhat participant-observer objectivity in the form of responses made to others.

In contrast to the scapegoat leader, is usually not able to engage in very much self-disclosing or to work on his or her own perceptions or representations of his or her own experience in the group context.

Leadership in this context refers to roles which have two primary characteristics: (1) each of these persons performs important and consistent maintenance functions across most of the group's life; and (2) these four persons take turns, usually in pairs, leading the dialectical discussion process by which group-level concerns are explored and resolved in each phase of the group. In a mature group at Phase 7, the significance of these roles dissipates and the functions are shared more freely among all of the members. We think of each of the four leaders as modeling, for the rest of the group, a conflict that everyone feels to some extent because of the very fact that they are members in a group. For example, the Task Leader models the conflict around exercising control in the group—i.e., taking and using power to direct the group task versus giving to or sharing this power with other group members. The Emotional Leader models the conflict between affiliation with other members and rejection of other members—i.e., the problem of whether to form deep bonds or to deny the need for deep bonds with others. The Scapegoat Leader models the conflict between assertion of the self and conformity to the group. Emotionally the struggle is between impulses of aggression and submission, a problem that is raised by the very act of joining with others. Finally, the Defiant Leader is usually a member of the group who openly expresses ambivalence about dependence and independence throughout the group's life, and models that struggle for the group as a whole. The Defiant Leader struggles with the problems surrounding the ability to trust others and the ability to take care of or protect oneself in relation to others.

It seems clear from these descriptions that group members who themselves have concerns about one or another of these emotional conflicts would tend to become candidates for the relevant roles. That is conjecture at this point, but it will ultimately be one of the questions for research to clarify.

Interplay with Phases 1-3

Before moving on to our research results, a brief description of the interplay between leaders and phases will be given for the first three phases in order to create a context for interpreting the results.

Phase 1 usually requires the settlement of membership composition because the members will not make a contract to become a group until they know who all the participants will be. An important aspect of Phase 1 is that members assess each other and estimate their own abilities to cope with other members. Some will leave at this point if they feel too uncomfortable to be able to work with the others present, or if they cannot find another member with whom they can connect (Dugo and Beck, 1982).

During Phase 1, the Task Leader (usually the therapist) plays a very important role in setting the emotional tone, the pace, and the structure of the group. In addition, he or she usually demonstrates the therapeutic work that will be done with individuals in the group. In this ongoing role, the Task Leader functions as the expert on communication and self-exploration and influences goal clarification, leadership selection, and many other dimensions of group life.

A second important person—the Emotional Leader—is selected during Phase 1. This is generally the best-liked member of the group, who acts as a monitor of the group's emotional processing, is ultimately perceived as the most important support person to other members, and—most important—becomes the model of the work they have all gathered to do.

In Phase 2, the group moves on to the actual testing of the assessments made in Phase 1. Major group organizational issues are worked out, such as the completion of leadership selection and the resolution of competitive needs. On the way to those two achievements, the group must establish an initial set of norms regarding its operation and a method for managing negative feelings. In addition, group goals must be clarified and an initial group identity formulated. Neither of these two latter issues is handled for all time, but they must be initiated at a level that engages the entire group in such a way that they can proceed in a cooperative manner beyond this point. This is the most difficult phase in group process. It is usually characterized by a conflict with one person in particular—the Scapegoat Leader—who serves as a reference point against which the rest of the group defines itself. The Emotional Leader and the Scapegoat Leader usually bracket the range of attitudes expressed by the group members regarding the formative structural issues of the group. The Task Leader often must be available either to mediate, to support, or to help clarify issues during this conflict. Ultimately, the primary responsibility lies with this leader to help the group to face and address the underlying anxiety that accompanies the enormously complex tasks of Phase 2.

After the conflict is presumed to be resolved, Phase 3 inaugurates a cooperative work process, during which members become more personally disclosing. This period allows a variety of therapeutic methods for dealing with personal change and growth in greater depth. Members take turns to discuss the issues that brought them to the group. As a result, the others see each member more clearly, and each member becomes more consciously aware of himself or herself. By the end of this phase, the members are really individuals once more, having established a kind of equality as clients by participating in this shared self-disclosure. The Emotional Leader has begun a significant growth spurt and become a model of the change process to the rest of the group; the Scapegoat Leader has worked toward reintegration into the group; the Defiant Leader has begun to participate more actively, sometimes assuming a therapist-like stance in relation to others while offering a minimal amount of self-disclosure; and the Task Leader/therapist has functioned most fully in the therapeutic role, helping individual members to explore their issues and the entire group to make this work a joint effort.

The individuals who take on the four leadership roles are not just serving a group-level function. Their personalities modify the roles in significant ways. The roles become vehicles for working on and, in a successful group, working through significant developmental issues. The roles described continue to be important through the sixth phase in group development. After that, however, they seem to dissolve and the members share the various functions in a more fluid way. Presumably, by this point in group life, the roles no longer serve a needed function for either the group as a whole or for the members who have filled them.

RESEARCH RESULTS

We shall now describe some of our research. We have been studying three time-limited psychotherapy groups which met for either 15 or 20 one-and-a-half-hour sessions each in an outpatient setting. Our research team has been designing a number of different measures which are aimed at illuminating group development. The goal has been to design measures subtle enough to track the group's process, but simple enough to be useful in a wide range of contexts.* The measures and their development have been described in greater detail elsewhere (Beck, Dugo, Eng, and Lewis, in press; Beck and Peters, 1981; Peters and Beck, 1982).

The results to be presented here grow out of the pilot work aimed at developing measures; they are not the outcome of hypothesis-testing research, which will be the next phase of the research program. Throughout this pilot study, clinical analysis of the material has been used as the criterion against which the measures were compared. As we close in on measures that promise some general usefulness, we spend more time going back and forth between clinical and empirical views in arriving at decisions. The data on the three groups in this pilot study were collected in the earliest phase of this work. Even at that time, however, we were concerned with finding an empirical measure of the emerging leaders. The sociometric approach was chosen because it represented the group member's own viewpoint and because of its history in the study of leadership. The goal in our sociometric study was to find a set of questions that consistently separated each of the four leaders from the rest of the group (Beck and Peters, 1981; Peters and Beck, 1982).

Empirical Measures of Leadership Roles

Over the years many questions have been used experimentally. At the time that the data were collected on the three groups in this methodological study, the following questions were asked of all the group members at the end of each group.

Editors' Note: The nature of Beck et al.'s instruments provides a good example of the merging of research and clinical interests. The measures show considerable originality, ranging from positive/negative behavior toward the scapegoat leader, through normative/personal content themes, to a frequency count of the pronoun "we." All of the measures are tightly connected to various aspects of the theory they have developed. At the same time, the measures are easily translated into clinical practice; with some experience, the therapist can readily monitor such behavior during a session.

1. The pleasure that you derived from their presence in the group.
2. The extent to which they influence or determine what actually takes place in the group meetings.
3. The degree to which you felt they understood you.
4. The degree to which you felt you understood them.
5. The degree to which you felt they were similar to you.
6. The degree to which they expressed themselves as feeling similar to you.

The data were summarized by computing the mean rank for each member of each group. The members were then rank-ordered within their groups.

Before we examine the results for the three groups in this study, we should note that Groups A and S each had six clients and two therapists; Group N had five clients and two therapists. Table 1 shows those results which had some pattern across the three groups. Thus, we see that the Task Leader was well-liked (Question 1) and was perceived as high in understanding the group members (Question 3). Of some interest is the fact that two of the three Task Leaders were in the middle of the ranks on influencing the group process (Question 2). The Emotional Leader was ranked quite high by all the groups on all the questions except for Question 6. The Scapegoat Leaders were perceived in a variety of ways across these three groups, except for the question on influence, where they consistently received high ranks. The Defiant Leaders were all placed in the bottom four ranks on pleasure, influence, who understood you, and expressing themselves as similar to you (Questions 1, 2, 3, and 6). As indi-

TABLE 1

Rankings of Leaders on Six Sociometric Questions by Groups A, S, and N

Question	Task Leader			Emotional Leader			Scapegoat Leader			Defiant Leader		
	A	S	N	A	S	N	A	S	N	A	S	N
1	2	2	1	1	1	2				5	8	7
2	4	4	1	1.5	1	3	3	3	2	6	7	7
3	2	1	1	1	2	2				5	8	7
4				1	1	1						
5				1	2	1						
6										5	8	7

TABLE 2

Major Differences between Phases 2 and 3

Phase 2		Phase 3
Movement from high tension, anger, criticism or discomfort	To	Relatively positive feeling and mutual support
Movement from relatively defensive (stereotyping, manipulating, deflecting behavior) "parallel play"-type communication	To	More open, mutually exploratory behavior; responsive communication
Movement from concern, apprehension, and struggle related to organizational and norm development issues	To	Focus on individual members and their personal concerns

cated earlier, these questions were administered after the groups terminated. The Defiant Leaders in all three of these groups left before their groups terminated. All of the groups had progressed far enough in phase development to have reintegrated their Scapegoat Leaders, but their problems with their Defiant Leaders were fresher in their minds and essentially unresolved. The most striking aspect of Table 1 is the strong positive image of the Emotional Leader that is reflected in the responses to this set of questions. From everything we have come to understand about group process, the Emotional Leader strongly engages the hearts and minds of all the group members, including the Task Leader.

Empirical Measures of Phase Development

Turning now to another aspect of our work—one of the major tasks of our program has been to find empirical measures of the phase development in groups. On the basis of a review of the literature on phases, and the use of Beck's theory, a list was made of the generally agreed-upon characteristics of Phases 2 and 3. By comparing these, it was possible to define the major changes that took place when the group moved from one phase to the other. Table 2 lists the critical changes that have been identified in this way.

We wanted to have measures that would show the group's process, so variables were designed or adapted for groups to track the dimensions of change. Figure 1 shows the first three measures of group process we

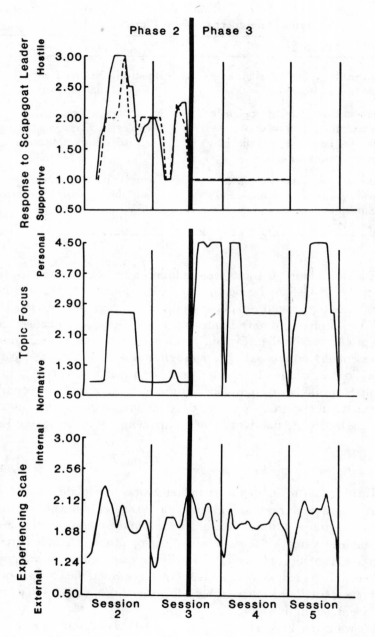

FIGURE I

IDENTIFYING THE BOUNDARY BETWEEN PHASES 2 AND 3

developed. These three measures were used to study the moment-to-moment process and to define the boundaries between Phases 2 and 3.

As noted earlier, the three groups we studied were all audiotape-recorded; then, typed transcripts were prepared for use in the ratings of the three variables. In Figure 1, all three graphs describe Group A. They show the same four sessions of the group (the second through the fifth), encompassing Phases 2 and 3. The thin vertical lines demarcate the sessions, while the heavy vertical line indicates the boundary between Phases 2 and 3. The second phase, as indicated earlier, is the competitive, scapegoating period and the third phase, the work-oriented cooperative period. Looking across each graph, one sees the group's behavior as it is described by that variable across time. Looking up and down across graphs, one sees the same behavior as it is described by three different views.

The top graph shows the verbal behavior of the members of the group, excluding the therapists toward the Scapegoat Leader (for a description of this variable — *response to Scapegoat Leader* — see Beck [in press]). Each statement was rated in terms of a three-category system: whether is was supportive (1.00 on the graph), mildly negative (2.00), or openly hostile (3.00). An average rating per page of transcript was computed. Figure 1 shows the data after they had been processed by a statistical smoothing procedure known as hanning, which is based on running medians. The smoother allows only major trends to be reflected in the final graph (Beacon and Tukey, 1974).

As can be seen, in Group A there was a generally negative response to the Scapegoat Leader during the second session and the first half of the third, after which the responses were all supportive in nature. This pattern is consistent with the idea that a group is in conflict during Phase 2, especially with its Scapegoat Leader; resolves that conflict; and moves on to a more cooperative period of work in Phase 3. This particular process measure therefore gives a picture of the Scapegoat Leader's role in these two phases that supports the description in the theory.

The middle graph in Figure 1 shows a measure of the *topic focus* of the group as a whole on either personal issues or on normative/organizational issues during the group's dialogue (Dugo and Beck, 1980). After the session transcripts were divided into units on the basis of the group's focus on a topic, the units were rated in terms of a primary focus on group-level normative or organizational issues (1.00 on the graph), a primary focus on personal issues of particular interest to individuals or dyads (3.00), or an equal focus on both personal and group norm or organizational issues (2.00). The last category is called "combination" as a shorthand.

Group A showed a pattern on this variable of being involved primarily with group norms and group organizational issues during the second session and the first half of the third, with a short period of focus on combined personal and normative issues. After that point in time, the group focus was either on personal issues of the members or combined personal and normative issues, with no sustained work on normative issues alone. This pattern again confirms the difference between Phase 2 (which is primarily involved with goal setting, norm creation, and leadership selection) and Phase 3 (which is primarily concerned with personal self-disclosure and setting personal goals for work in the group).

The bottom graph in Figure 1 shows a measure known as the *experiencing scale,* which was applied to every statement in the transcript (Lewis and Beck, 1980). Again, average ratings per page were computed and then processed with the statistical smoother. This scale assesses the individual speaker's degree of involvement in the process of self-exploration. The term "experiencing" refers to the ability to recognize and accept feelings and their meanings and impact. It also reflects the extent to which awareness of subjective experience is used as a referent for thought and action. The scale progresses from limited and externalized references (1.00 on the graph), to descriptions of events (2.00), to the expression of personal feelings about the events described (3.00), to a predominant concern with a description of inner feelings and reactions (4.00). The scale actually has seven points, but this graph only goes to 4.50, since none of these smoothed graphs showed levels higher than 4.00. There is also a Therapist Scale, which rates responses addressed to another person's issues in terms of the same categories (Klein, Mathieu, Gendlin, and Kiesler, 1969).

The graph in Figure 1 shows all the group members, including the therapists, averaged together. We think of this group-as-a-whole graph of the experiencing scale as a measure of awareness and integration of experience. The most interesting feature in this graph of Group A is that the scale peaks at the shift from Phase 2 to Phase 3. Clearly it also peaks at other times as well. For example, the highest peak in Session 2 is part of the group's shift from Phase 1 to Phase 2, and also part of the group's attack on the Scapegoat Leader. The highest peak in Session 5, near the end of the session, is the shift from Phase 3 to Phase 4.

Taken together, these three graphs are currently being used as the measure for the definition of the boundaries between Phases 2 and 3.

They also appear to be useful in defining the boundaries between Phases 1 and 2, and between 3 and 4. Our recent work has also included a detailed analysis of Phase 1.

Our results constitute the first empirical evidence of phase boundaries that has been produced. It has been gratifying for us that in the main the characteristics of the process fit our expectations based on the theory — namely, that the Scapegoat Leader is the object of hostile feelings during Phase 2, while the group is primarily working on normative and organizational issues, and that this hostility subsides when the group is able to resolve its Phase 2 group-level issues and move on to a cooperative period of self-exploration and self-disclosure. Also, we see from the experiencing scale that a high level of experiencing characterizes phase shifts, indicating that these are times when a heightened self-awareness accompanies an integrative group-level process.

Further Data Analysis

In addition to these observations, we have learned many *new* things from our data analysis. For example, looking at the graph for topic focus again, we find a period of time in Session 4, which continues in Session 5, when the group is rated as dealing with a combination of normative and personal concerns. A version of this period has been found in the midst of Phase 3 in all three of the groups. A check back to the transcripts reveals that during this period the group seems to be reprocessing the issues that came up during the conflict with the Scapegoat Leader in Phase 2, except this time they approach the issues from a position of greater self-awareness and, more important, they each own their individual part in the conflict. The quality of insight and resolution achieved at this point in the process is undoubtedly significant for the progress of the group and for the reintegration of this leader into the group. The basic early relationship between the Scapegoat Leader and the rest of the group offers many opportunities (including this Phase 3 period) during which the therapist can help the group members to understand the dynamics of the scapegoating process. Many clients have been scapegoated either in their own families or in peer groups, and this live, in-the-group relationship potentially makes it possible for everyone to explore his or her own version of the experience if the therapist is aware of and able to make use of the process in that way.

The process variable that assesses level of experiencing has proved to be a very productive measure. It is possible, for example, to produce graphs for individual members, or subgroups within the group. Figure 2

rs a comparison of graphs that specifically addresses the participation
leaders. It portrays the relationship between the behavior of the
imary therapist, or Task Leader, in the group, and the behavior of

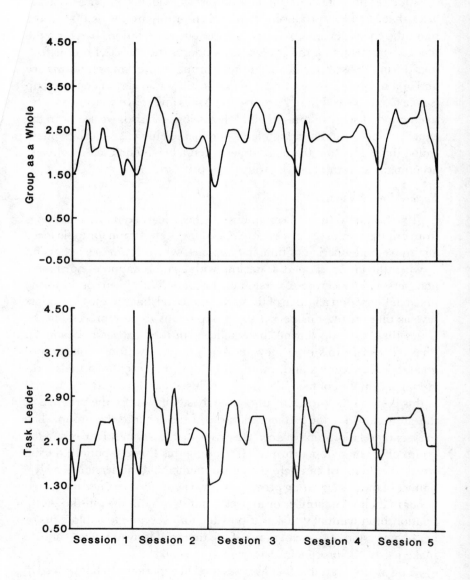

FIGURE 2
LEVEL OF EXPERIENCING IN GROUP A

the group-as-a-whole as this is expressed on the level of experiencing measure.

In Figure 2, based on Group A in our study, the level of experiencing of the group-as-a-whole is shown on top, with the graph for the Task Leader's level of experiencing below. Note that in each case the Task Leader (who was the therapist in all three groups) very closely follows the peaks and valleys of the group-as-a-whole. The same pattern was found in the other two groups as well. These three groups were conducted by client-centered therapists, with a senior therapist and a student co-therapist in each group. In Groups A and S, the therapist's statements tended to hang just below the level of the group-as-a-whole, while in Group N the therapist tended to be above the level of the group-as-a-whole. We have no way of knowing yet whether the pattern we observed relates to other variables or to the outcome of the group in a systematic way, or whether it is characteristic of therapists with a different orientation. At the very least, it seems to show a high level of attention on the part of the Task Leader to the main process of the group, and that is consistent with the role described in the theory.

Another analysis, based on the experiencing scale and measure of topic focus, gives interesting evidence of the function of the four leaders during the change periods of the group-level processes. We examined the proportion of these change periods in which leaders versus non-leaders participate with a significant contribution. ("Leaders" here refers to the four leadership roles identified by the theory.) A criterion has been defined for selecting the significant peaks in the group-as-a-whole curve for the level of experiencing. Similarly, a criterion has been defined for the significant shifts in the topic focus variable (see Figure 1). We are using these two criteria to identify important group level change periods in terms of the pages of transcript which are involved in the peaks and shifts (Lewis et al., 1981). As we have already indicated, the level of experiencing measures the degree of attention to inner experience and the quality of processing by the speaker. Broadly speaking, we think of it as a measure of the quality of the individual member's participation in the group therapy process. With this in mind, we recorded those participants whose individual experiencing ratings were above criterion during the significant change periods.

Table 3 shows the average proportion of leaders versus nonleaders whose individual peaks in experiencing coincide with significant group-level changes. The table further breaks down group-level changes into those that occur during the group shift from one phase to another and

TABLE 3

Average Proportion of Leaders' and Nonleaders' Participation in Experiencing Peaks and Topic Focus Shifts

	Experiencing Scale			Topic Focus		
	Peaks during Phase Changes	Peaks during Nonphase Changes	Overall Average	Shifts during Phase Changes	Shifts during Nonphase Changes	Overall Average
Group A						
Leaders	81.25	77.29	79.29	91.50	52.00	71.75
Nonleaders	68.75	53.57	61.16	75.00	50.00	62.50
Group S						
Leaders	81.25	71.15	76.20	75.00	55.36	65.18
Nonleaders	75.00	51.23	63.13	50.00	35.64	42.82
Group N						
Leaders	75.00	78.57	78.12	62.50	66.66	66.17
Nonleaders	66.66	71.42	70.83	33.33	40.00	39.21

those that occur at other times during the group's process. The data have been summarized for the three groups in our pilot study. The trend is clear that the four leaders have higher rates of participation at a significant level of experiencing during group-level change periods than nonleaders across both categories of change periods, and across all three groups.

Another aspect of our research program has focused on designing simple measures of verbal behavior, such as length of statements and number of pronouns, and these have proved useful in characterizing differences between phases, as well as differences between leaders (Eng, 1980; Eng and Beck, 1980, 1981, 1982). Each statement in the group therapy transcript is identified in terms of the speaker, the person or persons to whom it is addressed, and the person or persons it is about. The length of statement, the number of stammers, and the number of interruptions are also recorded. In addition, the number of times the pronouns "I," "you," and "we" are used is counted. Only some of these measures have been analyzed to date.

Table 4 presents a summary of the phases in which each of the four leaders appeared in the top four ranks on two of the verbal measures. The measure called "verbal participation" was assessed by length of statement. Operationally, this included a count of the words, pauses,

TABLE 4

Group Phase in Which Leader Appeared in Top Four Ranks on Verbal Measures in All Three Groups

Leader	Phase of Verbal Participation[a]	Phase of Use of "We"
Task Leader	1, 2	1, 2, 3
Emotional Leader	1, 2, (3)	—
Scapegoat Leader	(1), 2	1, 2
Defiant Leader	1, (3)	—

[a]Figures in parentheses refer to phases in which the leader was ranked in the top four ranks in two of the three groups.

laughs, and other verbal utterances in each statement. It was an estimate of the amount of group time taken by each participant. As can be seen, the Task and Emotional Leaders were primary contributors to group interaction in both the first and second phases. Indeed, in two of the three groups the Emotional Leader was in the top four ranks in the third phase as well. The Scapegoat Leader was in the top four ranks in Phase 2 and in two of the groups in Phase 1 as well. Again, this fits with previous results that point to the significance of this leader in Phase 2. The Defiant Leader was in the top ranks in Phase 1 and in two of the groups in Phase 3 as well, when this leader seems to begin to emerge in a more prominent role.

The other measure in Table 4 involves the use of the pronoun "we" to refer to the group itself or a subgroup within the group. This measure was calculated for each group member for each phase, and the members were then rank-ordered. It is of interest that in addition to the Task Leader, the Scapegoat Leader in all three groups was a significant contributor to the use of the pronoun "we" to refer to the group. Yet the Emotional Leader, whom we might have expected to be more active in this way, was not. This finding is, however, consistent with the idea that the Emotional Leader focuses on intensive personal change during the early phases. For groups that reach Phase 3 and beyond, our hypothesis is that the Emotional Leader will emerge as a user of the group "we" pronoun in the later phases.

We-group has also been summarized for the group-as-a-whole by phase. Table 5 shows the average number of group "we" pronouns per page of transcript in each phase. In all three groups there is a clear drop in the use of this pronoun in Phase 3, as compared with Phases 1 and

TABLE 5
**Average Number of "We" Statements
per Transcript Page per Phase**

Group	Phase 1	Phase 2	Phase 3
A	2.43	2.16	1.14
S	1.36	1.69	0.39
N	—[a]	1.24	0.97

[a]Data not currently available.

2 — as we might have expected from the theory. Phase 3 is dominated by work on personal issues by each of the group members, whereas Phases 1 and 2 deal primarily with group normative and organizational issues, drawing attention to the group-as-a-whole.

CONCLUSION

All of our work thus far has been theoretical or methodological. A major step ahead of us is to apply our measures to a new set of groups in a hypothesis-testing research design. We are designing tools that will allow us to identify some of the systematic aspects of group behavior, as well as some of the unique ones. Our model of group development, when combined with actual measures for defining phase boundaries, should create a basis for evaluating the success or failure of the group-as-a-whole, for illuminating those leadership behaviors which facilitate group process and development and those which do not, and for learning a great deal more about the potential and problems for each phase as a context for the growth of individual members.

In concluding, we would like to address the question: What is crucial about these leadership roles to the working group therapist? First and foremost, they exist in every group, so far as we know at this time. An effective Task Leader will make use of this knowledge to facilitate the emergence of these leaders and will learn to work collaboratively with them, having recognized their significance to the structural development of the group. Second, the four leaders perform — they give a good deal of themselves and they do a good deal of the actual work of the group. In fact, there is no group structure without their significant, focused contributions. Third, the four leaders mirror the conflicts of the group-as-a-whole, and they take turns bracketing the dialectical process by which group-level issues are addressed and resolved. Careful observation of that behavior should enable the therapist to help the group focus clearly on these issues and should facilitate their resolution.

From the perspective presented here, the best advice we can offer any Task Leader/Therapist is: Listen to the other leaders in your group, pay attention to the content issues which they raise, notice what it is they are attending to in the group's process or feelings, notice when their functioning peaks and over which issues they peak, engage them in a collaborative process, and finally, be glad they are there — you are not alone with the burdens of leadership.

REFERENCES

Beacon, A. E., & Tukey, J. W. (1974), The fitting of power series, meaning polynomials, illustrated on band-spectroscopic data. *Technometrics,* 16(2):147–192.

Beck, A. P. (1974), Phases in the development of structure in therapy and encounter groups. In: *Innovations in client-centered therapy,* ed. D. Wexler & L. N. Rice. New York: Wiley Interscience.

_____ (1977), On the development of a rating system for the identification of group phase boundaries. Presented at Annual Conference of Society for Psychotherapy Research, Madison, Wis.

_____ (1980a), Group development and emergent leadership. Presented at Annual Conference of Society for Psychotherapy Research, Asilomar, Cal.

_____ (1980b), Process variables for the analysis of group development. Presented at Annual Conference of Society for Psychotherapy Research, Asilomar, Cal.

_____ (1981a), Developmental characteristics of the system forming process. In: *Living Groups: Group Psychotherapy and General System Theory,* ed. J. E. Durkin. New York: Brunner/Mazel.

_____ (1981b), The study of group phase development and emergent leadership. *Group,* 5:48–54.

_____ (in prep.), A process analysis of group development. *Group.* A review of theories and research on group development.

_____, Dugo, J. M., Eng, A. M., & Lewis, C. M. (in press), Process analysis of group development. In: *The Psychotherapeutic Process: A Research Handbook,* ed. L. S. Greenberg & W. M. Pinsoff. New York: Guilford Press.

_____ & Keil, A. V. (1967), Observations on the development of client centered, time-limited, therapy groups. *Counseling Center Discussion Papers,* 13(5). Chicago: University of Chicago Library.

_____ & Peters, L. N. (1981), The research evidence for distributed leadership in therapy groups. *Int. J. Group Psychother.,* 31:43–71.

Coché, E., Cooper, J. B., Petermann, K. J., & Sillitti, J. (1981), Differences in the process of cognitive and interactional psychotherapy groups. Presented at Annual Conference of Society for Psychotherapy Research, Aspen, Col.

Dugo, J. M., & Beck, A. P. (1980), Development of a variable assessing group level focus on normative or personal issues. Presented at Annual Conference of Society for Psychotherapy Research, Asilomar, Cal.

_____ _____ (1982), Issues of intimacy and hostility viewed as group-level phenomena. Presented to American Group Psychotherapy Association, New York.

Durkin, J. E. (1981), *DEST Test of Group Leadership.*

Eng, A. M. (1980), Use of pronoun counts in the analysis of group development. Presented at Annual Conference of Society for Psychotherapy Research, Asilomar, Cal.

_____ & Beck, A. P. (1980), Speech interaction measures for the analysis of group development. Presented at Annual Conference of Society for Psychotherapy Research, Asilomar, Cal.

_____ _____ (1981), Use of verbal participation measures and pronoun counts in the analysis of group development. Presented at Annual Conference of Society for Psychotherapy Research, Aspen, Col.

_____ _____ (1982), Speech behavior measures of group psychotherapy process. *Group,* 6:37–48.

Hare, A. P. (1976), *Handbook of Small Group Research,* 2nd Ed. New York: Free Press.

Klein, M. H., Mathieu, P. L., Gendlin, E. T., & Kiesler, D. J. (1969), *The Experiencing Scale: A Research and Training Manual,* Vols. I & II. Madison: Wisconsin Psychiatric Institute.

Lacoursiere, R. (1980), *The Life Cycle of Groups: Group Developmental Stage Theory.* New York: Human Sciences Press.

Lewis, C. M., & Beck, A. P. (1980), An application of the experiencing scale to the analysis of group development. Presented at Annual Conference of Society for Psychotherapy Research, Asilomar, Cal.

_____, Dugo, J. M., & Beck, A. P. (1981), The application of two process research variables to the analysis of structural development in small groups. Presented at Annual Conference of Society for Psychotherapy Research, Aspen, Col.

MacKenzie, K. R. (1981), The concept of role as a boundary structure in small groups. In: *Living Groups: Group Psychotherapy and General System Theory,* ed. J. E. Durkin. New York: Brunner/Mazel.

Peters, L. N., & Beck, A. P. (1980), Research on distributed leadership in psychotherapy groups. Presented at Annual Conference of Society for Psychotherapy Research, Asilomar, Cal.

_____ _____ (1982), Identifying emergent leaders in psychotherapy groups. *Group,* 6:35–40.

Tuckman, B. W. (1965), Developmental sequence in small groups. *Psychol. Bull.,* 63:384–399.

7

The Clinical Application
of a
Group Climate Measure

K. ROY MacKENZIE, M.D., F.R.C.P.(C)

The description of a group along a series of interactional dimensions is termed the "group climate." It is an aggregate assessment which takes into account the behavior of all members. Data may be obtained from various sources, such as therapists, observers, and trained research raters. One may also examine the perceptions of group members through a Group Climate Questionnaire (MacKenzie, 1981). The results may be recorded either as individual members' impressions of the group or averaged into a group score based on the opinions of all members. Descriptive dimensions may remain constant over long periods of time, or they may shift significantly several times within a single group session.

Group climate measures identify features of the therapeutic environment that encourage compatible types of interpersonal events. These events, or "critical incidents," have an impact on individual members, in a positive or negative direction. A number of Yalom's (1975) "curative factors" may be seen as aspects of group climate—for example, universality and catharsis. Thus, a study of group climate dimensions may be directly related to the process of change in psychotherapy groups.

The behaviors evaluated in making group climate ratings are in part

This chapter is based on a presentation to the Annual Meeting of the Society for Psychotherapy Research, Aspen, Colorado, 1981. The research program from which this work originates is supported by operating grants from the National Institute of Mental Health (1 R03 MH 34901-01) and the Research and Development Fund of Foothills Hospital, Calgary.

shaped by group norms for expected behaviors in the particular group. Norms are influenced by a number of factors, including the context in which the group is meeting, the verbal and nonverbal cues from the leader, and the personal characteristics of each member. Norms exert an "environmental press," which can be quite powerful in determining social behavior (Bond, 1975; MacKenzie, 1979).*

The measurement of group climate is one application of a larger research interest in assessing social environments and the way they influence behavior. Moos (1974) has demonstrated that atmosphere dimensions on a psychiatric ward correlate with post-discharge adjustment and the likelihood of readmission. Lieberman, Yalom, and Miles (1973) suggest a similar relationship between the social atmosphere of encounter groups and outcome. Developmental stages are another important way of conceptualizing the group as a social system (Beck, 1974; Durkin, 1981; Hill and Gruner, 1973). In Chapter 4, Livesley and I described stages as dealing with specific types of interactional tasks. By successfully addressing these tasks, members develop closer and more complex relationships. Stages may be identifiable by sequential group climate measurements completed by group members. (An example of how such measurements can track group progress is presented later in this chapter.)

As I suggested above, one way of measuring group climate is through a questionnaire. I have elsewhere presented a 32-item Group Climate Questionnaire—Long Form (GCQ-L) containing eight scales (MacKenzie, 1981). Clinical application of this instrument has revealed major shifts in group climate dimensions from one session to the next. Consequently, the GCQ needs to be administered after every session if group events are to be adequately traced. GCQ scores may be used either for research purposes or in routine clinical work to alert the therapist to emerging trends in the interaction as perceived by group members. If studies are to be conducted in clinical programs, however, instruments must be devised which are practical from the standpoint of

Editors' Note: MacKenzie's research is based on that portion of the normative structure of the group reflected in overt *behavior,* a different approach from that taken in the next chapter by Bond, who looks at normative *expectations.* There are some potentially interesting connections between stage ideas and normative expectations. As Bond shows in his chapter, norms appear to be accepted as ideal expectations right from the start of a group. MacKenzie's work, on the other hand, might be taken to suggest that particular behaviors are only tried out when the group members are ready to do so, that is, when some preliminary interactional tasks have been achieved.

time and convenience. With this in mind, I shall present a short form of the GCQ, which is suitable for routine use in a group therapy program.

METHOD

Factor analysis of the original GCQ-L revealed the following scales: *engagement, support, practicality, disclosure, cognition, challenge, conflict,* and *control.* The shortened version presented here was derived from these scales by selecting high-loading items and collapsing the "work" scales for disclosure, cognition, and challenge. The Group Climate Questionnaire—Short Form (GCQ-S) contains 12 items (see Table 1) rated on a seven-point Likert scale, ranging from "not at all" to "extremely." Each item is couched in nontechnical language and describes a specific behavior. The GCQ-S takes five to ten minutes to complete and has been found acceptable for use on a routine basis following each session of a given group.

TABLE 1
Items on Group Climate Questionnaire—Short Form

1. The members liked and cared about each other.
2. The members tried to understand why they do the things they do, tried to reason it out.
3. The members avoided looking at important issues going on between themselves.
4. The members felt what was happening was important and there was a sense of participation.
5. The members depended on the group leader(s) for direction.
6. There was friction and anger between the members.
7. The members were distant and withdrawn from each other.
8. The members challenged and confronted each other in their efforts to sort things out.
9. The members appeared to do things the way they thought would be acceptable to the group.
10. The members distrusted and rejected each other.
11. The members revealed sensitive personal information or feelings.
12. The members appeared tense and anxious.

In practice, the GCQ-S is paired with a brief critical-incident form, which yields anecdotal data concerning issues in the session considered personally important by the individual. The instructions for the critical-incident portion read as follows:

TABLE 2
Varimax Factor Loadings for Sessions 1–5

	Factor			
	1	2	3	4
Percent of Variance	23%	14%	11%	10%
Item				
1. Liked/cared	– 0.52	– 0.07	0.18	– 0.02
2. Reasoned out issues	– 0.02	– 0.17	0.56	– 0.08
3. Avoided issues	0.30	– 0.14	0.01	0.13
4. Participation	– 0.61	– 0.03	0.26	0.04
5. Depended on leader	0.01	0.52	– 0.15	0.19
6. Friction and anger	0.68	0.27	0.16	– 0.46
7. Withdrawn	0.54	0.02	0.02	0.22
8. Confronted	– 0.10	– 0.05	0.64	0.07
9. Acceptable behavior	0.12	0.20	0.04	0.76
10. Distrust/rejected	0.56	0.32	0.08	– 0.11
11. Self-disclosure	– 0.03	– 0.53	0.35	0.17
12. Tense/anxious	0.09	0.49	– 0.02	0.06

> Please describe briefly the event that was most personally important to you during today's session. This might be something that involved you directly, or something that happened between other members, but which made you think about yourself. Explain what it was about the event that made it important for you personally.

The GCQ-S was completed at the end of each therapy session by 75 members from 12 therapy groups. The groups had an average of seven members each, and the therapy ran for approximately 35 sessions per group, with membership turnover of less than 10%. From those attending the 250 sessions, 1,435 ratings were possible. We actually obtained 1,150 GCQ-S responses — an 81% compliance rate. Approximately 60% of the members were women and 40% men. All were between the ages of 18 and 50 years, and they suffered from neurotic or personality difficulties of varying severity.

Since it is inappropriate to factor-analyze data containing repeated ratings by the same individual, scores were taken from all groups in clusters of five sessions, so that no sample contained more than one rating by any one individual. In this way five data pools were created, each containing an average of 44 ratings. The first set contained items from

TABLE 3
Varimax Factor Loadings for Sessions 23–33

	Factor			
	1	**2**	**3**	**4**
Percent of Variance	43%	15%	11%	9%
Item				
1. Liked/cared	0.67	− 0.03	− 0.28	0.44
2. Reasoned out issues	0.60	− 0.28	− 0.25	0.37
3. Avoided issues	− 0.20	0.75	0.12	− 0.03
4. Participation	0.83	− 0.37	− 0.13	0.14
5. Depended on leader	− 0.13	0.43	− 0.01	0.50
6. Friction and anger	0.00	0.04	0.81	− 0.21
7. Withdrawn	− 0.42	0.55	0.41	− 0.03
8. Confronted	0.75	− 0.30	0.19	− 0.24
9. Acceptable behavior	− 0.26	0.77	0.11	− 0.12
10. Distrust/rejected	− 0.28	0.24	0.69	0.09
11. Self-disclosure	0.77	− 0.19	− 0.21	0.05
12. Tense/anxious	− 0.23	0.27	0.08	− 0.68

one session of each group over Sessions 1–5, the second from Sessions 6–10, and so on. In order to obtain sufficient ratings for statistical analysis, the last data pool encompassed Sessions 23–33. Each data sample was subjected to factor analysis with varimax rotation using the *Statistical Package for the Social Sciences* (Nie, Hull, Jenkins, Bent, and Steinbrenner, 1975). This analytic process identifies clusters of items that move together during different ratings. The results are thus of use in the development of statistically sound scales.

RESULTS

The results of the factor analysis of the items obtained from early group ratings (Sessions 1–5) are shown in Table 2. Analysis of each of the other four sets of data yielded essentially identical factors and therefore only the results of Sessions 23–33 are shown in Table 3. In these two tables, the figures in each column indicate the contribution each item makes to the total factor, with a higher figure indicating that the item is more important. Some items load in a negative direction. "Percent of variance" is a statistical calculation showing how much of the difference

TABLE 4
Item/Scale Correlations

Item	Engaged	Avoiding	Conflict
1. Liked/cared	0.72*	− 0.33	− 0.31
2. Reasoned out issues	0.77*	− 0.28	− 0.07
3. Avoided issues	− 0.33	0.72*	0.30
4. Participation	0.77*	− 0.42	− 0.20
5. Depended on leader	− 0.14	0.66*	0.20
6. Friction and anger	− 0.07	0.11	0.88*
7. Withdrawn	− 0.45	0.76*	0.31
8. Confronted	0.76*	− 0.35	0.01
9. Acceptable behavior	− 0.36	0.75*	0.07
10. Distrust/rejected	− 0.25	0.44	0.81*
11. Self-disclosure	0.69*	− 0.27	− 0.15
12. Tense/anxious	− 0.30	0.44	0.31

*Items used in calculating scale scores

between the way items are answered is accounted for by each factor. Factors are always numbered in decreasing order of importance.

These results were used to develop three scales, using as criteria: (1) a factor loading greater than 0.50 and (2) deletion of items that loaded strongly on more than one factor. The entire data base of 1,150 completed ratings was then subjected to item/scale analysis. This procedure correlates each item with the score of each scale and provides a way of identifying items that should be included in a scale (see Table 4). The means and standard deviations on each scale for both members and therapists were compared using a *t*-test to establish if the mean scores differed significantly (see Table 5). The means and standard deviations are of use in deriving standard transformed scores. Finally, interscale correlations were calculated (see Table 6).*

Scale 1: Engaged

This scale is derived from the engagement, support, disclosure, challenge, and cognition scales of the original GCQ-L. Some items

Editors' Note: The practitioner can use MacKenzie's Group Climate Questionnaire without a knowledge of statistical methodology. Simple inspection of responses to individual items is often highly informative; the totals on the scales suggested by Table 4 and described below are perhaps even more useful. In the first chapter in this monograph, Dies suggests the potential value of such instrumentation.

TABLE 5
Scale Score Means and Standard Deviations

	Members		Therapists			Proba-
	Mean	S.D.	Mean	S.D.	*t*-Value	bility
Engaged	17.85	4.68	14.61	3.39	9.54	< 0.05
Avoiding	8.17	4.02	10.33	3.05	− 8.04	< 0.05
Conflict	2.54	2.46	3.85	2.28	− 7.76	< 0.05

reflect the importance of the group for the members and a sense of closeness between them. This portion of the scale is related to the concept of cohesion (Item 4), which has been identified as an important condition for effective group psychotherapy (Yalom, 1975). The scale also encompasses Rogerian dimensions (Item 1), which have a lengthy documented relationship to effective individual therapy (Rogers, 1961). In addition, items describing an atmosphere of constructive interpersonal investigation load on this scale. Self-disclosure (Item 11) has been found to be an important step in the process of change (Dies, 1977). Cognitive understanding of the meaning of behavior (Item 2) has been emphasized as an important process for maintaining behavioral change, labeled "meaning attribution" by Lieberman et al. (1973). Challenge and confrontation (Item 8) promote interpersonal learning. The merging of support and work dimensions was not originally anticipated, but is clearly indicated in the analysis, resulting in a scale that describes a positive working atmosphere.

Scale 2: Avoiding

This dimension is derived in part from the control scale of the original GCQ-L, which dealt with the degree to which the actions of the individual were influenced by group pressures. The present avoiding scale is centered on the idea of avoidance of responsibility by the

TABLE 6
Interscale Correlations

	Engaged	Avoiding
Avoiding	− 0.44	—
Conflict	− 0.18	0.30

members for their own change process. This includes such behaviors as avoidance of problems (Item 3), dependence on the leader (Item 5), and high adherence to group expectations (Item 9). In addition, an item dealing with interpersonal distance (Item 7) also loaded on this factor. Taken together, these items suggest that members are avoiding a significant encounter with themselves and their problems as well as with other group members.

Scale 3: Conflict

This scale deals with interpersonal conflict (Item 6) and distrust (Item 10). Such behavior would generally be considered unwanted by group members, but it is important in promoting an atmosphere in which defenses can be challenged. Conflict forces members to further self-disclosure so that differences can be explored. This process is an important mechanism for increasing the information members have about themselves and for exploring difficult issues.

DISCUSSION

The GCQ-S has been in routine use for several years in a general hospital outpatient group psychotherapy program. The 81% compliance rate reflects its acceptability to group members. This is undoubtedly influenced by the positive support for its use from the staff. Therapists report that they find the results of value as an additional viewpoint on the group process. They are forced by the GCQ-S scores to think of the group as a whole, and sequential group session results may alert them to evidence that the group is "stuck" in its development. They frequently find it reassuring to discover that group members are as aware of avoiding behavior as the therapists are. Responses of individual members are also of interest to the therapists, allowing them to identify members who are seriously out of step with the group view of events. For example, a patient locked in a "scapegoat" role may be experiencing the group in far more negative terms than the other members. GCQ-S results are not taken as an "absolute truth," but only as another source of information with which to understand group process and formulate appropriate interventions — an example of applied clinical research.

Most group participants seem able to assess and rate whole-group phenomena quite quickly. The process involved is a common one for anyone in a social situation, i.e., "There was a lot of tension in the air during that staff meeting." It should be borne in mind, however, that even the simple items of the GCQ-S require a significant amount of inference since the member must combine behavior of all members for the entire session to make a rating. Extreme behavior by one member may therefore skew the ratings. In addition, there may be major shifts of climate within a single session, producing difficulty in satisfactorily describing the whole. The presence of a particular type of behavior is the important issue, even though it may be expressed primarily by one member or for only a portion of a session. The relationship between this descriptive approach and the normative expectations of the members is complex, an issue discussed in depth in Chapter 8 by Bond. From a practical point of view, member reports of group climate serve as one useful method of studying whole-group phenomena over time.

The three factors emerging from analysis of the GCQ-S are closely related to dimensions therapists frequently use in describing groups: a close working atmosphere, resistive avoidance of issues, and friction. It is not surprising to find a modest negative correlation between the engaged and avoiding dimensions and a positive correlation between the two "negative" scales of avoiding and conflict. The engaged and conflict scales are not negatively correlated, indicating that group members do not necessarily see these behaviors as incompatible, that is, a particular session may be described as both "engaged" and "in conflict."

Members tended to rate groups as more engaged, less avoiding, and in less conflict than did the therapists (Table 5). These results are not surprising in that members tend to have a greater need for group cohesion and are more likely to evade the unsettling work of psychological change. Nevertheless, the findings are a reminder that perceptions of groups vary according to the perspective adopted. Preliminary work in our research program suggests that there is a similar systematic rating bias associated with specific group role positions.

The analysis of data from Sessions 1–5 contained in Table 2 indicates a factor structure markedly different from that obtained in data from later group sessions. For these early sessions, Factor 1 contains items from all three of the clinical scales on a bipolar dimension with "importance" and "caring" on one end, and "friction," "distrust," and "distancing" on the other. This factor seems to reflect a predominant concern with cautious orientation to a new social environment. The other three factors in the data pool from the early sessions have few strong item loadings.

These results are compatible with the idea that early in a group's life, resolution must be found to basic social anxiety before constructive work can occur. While this idea is familiar to clinicians, our data suggest that this entry tension significantly alters the criteria by which members perceive the group. They do not make the more complex associations characteristic of later reporting periods. For example, they have difficulty identifying the relationship between positive bonds and interpersonal work; they do not conceptualize the idea of avoidance of personal initiative; and friction is seen only in relationship to meeting group expectations. From a practical standpoint, these results mean that GCQ-S scores obtained early in a group's life will show a strong negative correlation between the engaged score, and both the avoiding and conflict scores. That is, it will appear as if the group were being described with only one dimension.

AN EXAMPLE OF THE APPLICATION TO THEORY

Descriptive reports from group members themselves constitute one source of validation for the group developmental hypothesis. Preliminary work with the GCQ-S suggests that the profiles obtained support the idea of sequential stages. Figure 1 presents sequential mean GCQ-S scores obtained from members over the first 14 sessions in one of the groups in this study.* The results shown in this figure are expressed in standard *t*-scores using the normative values from Table 4. The rising engaged score and low avoiding and conflict scores over the first four sessions represent a characteristic pattern for Stage 1 (engagement), when the group is dealing with basic involvement issues and cannot tolerate negative interaction (see MacKenzie and Livesley, Chapter 4). During Sessions 5 and 6 a shift occurs, signaled by a drop in the engaged score and a rise in the avoiding one. At the same time, the conflict score rises slightly above baseline levels. Session 7 reverses this with some strengthening of engaged, a drop in avoiding, and more conflict. Sessions 8 and 9 recapitulate on a grand scale the pattern of Sessions 5 and 6, with the avoiding score rising sharply, accompanied by a major drop in the engaged one. Finally, in Session 10, there is a steep increase in the conflict score, associated with a rise in the engaged score and a drop in the avoiding score. Sessions 11–14 indicate a more tranquil period, with an elevated engaged score and low avoiding and conflict scores.

Editors' Note: At this point in time these findings can be taken as suggestive only, since the question of specific criteria for stage identification has not been resolved. The task is one of complex pattern recognition which involves absolute levels of scale scores as well as changing levels and relationships between scales.

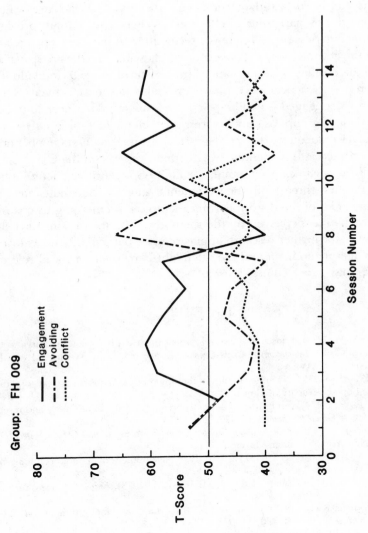

FIGURE I
SEQUENTIAL MEAN GCQ-S SCORES OVER 14 SESSIONS

When viewed from a stage perspective, it would appear that Sessions 5–10 represent this group's protracted efforts to master Stage 2 (differentiation). This stage is characterized by an emphasis on differences, accompanied by conflict and anger as members strive to establish their individuality in the group (MacKenzie and Livesley, Chapter 4). Sessions 5 and 7 suggest the emergence of these issues, which are dealt with by avoidance, particularly in Session 8. When conflict finally breaks into the open in Session 10, there is a recognition in the rising engaged score that the group is working once more. Following this, the group can settle into the positive working state characteristic of Stage 3 (individuation), when members begin to explore personal issues more actively. This sequence of engaged — avoiding — conflict — engaged has been found characteristic of groups as they progress through the first three stages. There is as yet inadequate data to determine if subsequent stage phenomena can be successfully identified by member reports on the GCQ-S.

From a clinical standpoint, the GCQ-S is sensitive enough to identify the first three group developmental stages. The results have been found to be of interest in alerting therapists to emerging trends in the interaction as perceived by the members. The instrument thus shows promise for further research application. In particular, studies focusing on stage phenomena and the attendant perception of social role occupants may prove clinically useful.

REFERENCES

Beck, A. P. (1974), Phases in the development of structure in therapy and encounter groups. In: *Innovations in Client-Centered Therapy*, ed. D. A. Wexler & L. N. Rice. New York: Wiley.

Bond, G. R. (1975), Norm formation in therapy groups. Unpublished doctoral dissertation, University of Chicago.

Dies, R. R. (1977), Group therapist transparency: A critique of theory and research. *Int. J. Group Psychother.*, 27:177–200.

Durkin, J. E., Ed. (1981), *Living Groups: Group Psychotherapy and General System Theory.* New York: Brunner/Mazel.

Hill, W. F., & Gruner, L. (1973), A study of development in open and closed groups. *Small Group Behav.*, 4:355–381.

Lieberman, M. A., Yalom, I. D., & Miles, M. B. (1973), *Encounter Groups: First Facts.* New York: Basic Books.

MacKenzie, K. R. (1979), Group norms: Importance and measurement. *Int. J. Group Psychother.*, 29:471–480.

——————— (1981), Measurement of group climate. *Int. J. Group Psychother.*, 31:287–296.

Moos, R. (1974), *Evaluating Treatment Environments: A Social Ecological Approach.* New York: Wiley.

Nie, N. H., Hull, C. H., Jenkins, J. G., Bent, D. H., & Steinbrenner, K. (1975), *Statistical Package for the Social Sciences.* New York: McGraw-Hill.

Rogers, C. (1961), *On Encounter Groups.* New York: Harper & Row.

Yalom, I. D. (1975), *The Theory and Practice of Group Psychotherapy.* New York: Basic Books.

8

Norm Regulation in
Therapy Groups

GARY R. BOND, Ph.D.

Recent work by MacKenzie (1979, 1981) on the conceptualization and measurement of group norms has renewed an inquiry long regarded as a key to our understanding of how psychotherapeutic groups induce change in their members. Empirical work on group norms has been characterized by a series of fits and starts in which promising studies have not been followed up by subsequent research (e.g., Bennis, Burke, Cutter, Harrington, and Hoffman, 1957; Jackson, 1965; Luke, 1972; Psathas and Hardert, 1966). Each of these studies, as well as those cited by MacKenzie, has generally ignored prior methodologies and has followed its own idiosyncratic definition and measurement strategy, making comparisons between studies difficult. Implicitly there has been dissatisfaction with both the conceptual models used and the ways these have been made operational. Whatever the reasons, no progress will be possible until there is shared agreement among researchers on an operational definition and a corresponding standardized method of assessment.*

Editors' Note: This chapter delineates Bond's work on fundamental characteristics of normative structure in small groups, a central and almost unexplored area of investigation. Its importance is reflected in the fact that a large encounter group study indicated important connections among leader behavior, the subsequent normative structure of the group, and outcome (Lieberman, Yalom, and Miles, 1973). Norms are central to the basic idea of what a group is; a group may be defined as an entity by how it behaves, the expectations its members have for such behavior, and the assessments made by them of behaviors that occur. The approach adopted by Bond is rooted in a simple but powerful two-dimensional theory of norms: behaviors considered acceptable and those expected to occur.

In spite of the confusion and ambiguity in the use of the norm concept, most agree that it is multifaceted, involving behavioral, expectational, and evaluative components. While behaviors, member expectations, and evaluations of behavior obviously have some relationship to each other, the imperfect correlations between the components have been the major stumbling block in our understanding of norm regulation. It has been repeatedly noted in the literature that members often behave contrary to the norms of the group and, conversely, that behavioral uniformity in itself does not imply norm regulation. Rather than pinning the definition of norms to a single component, therefore, it would seem a logical step to use two or more components in defining a model of norm regulation. Yet most researchers have measured norms along a single facet, resulting in a "flat," unidimensional portrayal of the group process, and essentially disregarding their own conceptualizations. MacKenzie (1981), for example, asks respondents to rate the frequency of occurrence of 32 behavioral patterns, thus keying on the *behavioral* component of norms. Luke (1972), on the other hand, assesses the normative environment of T-groups with "importance" ratings on a series of normative statements, making the *evaluative* component of norms the focus of his assessment.

A more complicated example is given in the work of Lieberman, Yalom, and Miles (1973), whose methodology suffers nonetheless from the same flaw of forcing a multidimensional phenomenon into a unidimensional rating scale. Lieberman et al. (1973) suggest this novel approach: that participants imagine how they would describe their group for a new member by rating the group's responses to specific behaviors. In essence, this approach requires that respondents make a complex judgment and summarize it in a single rating. None of these strategies is satisfactory, since all fail to take into account two frequently observed phenomena: *deviant* behaviors, i.e., behaviors that occur even though they are disapproved of by a consensus of the group (e.g., Stock, 1964), and *risky* behaviors, i.e., behaviors that are, up to the time of their occurrence, unexpected, and yet are readily approved of and accepted by the group once the "initiatory act" has occurred (Glidewell, 1974; Redl, 1942).

Another conceptual issue which has not been dealt with satisfactorily in the literature is the relationship between positive and negative norm regulation. Sometimes it is assumed that they are two sides of the same coin. Psathas and Hardert (1966), for example, have suggested that norms have a prescriptive element (e.g., "Members should express feelings openly and honestly") and a corresponding proscriptive element (e.g., "Members should not block the expression of feelings"). It is an empirical question whether such symmetry exists in norm regulation. An alternative view would be that the corresponding sanctions (encouragement or discouragement) are psychologically quite different and are employed for distinct types of behavior. In this view, some behaviors pertain to "system maintenance" norms and do not capture the attention of the group unless negative instances of the behaviors occur, in which case they are disapproved of publicly. Examples in therapy would include attendance, punctuality, and confidentiality, none of which is exceptional, barring departures from the expected behavior. In contrast, "task" norms involve behaviors that are regulated by praise and support when they occur, but are not always uniformly exhibited by every member of the group. Behaviors in relation to self-disclosure, intimacy, and affect expression would fit this latter description. Some evidence for this distinction comes from the work of the anthropologist Cancian (1972), who classified "member" norms and "ranking" norms in a pre-industrial society. Cancian observed that the member norms were followed by most men out of a sense of loyalty, whereas only some men, who were accorded the highest esteem and status, exemplified the ranking norms.

Finally, any measurement of norms should reflect the notion of group consensus rather than, as some researchers have assumed, a statistical mean of ratings. Further, the unit of measure should be the *group* rather than the individual respondent. The study most consistent with this conceptualization is that by Lieberman et al. (1973); the other studies cited appear to ignore these points in their measurement strategy. In their study of encounter groups, Lieberman et al. (1973) used as their criterion of consensus two-thirds agreement among participants in each group. One methodological problem with an arbitrary criterion, even when applied consistently within a study, is that the cut-off for consensus is artifactually more stringent in groups of a certain size. So, for example, to reach two-thirds agreement, a minimum of four members is needed in both a six-person group (67% agreement) and a five-person group (80% agreement). While the variability in the stringency of the cut-off criterion is relatively unimportant for groups of nine or more members (as was true in the encounter group study), it becomes more critical for smaller groups, as therapy groups tend to be. Accordingly, a procedure of randomly selecting an equal number of respondents from each group is suggested as a way to equalize probabilities and thereby standardize the definition of consensus. This strategy assumes that group members are all equally reliable informants, a premise that, while ignoring the possibility of distortion by deviant members or from other sources, is consistent with the view that norms are objective, consensually validated attributes of the group.

The above discussion has focused on the structural aspects of norms. The issue of content has been dealt with in a number of different ways. Recognizing that norms refer to *classes* of behaviors, some investigators have used relatively abstract summary statements as the items in their rating systems, so as not to be distracted by specific behaviors. The danger here is that respondents will read their own meanings into summary statements and will give socially desirable responses. Specific behavioral items are less susceptible to misinterpretation and to halo effects.

Lieberman et al. (1973) used a 48-item behavioral inventory with 171 respondents and this was factor-analyzed to yield six interpretable factors (examples of items are given in parentheses): *intense emotional expression* (cry, show sexual attraction), *open boundaries* (disclose information, bring friend), *hostile, judging, confrontation* (put down another member, interrupt), *counterdependence* (challenge leader, resist leader's suggestions), *dependence* (offer leader ride home, appeal to leader), and *peer control* (be absent often, say little or nothing). In two subsequent surveys building on this approach, Lieberman and I explored norm dimensions in Synanon-modeled groups in a drug rehabilitation program (Bond, 1972) and in women's consciousness-raising groups (Bond and Lieberman, 1980). In the first study, based on an item cluster analysis of a 54-item checklist with 505 respondents, three major content dimensions were obtained: *self-disclosure* (past experiences, dreams and fantasies, details of sex life), *affect expression* (cry, shout with anger, show sexual feeling), and *resistance* (show no intention of changing, insist the group is wrong). In the second study, based on a factor analysis of a 34-item checklist with 1,603 respondents, five factors emerged: *self-disclosure* (talk about feeling lonely, talk about feeling inadequate, share good things about self), *affective relationships* (show sexual attraction, shout with anger, tell group off), *turn-taking* (dominate discussion, interrupt), *membership criteria* (be absent frequently, say nothing), *judgmental behavior* (give advice, say another's behavior is wrong). A synthesis of these studies suggests several common content dimensions, which generalize across different settings and serve as the normative issues in the current report.

Factor-analytic approaches to derive norm content dimensions have two drawbacks. First, most studies have used the individual participant as the unit of analysis in order to maximize sample size, even though norms are conceptualized as a property of the group. To use the group as the unit of analysis would unfortunately require a prohibitively large sample. Second, in any given setting, there will be certain "universal norms" derived from the prevailing ideology. In the drug rehabilitation study, universal norms included the prescriptions that members ask for and give advice, and the proscriptions that members not hit other members, make threatening remarks, tell outsiders about what happened in the group, or leave the group without the leader's permission. Behavioral items relating to universal norms are given identical ratings by nearly all respondents and do not correlate highly with items that do vary. Thus, we have the paradox that the most strongly held normative beliefs are the least apparent through factor analysis.

A TWO-COMPONENT MODEL
OF NORM REGULATION

Norm regulation is dually determined by the shared evaluations and the shared behavioral expectations of group members. According to the model, a precondition for norm regulation is that a consensus agrees that the behavior is either acceptable or unacceptable. Without this consensus, the behavior is considered lacking in norm regulation, regardless of the expectations of members. Positive norm regulation occurs when (1) a consensus of group members thinks that a behavior is acceptable, and (2) a consensus also thinks that the behavior might occur in their group. This definition stipulates that *some*, though not necessarily all, members are expected to behave in the prescribed fashion for the behavior to be positively regulated. This "weak" meaning of norm regulation identifies *permissible*, not obligatory, behaviors in the group, and is compatible with the goal of group therapy — to create a noncoercive therapeutic environment in which certain behaviors are encouraged and supported.

Conversely, negative norm regulation occurs when (1) a consensus thinks a behavior is not acceptable, and (2) a consensus thinks it will not occur. In this case, if *any* member is expected to behave contrary to the behavioral proscription, then the behavior is not fully regulated. Unlike positive regulation, total conformity is necessary. This is also consistent with the rules of membership most therapists try to establish; a norm discouraging the disclosure of confidential information outside the group will not accomplish its intended purpose unless all members agree to it.

This operational definition accomplishes several things. First, it acknowledges the fact that these two components may not agree, as has been repeatedly noted in the literature. Second, it allows us to distinguish between different types of nonregulation and to suggest that some behaviors are "partially regulated," as seems to be the case for risky or deviant behavior. The term "totally unregulated" is reserved for instances when there is substantial disagreement regarding how the behavior is to be evaluated. These distinctions are schematized in Figure 1.

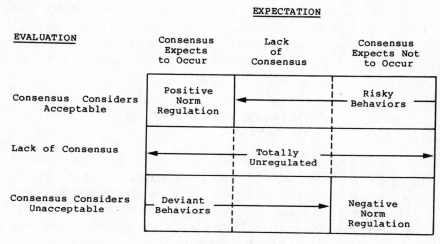

FIGURE I
Two-Component Model of Norm Regulation

A third advantage of the model is that it suggests a mechanism for the genesis of norms in therapy groups, if we include the additional postulate that the evaluation of behaviors generally precedes their occurrence. Risky behaviors, once they occur, are likely to be positively regulated due to the preexisting positive valence for the behavior in the group; deviant behaviors over time are likely to decrease in their probability of occurrence (and therefore become negatively regulated) due to the preexisting unacceptability of the behavior. By allowing for partial norm regulation, the model permits us to understand better the seemingly anomalous finding that the important norms are established early in the group's history and persist throughout the life of the group (Bennis et al., 1957; Lieberman, 1958). What may be established early in the group is an idealized version of the group and implicit, if not explicit, consensus about which behaviors are important and valuable; this idealized group structure may contrast with how the group actually functions, at least in the early stage of group formation.

APPLICATIONS OF THE MODEL

The norm model was applied to therapy groups in both early and later stages of development. Study 1 examined established groups that had formed at least two years prior to the study. They were open-ended groups which added new members over a period of time as old members dropped out. Study 2 examined the formation of norms in newly constituted groups, as assessed in the first and twentieth sessions.

A different checklist format was used in the two studies; the simpler format of Study 1 is recommended in future work. Also, the two studies used two different but overlapping sets of items; ideally, more items than those reported here might be used to map more fully the normative domain. The behaviors sampled addressed issues discussed extensively in the literature. A balance was sought between behaviors ordinarily prescribed and those usually proscribed. Some were chosen knowing that they would be nearly universally acceptable or unacceptable, while others were chosen to tap normative conflict or ambiguity.

STUDY 1

Method

Nine long-term, ongoing outpatient psychotherapy groups conducted at the Northwestern Institute of Psychiatry and the Adult Outpatient Psychiatry Center of Evanston Hospital participated in the study. Each group was led by a pair of co-therapists and had a stable membership of four to eight patients. The experience level of the therapists varied; five groups were led by psychiatric and psychology residents with little prior group experience, while four groups were led by therapists who had five or more years' experience with this modality. Every group had been in existence at least two years, and their current therapists had been leading the group for six months or longer. Patients completed a norm checklist at the end of a regularly scheduled therapy session as part of an ongoing study of therapy process.

Sample

Among the patients, 41% had attended over 50 sessions of their current group, 32% had attended 11 or more sessions, and 28% had attended 10 sessions or less. Most of the patients had a diagnostic classification of neurosis or character disorder. Fifty-three percent were male, and 47% female. Two-thirds were single, and only 9% currently married. Their median age was 30 years; the highest level of education attained included 58% who were college graduates, 35% with some college, and 6% who had completed high school; 85% were currently employed.

Normative Issues

Six normative issues were defined *a priori* using a 24-item inventory, as shown in Table 1. Inter-item reliability coefficients for ratings of evaluation and for ratings of expectations, respectively, were as follows: *self-disclosure* (0.71, 0.63), *support* (0.68, 0.59), *affect expression* (0.78, 0.77), *therapist relationship* (0.45, 0.24), *participation* (0.52, 0.51), and *boundaries* (0.66, 0.54).

Format

The inventory was presented twice with two different instructional sets, first asking: "How acceptable would it be to most members in your group if a member— —[did X]?" using a four-point *evaluation* scale; then asking "In the next four or five sessions, how likely is it that a member will— —[do X]?" using a four-point *expectation* scale. Consistent with the norm model, responses to the evaluation scale were dichotomized as either "acceptable" or "unacceptable," and responses to the expectation scale were dichotomized as either "expected" or "not expected."

In each group, four respondents were randomly chosen in order to make the definition of consensus equivalent for all groups; namely, agreement of at least three-fourths of the members.

Findings

Table 1 shows that an average of 60% of the 24 behaviors were norm-regulated in these established therapy groups, with 42% positively regulated and 18% negatively regulated. Twenty-six percent of the behaviors were partially regulated, and only 14% totally unregulated.

Norm regulation varied widely according to the normative issue under consideration. For two normative issues—self-disclosure and support—positive norm regulation was nearly universal. Conversely, negative norm regulation of boundary issues was generally achieved for three of four behaviors sampled. The remaining boundary item—"form personal relationships with member outside group"—was negatively regulated in only one group. This finding is at variance with the widely

TABLE 1
Norm Regulation in Established Therapy Groups

Normative Issue	Positively Regulated	Risk	Unregulated	Deviancy	Negatively Regulated
Self-Disclosure					
Reveal hateful feelings toward parents	100.0	– –	– –	– –	– –
Disclose shameful experiences	100.0	– –	– –	– –	– –
Plead for help	66.7	33.3	– –	– –	– –
Average percentage	88.9	11.1	– –	– –	– –
Support/Advice					
Defend another member	100.0	– –	– –	– –	– –
Give advice	88.9	– –	11.1	– –	– –
Say another's behavior is wrong	66.7	22.2	11.1	– –	– –
Average percentage	85.2	7.4	7.4	– –	– –
Affect Expression					
Show affection toward another	88.9	11.1	– –	– –	– –
Cry	66.7	33.3	– –	– –	– –
Shout angrily at another	44.4	22.2	– –	22.2	11.1
Tell group off	44.4	22.2	11.1	22.2	– –
Show sexual attraction	33.3	22.2	11.1	11.1	22.2
Scream	22.2	33.3	22.2	– –	22.2
Average percentage	50.0	24.1	7.4	9.3	9.3
Therapist Relationship					
Criticize therapists	44.4	33.3	22.2	– –	– –
Offer therapist ride home	– –	44.4	44.4	– –	11.1
Ask personal information of therapist	11.1	22.2	55.6	– –	11.1
Average percentage	18.5	33.3	40.7	– –	7.4
Participation					
Be frequently absent	– –	– –	11.1	55.6	33.3
Say nothing	22.2	– –	44.4	22.2	11.1
Do nearly all the talking	11.1	11.1	22.2	55.6	– –
Frequently joke	55.6	11.1	33.3	– –	– –
Say don't want to change	11.1	– –	11.1	33.3	44.4
Average percentage	20.0	4.4	24.4	33.3	17.8
Boundaries					
Share confidential information with outsiders	– –	– –	– –	33.3	66.7
Leave during group without explanation	– –	– –	11.1	11.1	77.8
Form personal relationship with member outside group	22.2	44.4	22.2	– –	11.1
Invite friend to group	– –	– –	– –	– –	100.0
Average percentage	5.5	11.1	8.3	11.1	63.9
Total percentage, all behaviors, all groups	41.6	15.3	14.4	11.1	17.6

Header note: Degree of Norm Regulation[a]

[a]Entries are percentages for nine therapy groups.

held opinion among group therapists that subgrouping should be discouraged on the grounds that it interferes with frank disclosure in the group. An average of 24% of the affect-expression items were classified as involving risk; these findings are consistent with the inhibitions most patients have in the direct expression of affect (such as crying, shouting at another member, or telling the group off). Similarly, one third of the therapist-relationship items, on average, were viewed collectively as involving risk, indicating some group approval combined with behavioral restraint in the expression of personal feelings toward the therapists. There was also considerable confusion and disagreement about how such behaviors would be received by the group. This dimension had the highest average percentage of behaviors for which no evaluative consensus of the group existed; 41% of the items were classified as unregulated. Finally, deviant behaviors were most common for the participation dimension, with five of the nine groups having some difficulty with regular attendance.

It should be noted that lack of norm regulation was not primarily a lack of agreement on how behaviors should be evaluated. For only 14% of the items, on average, was there any lack of consensus on the evaluation component, compared with the average of 41% of the items not fully regulated according to the two-component model.

STUDY 2

Method

Seven newly formed therapy groups at the Department of Psychiatry at the University of Wisconsin were assessed after their first, twelfth, and twentieth sessions.[1] Since the results from the two later assessments were similar, only the last assessment in each group was used. In addition, before the beginning of each group, both therapists and patients were asked to make predictions about norm regulation following a format similar to that of the norm checklist. Also, near termination of the group, therapists and patients completed a questionnaire indicating extent of "issue resolution" on a range of behavioral items paralleling the norm checklist. This instrument tapped the extent of perceived shared agreement in the group and whether issue resolution was seen as therapist-directed or part of a group decision-making process.

[1]The data from Study 2 derive from a study conducted by Morton A. Lieberman and used in my doctoral dissertation (Bond, 1975). I am indebted to Dr. Lieberman for his assistance.

Each group was led by a pair of co-therapists, who were either psychiatric residents or psychology interns. For most, this was their first experience leading groups. The groups ranged in size from six to eight patients in their initial membership. Six of the groups were long-term outpatient groups; one was a ten-session couples group. One group disbanded before the tenth session. The remaining five groups met for an average of 33 sessions before ending for the summer.

Sample

The sample consisted of 49 patients: 25 men and 24 women. The age range was from 19 to 42, with a median age of 23. All but eight were university students. Nearly all were single, except for participants in the couples group.

Format

Items were selected to assess five norm dimensions, four of which were similar to Study 1. An additional dimension, *member-group relationship,* concerned the degree of influence the group exerted over members.

For each item, respondents indicated: (A) whether the behavior had occurred, (B) how likely it was to occur in the future, (C) whether they would encourage or discourage the behavior, (D) whether they felt most people in the group would encourage or discourage it, and (E) whether the therapists would encourage or discourage the behavior. Norm regulation was defined by two-thirds agreement among patients to Rating Scales B and D. Rating Scale A, on which there was excellent agreement, was used to identify which behaviors occurred. The remaining two scales (C and E) were included to examine more fine-grained hypotheses regarding the formation of norms; they proved to be highly similar to Rating Scale D (Bond, 1975).

Findings

EARLY NORM REGULATION

Norm regulation for therapy groups following their first session is reported in Table 2. Several similarities may be noted between newly formed and established groups.

As early as the first session, the group had achieved a consensus on the acceptability or unacceptability of most behaviors. On average, 67% of the 25 behaviors were already positively evaluated by a consensus of the group and another 16% negatively evaluated by a consensus. Only 17% of the behaviors, on average, lacked this consensus. This suggests

TABLE 2

Norm Regulation in Newly-Formed Therapy Groups (First Session)

Normative Issue	Positively Regulated	Risk	Unregu-lated	Deviancy	Negatively Regulated	Subseq Occu rence Behav
Self-Disclosure						
Current life problems	100.0	— —	— —	— —	— —	100
Feeling inadequate	100.0	— —	— —	— —	— —	100
Feeling lonely	100.0	— —	— —	— —	— —	100
Sharing good things about self	100.0	— —	— —	— —	— —	100
Private or scary fantasies	85.7	14.3	— —	— —	— —	83
Homosexual feelings	— —	100.0	— —	— —	— —	50
Average percentage	81.0	19.0	— —	— —	— —	88
Affect Expression						
Cry	85.7	14.3	— —	— —	— —	83
Say which members dislike	85.7	14.3	— —	— —	— —	83
Say which members like	71.4	28.6	— —	— —	— —	100
Show sexual attraction	28.6	28.6	28.6	14.3	— —	33
Hug another member	28.6	71.4	— —	— —	— —	0
Scream	14.3	57.1	28.6	— —	— —	0
Shout with anger	— —	57.1	42.9	— —	— —	50
Average percentage	44.9	38.8	14.3	2.0	— —	50
Participation						
Be frequently absent	— —	— —	14.3	42.9	42.9	50
Say nothing	— —	— —	57.1	42.9	— —	100
Discuss politics	85.7	— —	14.3	— —	— —	83
Average percentage	28.6	— —	28.6	28.6	14.3	77
Boundaries						
Share confidential information with outsiders	— —	— —	42.9	42.9	14.3	16
Leave during group without explanation	14.3	— —	14.3	28.6	42.9	16
Form personal relationship with member outside group	28.6	28.6	28.6	— —	14.3	66
Members meet together socially	57.1	28.6	— —	— —	14.3	66
Average percentage	25.0	14.3	21.5	17.8	21.5	41
Member-group Relationship						
Defend another member	100.0	— —	— —	— —	— —	100
Refuse to go along with group	— —	14.3	85.7	— —	— —	83
Tell group off	42.9	28.6	28.6	— —	— —	83
Put down dominating member	42.9	14.3	42.9	— —	— —	66
Force member to stay	— —	— —	— —	— —	100.0	0
Average percentage	37.2	11.4	31.4	— —	20.0	66
Total percentage, all behaviors, all groups	46.8	20.0	17.1	6.8	9.1	64

[a]Entries are percentages for seven therapy groups.

[b]Entries are percentages for six groups over 20 sessions (five groups) or eight sessions (ti limited group).

that lack of norm regulation is not, even in the early stages of group formation, a function of widespread disagreement or confusion about the appropriateness or inappropriateness of behaviors. Moreover, members generally knew that the consensus of the group agreed with their own evaluation; for 79% of their responses to personal evaluations, they made the same rating for the group as a whole. "Pluralistic ignorance" (Schanck, 1932) was a rare phenomenon, even in the first session.

Self-disclosure, in addition to being highly acceptable, was nearly universally expected to occur. Disclosure of homosexual feelings, viewed as risky in all groups, was the sole exception to this principle.

Lack of norm regulation was common for the remaining normative issues. As with the established groups, disparity between evaluations and expectations was the major source of nonregulation. Risk was the major source of nonregulation for affect expression, while deviant and unregulated behavior accounted for most nonregulation of behaviors concerning participation, boundaries, and member-group relationship.

INITIAL NORM REGULATION AND SUBSEQUENT OCCURRENCE OF BEHAVIOR

One indication of the role of norm regulation in controlling behaviors is the fact that by the end of 20 sessions, 94% of the behaviors classified as positively regulated in the first session *had* occurred, compared with only 9% of the behaviors negatively regulated. The occurrence of nonregulated behaviors was less predictable. Among the partially regulated behaviors, 38% of the risky behaviors had occurred, compared with 64% of the deviant behaviors. Among the totally unregulated behaviors, 46% had occurred.

Acceptability of a behavior was not sufficient to assure its subsequent occurrence. Hugging, for example, was acceptable in all groups from the first meeting, but it never occurred in any group. Similarly, screaming was rated as acceptable in nearly all of the groups, but likewise never occurred. Conversely, unacceptable behaviors, such as frequent absences and silent members, did occur in all groups. Sharing confidential information was an example of an initially nonregulated behavior which occurred in only one group. Evaluation of behavior, by itself, is not highly predictive of future occurrence.

LATER NORM REGULATION

There was no overall change over time in the degree of norm regulation, as shown in Table 3. The percentage of positively regulated behaviors remained the same 47%); the percentage of negatively regulated behaviors changed from 9% to 10%. Within content dimensions, the changes were similarly unremarkable.

Risky behaviors, when they occurred, tended to become positively regulated. Of the ten risky behaviors that had occurred by the twentieth session, eight were now assessed as positively regulated (and only one was negatively regulated), compared with the 16 risky behaviors that had not occurred, none of which was positively regulated. Occurrence of behaviors where there is a preexisting consensus of appropriateness appears to be one mechanism for norm formation.

Deviant behaviors that did *not* occur, however, did not necessarily become negatively regulated, as shown by the example of sharing confidential information. There were too few such behaviors to make a conclusive evaluation.

OTHER FACTORS IN NORM REGULATION

Before the beginning of each group, both therapists and patients completed checklists indicating their predictions about what the norms would be. Overall, patients predicted 62% of the norms correctly (78% for positively regulated behaviors, 51% for unregulated, and 43% for negatively regulated); the therapists predicted 60% correctly (80%, 38%, and 48% respectively). Thus, both sources were reasonably accurate, but neither was more accurate than the other; their predictions overlapped considerably. The pre-group expectations and evaluations of both therapists and patients strongly influence the patterns of norm regulation.

There was considerable variation among groups in their change over time in norm regulation, with one group increasing the percentage of norm-regulated behaviors from 44% to 80%, while another group decreased from 80% to 48%. One possible explanation was suggested by difference in leadership style. The most autocratic co-therapists, as suggested by the highest percentage of leader-initiated decisions regarding normative issues as rated by members, led the group with the most *negatively* regulated behaviors. The most democratic co-therapists, as indicated by the highest percentage of group decisions regarding normative issues, ended with the greatest overall degree of *positive* norm regulation. While this was a *post hoc* analysis and limited to the two most extreme groups, it is consistent with the classic study by White and Lippitt (1968) and reinforces the notion that positive and negative norm regulation are distinct processes.

A serendipitous finding which emerged from a comparison of thera-

TABLE 3

Norm Regulation in Newly-Formed Therapy Groups
(Twentieth Session[a])

Normative Issue	Degree of Norm Regulation[b]				
	Positively Regulated	Risk	Unregu- lated	Deviancy	Negatively Regulated
Self-Disclosure					
Current life problems	83.3	— —	16.7	— —	— —
Feeling inadequate	83.3	16.7	— —	— —	— —
Feeling lonely	100.0	— —	— —	— —	— —
Sharing good things about self	83.3	16.7	— —	— —	— —
Private or scary fantasies	83.3	16.7	— —	— —	— —
Homosexual feelings	33.3	66.7	— —	— —	— —
Average percentage	77.8	19.4	2.8	0.0	0.0
Affect Expression					
Cry	66.7	33.3	— —	— —	— —
Say which members dislike	50.0	50.0	— —	— —	— —
Say which members like	66.7	33.3	— —	— —	— —
Show sexual attraction	16.7	16.7	66.7	— —	— —
Hug another member	16.7	66.7	16.7	— —	— —
Scream	— —	83.3	16.7	— —	— —
Shout with anger	33.3	66.7	— —	— —	— —
Average percentage	35.7	50.0	14.3	0.0	0.0
Participation					
Be frequently absent	— —	— —	— —	33.3	66.7
Say nothing	16.7	— —	33.3	50.0	— —
Discuss politics	66.7	16.7	16.7	— —	— —
Average percentage	27.8	5.5	16.7	27.8	22.2
Boundaries					
Share confidential information with outsiders	— —	— —	66.7	16.7	16.7
Leave during group without explanation	— —	— —	16.7	16.7	66.7
Form personal relationship with member outside group	66.7	— —	33.3	— —	— —
Members meet together socially	50.0	33.3	16.7	— —	— —
Average percentage	29.2	8.3	33.3	8.3	20.8
Member-Group Relationship					
Defend another member	100.0	— —	— —	— —	— —
Refuse to go along with group	16.7	16.7	66.7	— —	— —
Tell group off	66.7	16.7	16.7	— —	— —
Put down dominating member	50.0	50.0	— —	— —	— —
Force member to stay	— —	— —	— —	— —	100.0
Average percentage	46.7	16.7	16.7	0.0	20.0
Total percentage, all behaviors, all groups	46.7	23.3	15.3	4.7	10.0

[a]One group was time-limited and assessed after eight sessions.
[b]Entries are percentages for six therapy groups.

pist and patient ratings of how normative issues were resolved was that the patients perceived a significantly lesser degree of shared agreement than did the therapists. Therapists were more inclined to report implicit shared agreements, whereas patients saw a larger proportion of behaviors in the domain of individual choice. The analyses shown in Tables 2 and 3 would suggest that the therapists were more accurate in their judgments about the degree of shared agreement.

DISCUSSION

The norm model offers an objective method for measuring clinically observed phenomena of norm regulation, deviancy, and risky behavior. The results of these preliminary studies are generally consistent with clinical impressions, in that behaviors one would expect to fall within the respective quadrants of the norm matrix generally do so. By applying the model, it is apparent that lack of norm regulation is not primarily a result of confusion or disagreement about the appropriateness of the behavior, but rather reflects the disinclination or lack of opportunity of members to behave accordingly. The major issue in norm regulation is the lack of congruence between behavioral expectations and shared evaluations.

By applying this model of norm regulation to other groups and to a larger sampling of behaviors, it should be possible to gain a better understanding of the range of behaviors over which therapy groups exert control. The model helps to pinpoint the issues to which therapists should be alerted in their "social engineering."* Some issues appear to be settled from the first session, with or without the therapist's intervention. Knowing that self-disclosure is nearly universally approved of and expected, therapists may choose to focus their attention on other normative issues which are less easily resolved (though not relinquishing their responsibility to curb premature disclosures or to attend to less disclosing members). There appear to be a number of core issues, labeled "boundaries" and "participation" here, which therapy groups — whether estab-

Editors' Note: The two studies described by Bond suggest that members beginning group therapy have a high degree of agreement on what kinds of behavior are acceptable and that these expectations have reasonable predictive value. This work has important implications for the therapist. By understanding that there is inherent agreement on acceptable behavior, it should be easier to elicit behaviors that are positive for group development by specifically addressing them, i.e., "We all know that it would be a good idea if . . . ," and then press specifically for the enactment of constructive normative behavior.

lished or newly formed — often have difficulty with in achieving normative control. "Problem patients" — the monopolizer, the silent member, the nonattender, and the breacher of the group's confidence — are endogenous to groups at all stages of development, suggesting limits to the normative control therapy groups typically exert. While the groups reported here were successful in establishing some "counternorms" (norms contradicting the customs of everyday social intercourse), the transformation was obviously not complete. There was considerable ambivalence, as well as behavioral restraint, in expressing the full range of intense feelings, even though participants were highly accepting of these behaviors and were fully aware of widespread approval for these behaviors.

Early positive norm regulation is probably important for the success of a group from the standpoint of maintaining member involvement. In Study 2, in the two groups with most positive norm regulation in the first session (each had 16 positively regulated behaviors), there was only one premature termination. In contrast, for the three groups with the fewest positively regulated behaviors during the first session, one disbanded within the first ten sessions (it had eight positively regulated behaviors), a second (with 11 positively regulated behaviors) was beset with four premature terminations (the greatest number for any of the groups), while the third group with ten positively regulated behaviors) had no dropouts. (This last group later developed the greatest number of positively regulated behaviors.) While these *post hoc* associations are far from conclusive, they are consistent with the literature on role preparation (e.g., Heitler, 1973; Yalom, Houts, Newell, and Rand, 1967), which shows that patients participate more fruitfully when they receive pregroup training and therefore have a clearer idea what to expect. Similarly, when members of a group are all prepared to expect the same behaviors, they are more likely to stay. Intuitively this makes sense; participants need some assurance that the group is going to work, if they are to make a commitment. Ambivalence and anxiety are rampant in early group therapy sessions, and predictability is one antidote counteracting the impulse to flee.

Going beyond the data, we might speculate that *too much* positive norm regulation (with its attendant implicit pressure to perform) might also be counterproductive. The intrusive efforts at norm induction by charismatic encounter group leaders (Lieberman et al., 1973) is testimony that a confrontive, unempathic approach to the establishment of positive norm regulation can cause harmful effects. Rather, a collabora tive effort by therapists and patients is likely to result in the most wide-spread acceptance of norms, as the group decision-making literature suggests (Hoffman, 1979). One role that the therapist can play is to raise the consciousness of the group to the degree of norm regulation it has already achieved, often implicitly. The evidence suggests that members "know" more about norm regulation than they realize. Patients are likely to attribute their behavioral uniformities to individual choice and not implicit shared agreements. Conscious attention to the norms allows the group more influence over its direction.

REFERENCES

Bennis, W. G., Burke, R. L., Cutter, H., Harrington, H., & Hoffman, J. (1957), A note on some problems of measurement and prediction in a training group. *Psychother.,* 10:328–341.

Bond, G. R. (1972), A study of norms in groups at drug rehabilitation centers. Unpublished master's thesis, University of Chicago.

––––––– (1975), Norm formation in therapy groups. Unpublished doctoral dissertation, University of Chicago.

––––––– & Lieberman, M. A. (1980), The role and function of women's consciousness raising: Self-help, psychotherapy, or political activation? In: *The Evolving Female: Women in Psychosocial Context,* ed. C. L. Heckerman. New York: Human Sciences Press.

Cancian, F. (1972), What are norms? A study of beliefs and action in a Maya community. Unpublished manuscript, Department of Sociology, Stanford University.

Glidewell, J. C. (1974), A social psychology of laboratory training. Unpublished manuscript, Graduate School of Education, University of Chicago.

Heitler, J. B. (1973), Preparation of lower-class patients for expressive group psychotherapy. *J. Consult. Clin. Psychol.,* 41:251–260.

Hoffman, L. R. (1979), *The Group Problem Solving Process: Studies of a Valence Model.* New York: Praeger Publishers.

Jackson, J. J. (1965), Structural characteristics of norms. In: *Current Studies in Social Psychology,* ed. I. Steiner & M. Fishbein. New York: Holt, Rinehart & Winston.

Lieberman, M. A. (1958), The relationship of group climate to individual change. Unpublished doctoral dissertation, University of Chicago.

––––––– , Yalom, I. D., & Miles, M. B. (1973), *Encounter Groups: First Facts.* New York: Basic Books.

Luke, R. A., Jr. (1972), The internal normative structure of sensitivity training groups. *J. Applied Behav. Sci.,* 8:421–437.

MacKenzie, K. R. (1979), Group norms: Importance and measurement. *Int. J. Group Psychother.,* 29:471–480.

––––––– (1981), Measurement of group climate. *Int. J. Group Psychother.,* 31:287–295.

Psathas, G., & Hardert, R. (1966), Trainer interventions and normative patterns. *J. Applied Behav. Sci.,* 2:149–169.

Redl, F. (1942), Group emotion and leadership. *Psychiatry,* 5:573–596.

Schanck, R. (1932), A study of a community and its groups and institutions conceived of as behavior of individuals. *Psychol. Monogr.,* 43(2).

Stock, D. (1964), A survey of research on T groups. In: *T-Group Theory and Laboratory*

Method, ed. L. P. Bradford, J. R. Gibb, & K. D. Benne. New York: Wiley.

White, R., & Lippitt, R. (1968), Leader behavior and member reaction in three "social climates." In: *Group Dynamics,* 3rd Ed., ed. D. Cartwright & A. Zander. New York: Harper & Row.

Yalom, I. D., Houts, P. S., Newell, G., & Rand, K. H. (1967), Preparation of patients for group therapy. *Arch. Gen. Psychiat.,* 17:416–427.

9

Comparative Analyses of Change Mechanisms in Groups

MORTON A. LIEBERMAN, Ph.D.

Most accounts by people who find something of value to take away from group treatment attribute this to a limited set of discrete events and experiences. If we were to station ourselves outside the doorway of a psychotherapeutic group meeting, an encounter session, a women's consciousness-raising group, or a group of widowers who belong to a mutual aid group, what would we hear as they left the session? A goodly proportion would tell us, in the language associated with that particular type of group, that something positive had occurred. If we inquired about the ways they had been helped, we would in all likelihood hear such statements as: "I felt accepted for the first time in my life," "I was able to say things about myself I had never told anyone else before," "I finally understood what was bothering me and how it was I came to have such a difficulty," "I found people really understood my problem," "I reached out to others and they didn't move away from me," "I saw things in a new light," "I was able to get all of those angry feelings out." Rarely would we hear a participant state: "Although I feel I am better, I am not sure what happened or how it is I came to feel better."

Is this simple linkage by group participants between felt change and their reports about the nature of the group learning context anything

Studies referred to in this chapter were supported by the University of Chicago Cancer Control Center (PHS #3, R18-CA1640-0151), National Institute of Mental Health (Self-Help and Urban Problems: Alternative Help Systems, PHS #5, R01-MH30742), the Spencer Foundation, and a Research Scientist Award (Processes and Outcomes of People-Changing Groups, #1, K05-MH20342).

191

more than a common-sense labeling serving to reduce ambiguity? We rarely question the meaning of such connections, taking them at face value as representing an important, if not crucial, perspective for understanding change procedures.

This chapter critically reviews the findings from a series of change-mechanism studies, considering methodological perspectives on data generation, as well as the effects of group context on client perceptions of beneficial mechanisms. In addition, it examines change-mechanism research from an epistemological perspective to test the limitations of perceptually derived data for developing a theory of change processes.

Interest in the characteristics of change mechanisms has been apparent from the beginning of systematic group treatment. Corsini and Rosenberg (1955) published the seminal paper on change mechanisms. After questioning professionals who conducted and theorized about group psychotherapy, they produced long lists of items, from which a limited set of middle-level abstractions was generated. The categories have remained remarkably stable—concepts such as altruism, universality, insight, catharsis, and feedback are still prime ideas which appear with unending regularity in theoretical treatises, empirical studies, and everyday conversations of psychotherapists. The correspondence between theory, our experience as psychotherapists, and patients' reports reinforces the "correctness" of such a view. We are at peace because our common-sense perceptions of the therapeutic world make theoretical sense and are echoed in the perception of those who are the recipients of our treatment.

PROBLEMS OF STUDYING THERAPEUTIC MECHANISMS

The critical choice facing investigators is whether to use an external or internal frame of reference. They may choose to gather information relevant to change mechanisms by observing group participants, or they may choose to inquire directly about participants' personal experiences. Several considerations are worth noting. An external perspective provides a sensitive indicator of behaviorally embedded transactions. For example, information exchanges leading to insight or perspective building can only reflect attempts by others in the group to provide such information. The observations cannot directly assess insight or the development of a participant's altered perspective. What observations can do best is sensitively assay both the intensity and frequency of certain classes of behavior. If the investigator's hypothesis states that the frequency of a certain behavior is critical, then the observational mode is the method of choice.

Many of the events and experiences reflective of therapeutic mechanisms are not, however, behavioral. For example, universality, expressed in terms of finding out that there are many others like oneself, that one's problems, feelings, and fears are not unique, represents a state of mind and cannot be specifically linked to particular behaviors. Even for some behaviorally linked events, such as self-revelation, the indexing of the event may ultimately rest on the phenomenological set and not the observational one. Although often trivialized by experienced "groupies," who are masters at revelations that have been practiced frequently, what is revealed is not specific information but rather the sense that the individual has said something or is able to say something that heretofore was hidden. These considerations, as well as the difficulty and cost involved in observational measurements, have led most investigators studying therapeutic mechanisms to a phenomenological approach.*

INFLUENCES ON CHANGE-MECHANISM REPORTS

Although phenomenological information can be developed quickly, is low in cost compared with observations, and more adequately reflects the range of mechanisms that have been theoretically linked to change, it has its pitfalls. With Borman, I have shown that participants' reports of beneficial therapeutic mechanisms are influenced by the group therapist/leader, the group's ideology, specific properties general to all small face-to-face intensive groups, the complaint or affliction that brings the patient to a helping group, and by general societal values and beliefs about help (Lieberman and Borman, 1979). We developed information about change mechanisms from comparisons among various group systems: group psychotherapy, encounter groups, consciousness-raising groups, and self-help groups.

The most pronounced source of influence we found was the professional leaders. Despite differences in ideology between formal psychotherapy groups and encounter groups, these two settings shared remarkably similar respondent reports of helping experiences and events, which

*Editors' Note: Several of the earlier chapters in this monograph show that the "phenomenological" approach has been the most popular. In his chapter on leadership, Dies indicates that client reports have been used most often in the leadership literature. The chapters by MacKenzie and Beck and their colleagues also show a preference for assessing client perceptions, although Beck does incorporate more behavior-oriented measures as well.

sharply contrasted with those reported by participants in settings not containing identifiable leaders, such as consciousness-raising and self-help groups. Therapists of widely diverse theoretical persuasions appear to emphasize events and experiences that are under their control. We found that insight or other cognitive processes, feedback, the expression and experience of strong affect, self-disclosure, and experimentation were the common elements stressed by therapeutic and encounter group theory. Events and experiences reflecting these emphases appeared in the items that patients reported were characteristic of their learning experiences. They were subject to specific leader interventions, in contrast, for example, to altruism. Evidence was also found, although not with the same order of certainty, that ideological beliefs associated with particular self-help groups influenced the change events that participants stressed.

Beyond these influences, certain conditions characteristic of all intensive, change-oriented, small face-to-face groups have a profound influence on experiences reported as helpful. Individuals enter such settings in a high state of personal need and are required to share with others information and feelings that are ordinarily considered personal and private. Each participant is immediately faced with a number of strangers, dissimilar except for one critical characteristic — the shared status of being a patient in a psychotherapy group, the shared societally devalued role or status in a consciousness-raising group, or the shared affliction in a self-help group. The basic group requirement is to share something personal, no matter how banal, about the real or perceived similarity of one's suffering, whether it be in terms of behavior, role, life crisis, or the need for growth or change. The enactment of this requirement leads to high levels of cohesiveness, experienced instantaneous similarity, and the common perception that participants are different from others outside the group refuge. These conditions, as well as the manner in which they are expressed in the uniquely created social microcosm of a group whose purposes are change and aid, lead directly to the normalizing and support experiences judged to be so highly useful by all participants, no matter what kind of group. The requirement that some aspects of their painful affliction be shared in public not only leads to such normalizing and support experiences, but also provides a fertile context for making comparative judgments, a valued "change mechanism."

The particular dilemma or problem that brings a person to a group setting appears to influence the processes perceived as helpful. To illustrate, Compassionate Friends (a self-help organization) offers a setting where individuals who have lost offspring can seek solace from this tragedy. Such a loss appears to confront individuals with fundamental questions about their existence and the need for a reappraisal of basic life values. Experiences and events associated with existential concerns occur in meetings of Compassionate Friends and are seen by the participants as a critical change mechanism. We have not observed similar reporting in a variety of other groups, even those professionally conducted by existentially oriented leaders.

These observations about sources of influence on the experiences participants report as being instrumental in helping them learn, grow, change, and obtain relief call into question the nature and meaning of change-mechanism data generated from self-reports. It is well nigh impossible to link phenomenological data with observed frequencies of such events. What then are we, as investigators, studying? Obviously, the reason we have been intrigued for over 30 years with an examination of events and experiences that are proximally linked to therapeutic change is the belief that such events are intrinsic to therapeutics and are not merely the product of particular conditions or influences. The goal has been to develop general theories concerning therapeutic settings that produce change in those who participate. This dilemma could be resolved if we were able to link patients' reports of useful events to objective measures of benefit. Such a finding, combined with information that successful change mechanisms were those influenced by group leaders or group ideology, would go a long way to diminish our disquiet about the nature of the change-mechanism data generated through self-reports.

THERAPEUTIC MECHANISMS AND OUTCOME

This strategy of linking self-reported change mechanisms to outcome was pursued in the encounter group study I conducted with my colleagues over a decade ago (Lieberman, Yalom, and Miles, 1973). Outcome classification into learners, those unchanged, and negative reactors was based on a wide variety of information: self-reports; third-party, therapists', and co-participants' reports; and a host of psychological tests measuring changes in attitudes, value orientation, coping styles, self-perception of self-esteem, conceptions of others, interpersonal adequacy, and sociometric status within the group itself.

Two approaches, both relying on participants' perceptions, were used to assess the occurrence, as well as the importance, of various "change mechanisms." At the end of every meeting, each participant was asked to respond to a brief question: "What was the most important event for you personally in the group today and why was it important?" The events were coded by raters into 22 different categories, based on the type of change mechanism, who was involved in the event, and the nature of the person's response to the event. The other major source of data was provided by a questionnaire administered at the termination of the entire series of meetings. This questionnaire assessed the relative importance of 14 different change mechanisms. The mechanisms explored through the two methods included expression of both positive and negative feelings, self-disclosure, feedback, experiencing intense emotions (both positive and negative), a variety of cognitive events or experiences (insight, information, and understanding), communion or similarity, altruism, spectatorism, involvement, advice getting, modeling, experimentation with new forms of behavior, inculcation of hope, and reexperiencing the group as a family.

The encounter group study provided an ideal setting for examining change mechanisms, since it was predicated on random assignment of participants to different types of learning environments, created by different theoretical orientations. Included in our study were leaders who conducted sensitivity training, Gestalt, Psychodrama, psychoanalytically oriented, Transactional Analysis, Rogerian, marathon, Synanon, and personal growth groups, as well as leaderless groups that used a preselected tape program. We hypothesized that this diversity would provide a range of therapeutic mechanisms. Theoretical orientations, however, were not predictive of either leader behaviors or participant experiences, although an empirically devised typology of group leaders did provide a model of leader style.

We found: (1) wide variations in leader effectiveness; (2) some, albeit small, systematic differences in change mechanisms among participants under different leader types; and (3) considerable variation in change mechanisms among those who learned, those who remained unchanged, and those who experienced negative consequences. Most of the differences in change mechanisms associated with outcomes were due, however, to the negative change group. In other words, those who learned and those who remained unchanged (but not negative) resembled one another on critical change mechanisms. Furthermore, the significant change-mechanism differences among leader types were not the same ones that were critical to learning. Group differences in mechanisms explained "failures in learning."

Thus, from the macro-perspective provided by comparative analyses of various group change-induction settings — self-help, encounter, psychotherapy, and consciousness-raising groups — our findings suggest that system properties do have a major influence on the type of events or experiences participants report as being useful. When we shift to examining one system, even when the theoretical perspectives of the leaders differ widely, we are hard pressed to find precise linkages among specific leader behaviors, change mechanisms, and outcome.* The influence of leaders on participants' reports of therapeutic experiences appears to reflect generalized expectations about therapy and professionals, rather than the particular therapist behavior. We were able to show some differences in influence among the various leader types, but these were not the events that were critically related to productive learning. In short, our findings from the encounter group study suggest that we can be more articulate when leaders fail (their groups have a preponderance of negative outcomes). Most of the variance in our analyses presented in the book *Encounter Groups* comes from the failed leaders and the failed members.

How can we account for lack of substantive findings? Perhaps the global model of outcome used in the encounter group study, which rests on the summation of a wide variety of specific change indices, makes it difficult to connect mechanisms to outcome. Precision might be achieved if we were to specify particular outcome criteria, and determine whether there is a precise link between a particular benefit and specific therapeutic mechanisms. This question is addressed in the next study.

TESTING THE HYPOTHESIS OF INVARIANT RELATIONSHIP BETWEEN CHANGE MECHANISMS AND OUTCOME

Our final study of change mechanisms examines the links between change mechanisms and a specific type of benefit. The data for this study

---

Editors' Note: Chapter 2 by Dies shows that clients' perceptions of the group therapist significantly influence their reactions to the group experience. Lieberman is essentially correct, however, in asserting that specific links between group therapists' behaviors and particular therapeutic outcomes have not been established with a sufficient degree of clarity. The fact that group members report certain connections between their perceptions of leadership and their experience of outcome does not guarantee that this correlation is indeed reliable. Measurement problems, the complexity of the therapeutic process, and the client's inability to identify subtle influence processes all contribute to the ambiguity.

originated from a large investigation of self-help groups, involving several thousand individuals, and eight self-help organizations. We chose three organizations for our test. All three organizations dealt with significant personal losses — widowhood in two of them (Theos and NAIM), and child loss by parents in the third (Compassionate Friends). A 31–item change-mechanism questionnaire was administered after at least one year's participation.* Members were asked how helpful, on a three-point scale, each of the 31 items had been in their learning. Categories used to generate the items were: *universality, support, self-disclosure, catharsis, insight, social analysis, advice-information, perspective, feedback, comparative-vicarious learning, altruism,* and *existential experimentation* (Lieberman and Borman, 1979).

A single change dimension that reflected a common central issue of participants in each of these three different self-help organizations was selected. After a year's participation in the group, participants were asked to indicate, on a series of scales, the ways they had changed. Separate factor analyses of the responses to this questionnaire for each of the self-help organizations yielded a factor concerned with guilt and anger which had low correlation with standard depression and self-esteem scales.

General Examination

Initially we examined the change mechanisms of these three, rather distinct self-help organizations. Table 1 shows the top- and bottom-ranked mechanisms, i.e., those items that individuals indicated were very important or unimportant in being of help to them.

An examination of Table 1 indicates a rather remarkable correspondence among the three self-help organizations, which have different stated goals, ideologies, and norms. The prototypical experience for almost all individuals in these three self-help groups was universality — the feeling that you are with others who have been through the same experience, that you are not unique. Indeed, we found this experience characteristic of all eight self-help organizations we studied. This simple yet apparently powerful experience is the core to what members most value.

*Editors' Note: A critical issue here is the long delay between the beginning of treatment and the administration of the change-mechanism questionnaire. Chapters 2, 6, and 7 (by Dies, Beck et al., and MacKenzie) emphasize the importance of regular assessment of clients' perceptions of leadership and group process. What is viewed as helpful or "curative" after two months of participation may differ dramatically from the perceptions of curative factors gathered after a year of group work. Also, condensing one year of work into 31 simple items is an enormously complex feat.

TABLE 1

High- and Low-Change Mechanisms

Most Helpful

NAIM		Theos		Compassionate Friends	
Item[a]	Percent Respondents Endorsing	Item	Percent Respondents Endorsing	Item	Percent Respondents Endorsing
1. Being with other people who have been through the same thing (Un).	89%	1. Being with other people who have been through the same thing (Un).	79%	1. Finding out there are many others who have also lost a child (Un).	83%
2. Finding that I am pretty much like other people (Un).	79%	2. Learning that my problems, feelings, fears are not unique (Un).	77%	2. Being with other people who have been through the same thing (Un).	82%
3. Finding out there are many others who have also lost a spouse (Un).	76%	3. Finding out there are many others who have also lost a spouse (Un).	74%	3. Learning that my problems, feelings, fears are not unique (Un).	80%
4. When I hear others' pain I feel less sorry for myself (Comp).	68%	4. Getting a perspective on my problems (Cog).	69%	4. Sharing thoughts and feelings about my child's death (Un).	78%
5. Learning that my problems, feelings, fears are not unique (Un).	68%	5. Sharing thoughts and feelings about my spouse's death (Un).	67%	5. Getting a perspective on my problems (Cog).	72%

[a] Abbreviations for items are: Universality (Un), Comparative Judgments (Comp), Support (Sup), Altruism (Alt), Cognitive (Cog), Catharsis (Cath), and Self-Disclosure (SD).

TABLE 1 (*Continued*)
High- and Low-Change Mechanisms

Most Helpful

NAIM		Theos		Compassionate Friends	
Item[a]	Percent Respondents Endorsing	Item	Percent Respondents Endorsing	Item	Percent Respondents Endorsing
6. Feeling understood (Sup).	65%	6. Reaching out to others in need (Alt).	65%	6. Being able to say what bothered me instead of holding it in (Cath).	70%
7. When I listen to the experiences of others, it helps put mine in perspective (Comp).	65%	7. When I hear others' pain, I feel less sorry for myself (Comp).	65%	7. Reaching out to others in need (Alt).	67%
8. Reaching out to others in need (Alt).	64%	8. Feeling understood (Sup).	64%	8. Feeling understood (Sup).	64%
9. Helping others (Alt).	63%	9. Being supported and valued by the group (Sup).	64%	9. Knowing that I can call on another member when I am discouraged (Sup).	62%
10. Knowing that I can call on another member when I am discouraged (Sup).	61%	10. Knowing that I can call on another member when I am discouraged (Sup).	63%	10. Helping others (Alt).	62%
		11. Helping others (Alt).	61%	11. Seeing the ways that men and women grieve differently (Comp).	60%

[a] Abbreviations for items are: Universality (Un), Comparative Judgments (Comp), Support (Sup), Altruism (Alt), Cognitive (Cog), Catharsis (Cath), and Self-Disclosure (SD).

TABLE 1 (*Continued*)
High- and Low-Change Mechanisms

Least Helpful

NAIM		Theos		Compassionate Friends	
Item[a]	Percent Respondents Endorsing	Item	Percent Respondents Endorsing	Item	Percent Respondents Endorsing
1. Venting my anger (Cath).	15%	1. Venting my anger (Cath).	20%	1. Venting my anger (Cath).	30%
2. Understanding more about the causes of my problems (Cog).	24%	2. Feedback: others telling me what they think about the way I'm handling my loss (Cog).	32%	2. Feedback: others telling me what they think about the way I'm handling my loss (Cog).	34%
3. Revealing things about myself (SD).	25%	3. Discussing how bereaved spouses are unjustly treated by society (Cog).	35%	3. Discussing how bereaved parents are unjustly treated by society (Cog).	38%
4. Feedback: others telling me what they think about the way I'm handling my loss (Cog).	25%	4. Revealing things about myself (SD).	39%	4. Revealing things about myself (SD).	37%
5. Discussing how bereaved spouses are unjustly treated by society (Cog).	28%	5. Understanding more about the causes of my problems (Cog).	41%	5. Others helped me face my situation (Sup).	43%

[a] Abbreviations for items are: Universality (Un), Comparative Judgments (Comp), Support (Sup), Altruism (Alt), Cognitive (Cog), Catharsis (Cath), and Self-Disclosure (SD).

At a theoretical level, it bespeaks normalization, a process influencing perceptions that one's thoughts, feelings, and behaviors are not aberrant or unusual, but rather common to those who have experienced the same affliction or dilemma. Normalization is probably the prime and most immediate impact that self-help organizations have on their members. Three other mechanisms can be seen in the list of items characteristic of all the loss groups: support, comparative judgment, and altruism.

Equally instructive are those events or experiences that participants perceive as least helpful. Although the correspondence among the three organizations is lower than for those items seen as helpful, the expression of strong negative emotions, the revelation of personal material, and the receipt of information or reactions from others (feedback) are not viewed by the majority of participants as helpful. These least-helpful items are not a simple product of social desirability. Other types of groups such as encounter, sensitivity training, and, to a certain extent, psychotherapy groups, when studied in a similar fashion, demonstrate that many of these unvalued items may be perceived as among the most helpful (Lieberman et al., 1973). For example, in our study of encounter groups, we found that feedback was ranked first, as the most useful learning experience, and that the expression of negative affect was ranked third. Among group psychotherapy patients, these same two items were ranked, respectively, fifth and seventh.

The findings reflected in Table 1 suggest that there is a common prototypical experience in loss-oriented self-help groups. It does not of course tell us about the link between such events or experiences and the benefit individuals take away from such groups. To accomplish this, we need to turn to our next analyses.

Comparison of High and Low Learners

Required was a division of our samples into those who showed high and low benefit attributable to the self-help group experience. We chose the aforementioned guilt dimension for this analysis since it represented a common and important psychological dimension. Each individual in the three populations was given a score based on guilt dimension factor loadings. Those who decreased in guilt, defined as that group of people who had scores one standard deviation below the group mean, were defined as a high-benefit group; those one standard deviation above the group mean were defined as a low-change group. For each of the three organizations (NAIM, Theos, and Compassionate Friends), a separate linear discriminant analysis was computed. We chose this method since it maximizes differences, recognizing that such statistical procedures, without replication, are, at best, only suggestive. We asked the question: What events or experiences judged to be helpful would maximally distinguish the high and low learners? Table 2 shows the results of this analysis.

Contrasting Table 2 with Table 1 suggests that unlike Table 1, which showed similarity among the three groups, Table 2 shows that the particular sets of events distinguishing those who decreased in guilt and those who increased in guilt are unique for each system! The "predictive power" of the linear discriminant analysis is quite high, correctly identifying 76% of the participants in NAIM, 77% in Theos, and 88% in Compassionate Friends, and thus indicating that there are real differences (at least in a statistical sense) in the perception of important change mechanisms between those who benefited and those who did not. If such perceptions reflect actual experience, those who benefited had a different experience in the self-help group than those who did not. It would be difficult to state that there is a common set of mechanisms related to guilt reduction.

What can we learn about change processes by examining the events and experiences cited by participants in each of the three systems that maximally discriminated between those who showed a reduction in guilt compared with those who showed a slight increase in guilt? To recast the question for analysis, we asked: What unique experiences did those whose guilt was reduced have as participants? For the widows in NAIM (and an occasional widower),[1] the core experiences associated with guilt reduction were the sharing or revelation of troublesome feelings, normalization (not feeling out of place), the redirection of anger by externalizing it (seeing problems as being a product of an insensitive world), as well as reaching out to others in need. Those items seen as not characteristic for those who changed provide a clue to the underlying processes. The avoidance of hostile impulses by not venting anger, was characteristic of those who showed guilt reduction. The externalization of feelings, as well as catharsis in a setting that signifies that their feelings, behaviors, and thoughts are normal, could certainly be seen as consonant with the generally accepted theory of guilt and its reduction in cases of loss of a spouse.

Turning to the other widowhood organization, Theos, contrasting results were found. The normalization aspects were certainly there, but

[1] Sex differences were examined as a possible source of variation, but no variation was found.

TABLE 2

Discriminant Analysis: High and Low Learners

High Learners

NAIM		Theos		Compassionate Friends	
Item	Loadings	Item	Loadings	Item	Loadings
1. Seeing that some things are caused by the insensitivity of others and are not my fault.	0.36	1. I don't feel like I'm a "fifth wheel" when I'm at Theos.	0.47	1. Others helped me face my situation.	0.68
2. I don't feel like a "fifth wheel" when I'm at NAIM.	0.52	2. Reaching out to others in need.	0.36	2. Others gave me hope.	0.49
3. Reaching out to others in need.	0.26	3. Seeing how others coped gave me ideas.	0.33	3. Revealing things about myself.	0.43
4. Being able to say what bothered me instead of holding it in.	0.33	4. Being able to try out new ways of solving my problems in a supportive setting.	0.31	4. Being supported and valued by group.	0.34
5. Sharing thoughts and feelings about my spouse's death.	0.30	5. Finding out there are many others who have also lost a spouse.	0.23		
		6. Understanding more about the causes of my problems.	0.23		
		7. Being supported and valued by group.	0.22		

TABLE 2 (*Continued*)
Discriminant Analysis: High and Low Learners

NAIM		Theos		Compassionate Friends	
Item	Loadings	Item	Loadings	Item	Loadings

Low Learners

NAIM Item	Loadings	Theos Item	Loadings	Compassionate Friends Item	Loadings
1. Venting my anger.	- 0.24	1. When I listen to the experiences of others, it helps put mine in perspective.	- 0.58	1. Venting my anger.	- 0.42
2. When I hear others' pain, I feel less sorry for myself.	- 0.17	2. Getting a perspective on my problems.	- 0.45	2. Expressing sorrow.	- 0.38

rather than the emphasis on expressiveness, revelation, and externalization onto objects outside of self, we found an emphasis on cognitive mastery and the use of the group context for experimentation. Certainly it would be possible to see this set of experiences as consonant with some views of guilt, and many professionals could readily accept that these processes are linked to guilt reduction. The dilemma is why different processes lead to similar change in comparable populations. Frankly, no reasonable systematic explanation exists in our present data. The ideologies and characteristics of these two widowhood organizations are distinct, and there is no reason to assume that we should expect similarity in processes, given the characteristics of the groups. However, the purpose of our study was to test the idea that there *is* some unique set of experiences that individuals have that can be linked to a specific outcome. The findings on the two widowhood groups would not support such a view, although *post hoc* explanations of the change mechanisms could fit into an understanding of guilt as a dynamic process and "account" for how experiences could reduce guilt.

Among parents who have lost children, the change mechanisms differed from either of the two widowhood groups. Although normalization was common to all three groups, in Compassionate Friends guilt reduction is associated with existential considerations, the inculcation of hope, and confrontation with the situation. Unexpected loss of a child through illness, accident, or suicide was uniformly accompanied by bitterness and fury at society. The experience of isolation from others was a distinct psychological state, different from that seen among widows and widowers. Perhaps the dilemma facing those who have lost a child, and the consequent experience of acute guilt and responsibility, can best be resolved through confrontation with the ultimate meaning of their lives. Such a *post hoc* explanation could fit the particular circumstances of this group, but again we are faced with the dilemma that despite the appearance of such a fit, we are unable to provide reasonable generalizations regarding the link between change mechanisms and a specific type of change.

Although, as an examination of Table 2 reveals, the change mechanisms singled out by those who showed guilt reduction were not shared across the three systems, at least one generalization can be made. An examination of the entire array of items (not shown in Tables 1 or 2) reveals that those who showed change were more likely to endorse as "important" a larger number of change mechanisms than those who did not show change. This finding is similar to the encounter group study finding that high learners used a wider variety of change mechanisms than did unchanged participants. In the present study, the increased endorsement of a wide variety of change mechanisms may represent response bias, with high endorsement of all scales. In the encounter group study, however, since only one critical incident was collected per group session, the results were not open to such a potential artifact.

Given the confluence of these two studies representing different populations and group conditions, it seems reasonable to suggest that a diversity of change events is critical for success. The number of items endorsed as important by those who changed was more than twice the number endorsed by those who did not change. Therapeutic change does not appear to be maximized by the idiosyncratic match between an individual's specific group experience and particular events. Rather, it appears that the sheer number of different kinds of experiences or events a person encounters in a change-induction group will, on the average, lead to an increased likelihood of change.

CONCLUSIONS

Such observations concerning the way in which individuals use a group context for change, learning, or growth could lead to alterations in how we conduct such groups. Successful therapists appear to be those who are able to create a wide range of learning experiences for patients. Therapists or leaders thus might direct their attention toward maximizing a wide range of events or experiences thought to be therapeutic. In a sense, this would become a therapy of opportunity, in which members attempted to take advantage of as many different kinds of learning experiences as possible. Matching specific experiences to particular members would become less critical.

What are the implications of our observations for the study of therapeutic mechanisms?* Faced with such an array of findings, the easiest

Editors' Note: The idea of specific change mechanisms is an important one for the group therapist, and has been widely acknowledged in the group therapy literature, particularly by Yalom. The members' perceptions of critical events constitute one important source of data—the "experienced reality" of the group for the participants. Lieberman presents provocative findings in this chapter, indicating that groups with very similar functions used quite different mechanisms, despite the fact that the majority of members of all the groups perceived them as useful. Lieberman appropriately questions why there should be such a variation. Are the correct questions being asked? Are members really unable to identify what is useful for them? Are there other common underlying issues? These are some of the questions that need to be addressed.

response is to raise the question of methodology. Does the particular form of instrument used in these studies lead to artifacts related to social desirability or lack of sensitivity to the subtlety of change? The checklist method has been used in a variety of settings, and is open to stereotyped responses. The correspondence, however, with findings generated in the encounter group study, in which much more sensitive, specific, and detailed measures were used, suggests that technical considerations are not central.

A more serious concern may be raised in regard to the process of asking participants, either with a standard checklist or in the more open-ended post-meeting form of questionnaire used in the encounter group study, to assess their experiences. The influence of professional leaders on group ideology or the special demands of the affliction may override all other considerations. There may in fact be a unique set of events or experiences associated with change, but given the context of such studies, any approach that relies on phenomenological data will be shaped more by the context than by the specificity of change. Perhaps participants are fundamentally incapable of reflecting sensitively on particular experiences they have had in a change context. Psychological experiences in a therapeutic setting may be "preconceptual" and our demand that participants structure the events may fly in the face of their experiential reality. To state this another way, patients can provide us with answers only for the questions we as researchers ask, and therefore we end up studying reflections of our own theories. This chapter was written to stimulate a reexamination of the issues, not to provide solutions to the dilemma.

REFERENCES

Corsini, B., & Rosenberg, B. (1955), Mechanisms of group psychotherapy: Processual dynamics. *J. Abnorm. Soc. Psychol.*, 51:406–411.
Lieberman, M. A., & Borman, L. D. (1979), *Self-Help Groups for Coping with Crisis*. San Francisco: Jossey-Bass.
————, Yalom, I., & Miles, M. (1973), *Encounter Groups: First Facts*. New York: Basic Books.

Conclusion

This monograph is intended to encourage clinicians and researchers to establish links for effective communication. The various chapters were written for the practitioner, and contain many suggestions for improving clinical practice. This clinical emphasis should *not* be construed as implying that the practitioner is primarily responsible for the gap between research and practice. On the contrary, Chapter 1 by Dies demonstrated that clinicians and researchers are equally accountable, and that both parties must evaluate their contributions to the split within the field. Our choice to address the group psychotherapist reflected the view that much of the empirical literature has not adequately attended to the needs of the clinician and as a result has been disregarded as "irrelevant." As research-oriented clinicians, we hoped to avoid this pitfall by making the empirical findings and methods summarized here more meaningful to the practitioner.

Dies initiated this effort in the first chapter by outlining how group therapists can use research instruments to improve their clinical practice. He cited the recent literature to show that empirical and clinical modes of understanding actually overlap quite substantially (Hayes, 1981; Kiesler, 1981). The stereotyped view of the clinician as uninterested in empirical methodology and of the researcher as unaware of the practical realities of the clinical setting is no longer tenable. Clinicians who incorporate systematic evaluations of therapeutic process and outcome into their treatment programs can do much to reduce the breach between research and practice.

In his chapter on leadership, for example, Dies demonstrated how research has led to a greater understanding of this aspect of group treatment. His review of the research literature pointed to the usefulness of considering therapist behavior along a relatively small number of dimensions. In particular, these dimensions emphasized the function of the group therapist in creating a group atmosphere that will have a therapeutic impact on the participants. The findings Dies cited have considerable relevance for good training programs, suggesting that non-specific therapist activities must receive adequate attention. This view of the therapist as a "milieu manager" would counterbalance to some degree the emphasis on theory that characterizes many training programs. Moreover, this orientation is complementary to the view of the group as a social system discussed elsewhere in this monograph. The conclusions offered by Dies are also highly compatible with much of the group dynamics literature, particularly regarding the interaction of the therapist's task and relationship behaviors. In that literature, too, the importance of a positive, moderately structured leadership style, which stresses the significance of the group as the vehicle for change, is underscored (Hersey and Blanchard, 1977; Johnson and Johnson, 1982).

The chapter on change measures by Coché is directly related to the CORE Battery project sponsored by the American Group Psychotherapy Association (MacKenzie and Dies, 1982). It presented tools that can be easily employed in clinical settings to enhance therapeutic understanding. The utilization of a multidimensional change-measures battery need not be seen by the clinician as a threat to or a replacement for regular clinical assessment. Rather, it offers an alternative route to information that frequently provides additional insight and complements the type of material obtained in a clinical interview. Such an interweaving of data sources can be a useful experience for the clinician. Although in the development of any battery or test, controversy is bound to arise, Coché tried to show that such a battery can be used even in a busy clinical service and can result in information of value both for individual case understanding and for program assessment.

The final six chapters in this monograph looked at various aspects of group process and how this influences and is influenced by the group members. All of these chapters originated from a theoretical view of the group as a social system. Several of these contributors have found general systems theory a valuable organizing approach to the understanding of small group function (Durkin, 1981). One basic principle of general systems theory has to do with the importance of distinguishing varying levels of organization within complex systems. In regard to group psychotherapy, the group is seen as a system and the individual members as subsystems. The creation of a hierarchy could continue upwards to include the clinical setting within which the group occurs, the surrounding sociocultural environment, and so on. In the other direction, the hierarchy could move down to varying types of internal psychological dimensions and on to the connections between psychological constructs and physiological functioning. The appropriate terms for considering the organization of the group include developmental stages (Chapter 4 by MacKenzie and Livesley), social roles (Chapter 5 by Livesley and MacKenzie and Chapter 6 by Beck et al.), group climate (Chapter 7 by MacKenzie), and normative expectations (Chapter 8 by Bond). The goals contemplated by the members and the therapist contribute to these variables. The effects of such context variables will be reflected in a variety of therapeutic mechanisms and in positive or negative critical incidents.

It is important that the descriptive terms used are appropriate to group-level concepts. There has been a tendency to apply language suitable to the individual, primarily psychoanalytic in origin, to the group-as-a-whole. Indeed, Bednar and Kaul (1978) have identified this tendency as a major cause of the "conceptual malaise" afflicting group research. The borrowing of concepts from individual therapy to describe group treatment blurs the distinction between the mechanisms by which an individual organizes thoughts and emotions and how a group organizes its relationships. By clearly defining both levels with appropriate terminology, it is possible to look more clearly at the relationships between group events and individual behavior. The collection of articles in this monograph has provided a combination of theoretical and empirical data in this regard.

Several of the chapters dealt with the importance of information processing for understanding group events, particularly in terms of the kinds of information that tend to predominate at different developmental stages. Various critical dimensions for assessing interpersonal events were described, involving ideas about both the group as a collective entity and each individual member and the therapist. This emphasis is in keeping with the current interest in interpersonal constructs as the mechanism by which an individual develops his or her own view of the interpersonal environment (a view also colored greatly by personal perception). The focus on the interpersonal meaning of behavior provides an important theoretical link for the impact of previous experience on the interpretation of present reality.

It was appropriate that the final chapter in this monograph should have been that by Lieberman, regarding the manner in which members perceive their group experience as having been helpful. His observation that two groups of participants, both selected for the same type of stress situation, benefited in quite different ways is highly provocative. From a research standpoint, Lieberman's findings challenge the validity of participants' perceptions regarding what is useful about their therapeutic experience. Are members in fact blind to many aspects of their therapy experience, and do they construct their views of it only in retrospect? Are initial expectations the prime determinants of how members view the therapy experience? Does the philosophy of a particular group indoctrinate the participants to use a common language of explanation? Do complex theories of personality and interpersonal functioning obscure more than they reveal about the mechanisms of change? Perhaps the reader should review such questions in the light, not of research, but of everyday clinical practice. It is not at all uncommon for major discrepancies to exist between the therapist's views of the therapeutic process and those of the recipients (Strupp and Hadley, 1977).

Both the theoretical and the empirical chapters in this monograph dealt with dimensions of group phenomena that can be measured. As the editors, we feel that this monograph will have made a useful contribution if its serves to stimulate therapists to think in new ways about their clinical work and particularly if it encourages them to consider how their clinical hunches might be tested. The wide range of process, leadership, and outcome measures presented in this volume provides a rich source of instruments for evaluating group treatments. The systematic application of empirical measures to improve clinical service may eventually result in a narrowing of the gap between research and practice, especially if clinicians and empirical investigators work together to develop increasingly sensitive and sophisticated measures and methods for data collection.

REFERENCES

Bednar, R. L., & Kaul, T. J. (1978), Conceptualizing group research: A preliminary analysis. *Small Group Behav.,* 9:173–191.

Durkin, J. E., Ed. (1981), *Living Groups: Group Psychotherapy and General System Theory.* New York: Brunner/Mazel.

Hayes, S. C. (1981), Single case experimental design and empirical clinical practice. *J. Consult. Clin. Psychol.,* 49:193–211.

Hersey, P., & Blanchard, K. (1977), *Management of Organizational Behavior: Utilizing Human Resources,* 3rd Ed. Englewood Cliffs, N.J.: Prentice-Hall.

Johnson, D. W., & Johnson, F. P. (1982), *Joining Together: Group Theory and Group Skills.* Englewood Cliffs, N.J.: Prentice-Hall.

Kiesler, D. J. (1981), Empirical clinical psychology: Myth or reality? *J. Consult. Clin. Psychol.*, 49:212–215.

MacKenzie, K. R., & Dies, R. R. (1982), *The CORE Battery: Clinical Outcome Results.* New York: American Group Psychotherapy Association.

Strupp, H. H., & Hadley, S. W. (1977), A tripartite model of mental health and therapy outcomes. *Amer. Psychologist,* 32:187–196.

Name Index

215

Subject Index

DATE DUE

DEMCO 38-297